CASTING SHADOWS

GENEVIEVE MCKAY

CHAPTER 1

ALICE

"*A*lice, I'm leaving. Dad's driving me to the airport so this is goodbye." The bed tilts as my sister, Isabelle, flops down beside me.

I don't look at her. Instead, I stare out my open window at the dull blue sky, wishing like anything that I was out there now, not trapped inside.

"Alice?" She nudges my knee when I don't respond. "Come on. I know this is bad, but it's not the end of the world. You won't be grounded forever. And the doctors say that you can have a nearly normal life if you put your mind to it. You can't sulk forever."

Nearly normal. I tighten both hands around the pillow in my lap, giving it an angry twist. There is nothing *normal* about the way things are now.

The extent of the tumour was much greater than we anticipated, the specialist had said gravely, when I woke up from surgery unable to see anything in front of me. *Your central vision is no longer func-*

tioning. You should retain much of your peripheral vision but, Alice, I'm afraid that you have some life-altering challenges ahead of you.

Life-altering challenges? That was his way of saying that my life is completely ruined. I won't be on a future Olympic show jumping team like I'd planned. Or even be able to drive a car or get a motorcycle. I can't even read or put on my damn makeup properly. And, worst of all, I'm not allowed to ride.

Sell the ponies, sell the ponies. Dad's voice runs through my head like an endless mantra, and I bite back tears of rage. Two of my ponies are already gone, and Jiggs will most likely be next. All those hours of hard work and schooling up in smoke. Only my ancient, retired pony, Checkers, has been spared.

"You should be thankful, Alice," Isabelle presses on, oblivious to my inner turmoil. "You could have died. We were so scared when you went in for surgery."

Her voice wobbles and I let out a sigh. There's no point in staying angry with *her*, after all. None of this is Isabelle's fault.

"I didn't almost die," I mutter. "It was a benign tumour. It wouldn't have killed me, Isabelle. *This* is killing me."

I'd been relieved when they'd discovered the tumour in my brain. It wasn't cancerous after all and I assumed that once they removed it, I'd spend a few weeks healing and then my life would go back to normal.

But, of course, it couldn't be that simple. The tumour was larger than the surgeons had first thought, a hulking mass with multiple tendrils pressing on the parts of my brain responsible for vision. And when they'd taken it out, they'd taken most of my eyesight too.

A sharp breeze curls around me from the open window, ruffling the choppy remains of my hair and tapping against my cheeks like tiny fingers. Even though the air is cold, I love keeping the window open at this time of year. The nippy temperature suits me.

Fall is normally one of my favourite seasons. That extra zing in the air makes the horses fresh and feisty. This is galloping weather, riding on empty beaches weather, time for the horses to shake off their tame, show-ready personalities and be the wild creatures they are meant to be.

"Alice, did you even hear what I said?" Isabelle demands, and despite my internal misery, I bite back a smile. Irritating my sisters is something I've always done well, and it's nice to know I haven't lost my touch.

"Not really." I shrug.

"I'm sorry about the ponies, but you know that Dad's doing this because he loves you, right? He doesn't want you to get hurt. Or *killed*."

"It wasn't his decision to make," I say, turning toward her for the first time.

She's sitting too close for me to make out her features. She's just a blurry outline that I can't even see unless I tilt my head sideways at exactly the right angle.

I don't need to see Isabelle to know what she looks like, though. She has had the same blunt, shoulder-length blond hair style since she was twelve and her blue eyes always look slightly bored when she's talking to me. As if there isn't a single word I could say that might interest her. Honestly, I've never been her favourite sister. The fact that she's been so nice to me since the surgery has been a pleasant surprise.

"Look," she says with forced patience, "I totally understand how you must feel. I get it. But Dad is trying to protect you. You rode that psycho, Jiggs, when you'd barely recovered from surgery, even after you'd promised not to. And you jumped him even though you *knew* how dangerous it was. You both could have been permanently wrecked when that jump went down. Dad didn't have much of a choice but to sell the ponies and ground you."

"He had a choice." My voice hardens, even though I would do anything to take back my stupid decision to jump Jiggs that day. Sometimes I can still hear the horrible groaning noise he made when he hit the ground. "He had a choice not to sell the things that mean the most to me. Without even *asking*. I hate him."

"Your ponies are much too spicy and unpredictable for someone with limited vision," Isabelle says, using her most reasonable, big-sister voice. The one that makes me want to punch her. "Dad isn't even asking you to give up horses completely. He just wants you to stick with flat work on something safe for a while. I offered to lease you Shamus."

"As if I'd want a boring plodder like Shamus," I say, giving her what I hope is a scathing look. "He drags around in mindless circles like a robot. He's barely a horse. I don't know how you can stand to ride something that's half-dead."

"That's not true," she snaps, her anger rising to the surface just as fast as mine would if someone insulted *my* horse. "Shamus is kind and sensible and cleaned up at the dressage shows this year. At least he's sane, unlike all the haywire ponies you've ruined with your crazy riding."

She breaks off abruptly, as if realizing that she's gone too far.

"Get out." Hot rage engulfs me and I lean over suddenly and give her a hard shove with both hands that nearly sends her flying off the bed. "Go to your stupid university and leave me alone."

"Ow, you little brat." Isabelle jumps to her feet and I can feel her glaring at me. "Fine, see if I try to help you anymore. You deserve everything you get."

I suck in my breath, shocked out of my anger for a second. Nobody has said anything like that to me so far, although I'm sure more than one person is thinking it. I know how people talk about me behind my back. Alice is the mean sister. Alice hurts people's feelings. Alice is too hard on her ponies. They don't think I hear them, but I do.

Isabelle marches to the door and throws it open so hard that the handle hits the polished log wall with a loud crack that makes me jump. I expect to hear her stomp down the hall and right out of my life, but instead she hesitates.

"I didn't mean that," she says quietly from outside the doorway, sounding more sad than angry now. "You don't deserve any of this. You *are* a nightmare sometimes, Alice, but I do love you. You know that, right?"

"Isabelle, wait." I scramble to my feet, not wanting to leave things like this between us. "I shouldn't have shoved you or said bad things about Shamus, even if he is boring. I'm sorry. I *am* going to miss you while you're at school. Things will be awful around here without you."

It's the closest I've come to admitting how scared I am about this upcoming year. I don't want to be alone with only my dad and his annoying fiancée to keep me company. With Isabelle at university and my little stepsister, Triniti, about to start at a local boarding school, I will be left mostly alone in this massive house with only my dark thoughts to occupy my time. The idea terrifies me.

"Yes, I don't know how you'll survive without my charming personality." The humour is back in her voice. "But, honestly Alice, I think you should really think about what Dad said, about getting you a companion, a tutor to keep you company."

"What, am I ninety? As if I want some sort of paid assistant hovering over me. Go away. You're wrecking our touching moment here."

"Well, what about having Fina spend a few hours a day here? She offered to come hang out with you when she's not riding or looking after the farm."

"She's *always* riding and she has the foal to take care of now. Look, I don't need someone to sit with me like I'm an invalid. And I don't need charity from your weird friends. Especially not

Fina. She'd start trying to make me dress in rainbow leggings and fur capes or something. No thanks."

"You love her weirdness." Isabelle laughs. "Okay, not Fina then. But what about someone else? Elliot says she knows a girl...."

"Yuck, I'll pass on anyone Elliot recommends. Go on, you'll miss your plane."

"Fine. But I'll be home for Christmas," she says firmly. "And I'll email you all the time."

"I'll be sure to read every word." I grin in her direction. Literally, the only side benefit to this blindness thing is making other people feel uncomfortable from time to time.

"Brat, you know what I mean." She pauses, and when she speaks again it's so soft that I strain to hear her. "I wish Dad would have let Clara come home. She could have been your companion."

I freeze, concentrating on keeping my breathing steady so Isabelle doesn't see me freaking out inside.

"Yep," I say evenly. "It's a shame."

The truth is that my oldest sister Clara *could* have come home for a visit, but she'd chosen not to. I'd overheard Dad talking to her on the phone right after I'd come home from the hospital. He'd practically begged her to visit me. But she'd refused. In fact, she'd told him she'd rather die than step foot in this house or speak to me again. And she hasn't bothered to call or message me either, not once. Because she still hasn't forgiven me for betraying her.

"See you around, Alice."

The door closes behind Isabelle and I half-listen as her footsteps thud down the stairs, but in my head, I'm still thinking about Clara.

I'd spent my whole life practically worshipping my oldest sister. She'd pretty much raised me and Isabelle after Mom died. Dad had fallen apart, and it had taken years for him to be a parent to us again, so Clara had taken over even though she wasn't much older than us.

Sure, she was bossy and could be cruel. But she'd always protected me, even when I hadn't deserved it. Her only rule was that we sisters had to stick together no matter what.

That had been easier when I was little. But as I'd gotten older, I started to see that maybe Clara wasn't so perfect after all. That perhaps there was something a little disturbing about the way she treated people and the cruel things she did.

Finally, she'd taken it way too far. People, and horses, had been hurt after a series of mean pranks she'd pulled and I couldn't take her side anymore. And breaking our sister-code is something she will never forgive me for.

Part of me understands why she does the bad things she does, because every so often I can feel that thread of chaos running through me too. It's like a pulse of angry electricity zapping under my skin, making me want to smash things or hurt people. And to make bad decisions that I later regret.

Things like hide the fact that I *knew* there was something wrong with me long before they discovered the tumour, and I hadn't told anyone. I'd hidden the headaches, the blurry vision that came and went, and the dizzy spells from everyone until it was too late.

"If we had caught the tumour sooner then things might have been much different for you," one specialist had said, not bothering to mask his irritation and disgust. "The surgery would have been less invasive, and there are therapies and treatments you could have done to save more of your vision. I can't imagine why you wouldn't tell anyone. That was so irresponsible."

He was only the first in a long line of people to lecture me about that, as if I didn't already feel stupid enough. As if I wasn't the one now suffering. Nobody could understand when I tried to explain that I'd been too busy riding to get my eyes checked out.

And then there'd been that disastrous day, shortly after the surgery, when I'd crashed with Jiggs.

Jiggs is one of the best ponies I've ever ridden, but he's not easy. You have to ride him every second, channelling your breathing and controlling every inch of your body in order to keep him calm and get the best out of him or he will melt down and fall apart.

He and I fit together so well that I didn't see the harm in riding him that day where there was nobody around. I'd only planned to do flat work. The sun was blazing and I could see reasonably well. Or at least I thought I could.

Everything had gone brilliantly at first; if anything, Jiggs had acted even better for me than normal. More relaxed and happy. So, I'd figured, why not pop him over a small rail?

In hindsight, it was a terrible decision. Jiggs jumped the vertical but then plowed into the blue oxer and threw me right into the fence just as my dad and his fiancée, Tiffani, were driving past the ring.

Neither of us were badly hurt, but Jiggs had been rattled and wouldn't let anyone catch him for an hour afterwards. And even now, after weeks of turnout to decompress, he is still acting spooky and out of sorts. At this rate, nobody will ever want to buy him.

That minor accident had been enough for my dad. He grounded me and put the ponies up for sale that day. Mavis and True had sold right away, within days of them being listed. Somebody will eventually snap up Jiggs and then that entire part of my life will be over for good.

And yes, my dad already offered to buy me another horse someday, as long as it is a safe, boring plodder, but it isn't the same. The whole point of riding is the excitement, the adrenaline, and knowing that you have the best pony in the ring that you brought along yourself.

Riding a jaded old schoolmaster wouldn't be the same at all. Because what would even be the point?

"There is no point," I say out loud, flopping down on my bed again. The entire rest of my life stretches out in front of me like an endless stretch of grey. No excitement, no adventure. Just dull, unending boredom and *safety*.

I might as well not exist at all.

CHAPTER 2

SIDNEY

"Hey, Barb?" I hover outside the dingy office doorway, pressing my damp palms nervously together. "I'm sorry to bother you. It's about the ring."

Barb, owner of Happy Acres, the world's worst stable, doesn't bother to glance up from her oversized phone. She runs a finger slowly across the screen, grey ash drifting from the smoldering cigarette dangling forgotten in her other hand.

A smear of mascara sits under her left eye like an old bruise. Her short hair stands upright in a stiff halo and she's wearing a pair of vibrant pink leopard-print leggings. So, either she recently crawled out of bed, even though it's well past noon, or just made it home from the bar. Anything is possible with Barb.

"Go away, I'm busy," she snaps, not looking up.

I gulp and fix my gaze on the wall over her head, counting slowly downward from ten until I have my nerves under control.

Dozens of faded pictures cover the dusty walls. Most of the frames are layered so thickly with dirt and old spider webs that I can barely see the photos anymore. But I know what they are. Barb and her family had once bred fancy Quarter Horses and had shown all over North America. They were long-legged, elegant show horses with tails flowing past their hooves and freshly clipped coats. The pampered runway models of the western horse world.

Barb and her twin sister starred in half the photos; first as kids and then teenagers in heavy makeup and sparkly, bedazzled outfits, standing next to one impeccably bred horse after another. Both grinning at the camera while they held up their many ribbons.

I don't know what dramatic event made Barb into the snarly, depressed person she is now, but there is nothing happy or sparkly about her these days. A bitter alcoholic with a temper is more like it.

Across the room, a small heater whirs steadily, blowing hot air directly at the wooden desk, making the stacks of unpaid bills flutter. It's so stifling in here that I can barely breathe, which is a stark contrast to the nippy September weather outside.

Barb always complains that she's freezing. But that's probably because she survives solely on a diet of alcohol, animosity, and the many boxes of Pop-Tarts she keeps in her desk drawer.

"It will only take a minute." I finally push the words out, struggling not to inhale the awful stale smell of cigarette smoke and unwashed human.

Barb swears under her breath, but doesn't yell, so I plow onward.

"The ring needs to be harrowed. There are ruts. And rocks. One of the horses will get a stone bruise or injure a tendon It's a safety concern."

Basic stable management, really. I don't say that part out loud. This last, disastrous year has at least taught me to keep my mouth shut. Most of the time.

Taking a long drag from her cigarette, Barb finally looks

blearily at me, blinking hard like she's having trouble focusing. "If it's so much of a problem, then go take care of it yourself, *princess*. I'd hate for our humble ring to not meet your high standards."

Eyebrows raised, she locks her gaze on my custom leather boots, working her way upward to my tailored breeches and fitted Anky thermal jacket.

Under her withering stare, heat burns slowly up my neck and onto my cheeks. Barb makes no secret that she thinks I'm a spoiled, high-maintenance princess who complains about everything. But that couldn't be further from the truth. Yes, my gear is fancier than what the rest of the boarders at Happy Acres wear. But it's all I've got. They're leftover things from a much different, much happier, time in my life.

"The tractor that pulls the harrow died," I say, my voice coming out a squeak. "It hasn't worked in weeks. It needs to be fixed."

"You're treading on thin ice," she tells me, her lips curving in a humourless smile. "If you have a problem with the facilities, then you can *get out*. I've warned you before."

Underneath my nerves, anger flares in my chest, but I squash it down ruthlessly. *Don't make her upset. Don't make waves. We need this place.*

Barb watches me closely, eyes glittering in challenge, as if she knows exactly what I'm thinking. She's just waiting for me to snap back at her and give her the excuse she needs to kick me out for good.

Do it, a small, angry part of me urges, except that if Oriel and I get kicked out then we don't have anywhere else to go.

If it were up to me, we would both be back at perfect Capriole Farm where I'd spent my entire riding career, right until my life had exploded last year.

My old stable had been like a beloved second home to me, so the contrast between it and Happy Acres is like heaven and hell. Capriole had been immaculate, and Pablo, the owner, had overseen the care of the horses with an eagle eye. The ring was always perfect. The fence boards didn't sag and break, and the horses weren't left in dirty stalls for days.

Pablo would have never sat in a filthy, cluttered office smoking in yesterday's clothes when there were so many chores to be done.

Stop thinking about it, I tell myself firmly. *Pablo will never let you step foot in that place again after what happened. This is your life now, so you might as well get used to it.*

The absolute unfairness of it hits me all over again and for a second my lower lip trembles like I'm about to cry.

"Oh, for heaven's sake," Barb snarls, rolling her eyes. "Grow up. Get a few of the kids to hand-rake the ring if you're too precious to do it yourself. If they're desperate enough to ride, then they'll do it. Now get out, I'm busy. Don't bother me again."

She turns her back on me deliberately, holding her phone up close to her face as she swivels around in her chair. I've been dismissed.

"But..." I open my mouth in a last-ditch effort to make her care about this place, to care about the horses.

"Shut the door!" she bellows suddenly, making me jump. "You're letting the heat out."

I stumble backwards and slam the door shut, seething with a mixture of embarrassment and frustration. Why does Barb even stay at Happy Acres if she doesn't want to run the barn properly?

I march down the aisle, past the rows of crumbling stalls, not stopping until I'm outside in the fresh air.

"Well, that was a mistake," I say out loud. There is nobody around to hear me. All the horses have been turned out already. And the wild, unruly pack of barn kids that practically run this place in the holidays have gone off on a day-long trail ride. Only Archie, the orange barn cat, stretches out nearby, washing himself on the cracked concrete aisle. "I guess I should have just taken care of the ring myself."

Only the trouble with Barb is that anything you do can back-fire on you. She probably would have been equally annoyed if I'd gone ahead and dragged the ring without asking her first. You can't win with a completely irrational person like that.

But what to do about the ring now? I stare out over the parking lot, my gaze coming to rest on my little blue Audi wagon. *Yes, that might work.*

It is a beautiful car, although the blue metallic paint is already chipped in spots from driving the long gravel road to the barn every day. It has a glistening leather interior, heated seats, and best of all, it has a small hitch for towing things.

I don't technically own it since it's a lease, and I'm pretty sure that the dealership would not approve of me rigging up a rusted metal harrow to the tiny hitch and dragging it through a bumpy sand ring like I'm about to attempt. But I guess what they don't know won't hurt them.

They also don't need to know that I've learned how to stuff a bale of alfalfa in the hatch or pile a hundred pounds of bagged grain and shavings onto the back seat. It pretty much smells like a horse stable now and always has stray pieces of hay and shavings floating around.

My best friend Zara had flat-out refused to drive to school with me last year because she complained my car smelled like animals. At least that's one of the many lame excuses she came up with when she stopped hanging out with me so much.

"Sorry, girl," I pat the hood, feeling a twinge of guilt, "I know you were made for better things."

I slip inside, push the button to start the engine, and drive carefully around the rutted stable yard before stopping in the shadow of the towering, out-of-control manure pile that looms over the farm in a steaming mountain.

Most stable owners would make some effort to get rid of their extra manure, but not Barb. The little kids, who do most of the stall and paddock cleaning, have long given up pushing their heavy wheelbarrows to the top of the steep pile. So now the over-sized heap sprawls halfway across the yard, nearly as wide as it is tall. An eyesore that we all do our best to ignore.

The chain harrow is half-buried in the overgrown grass and I have to tug on it and give it a few kicks before it finally breaks free. I back the car carefully and then get out and drape the heavy chain over my tiny hitch.

"Come on little engine," I encourage, stepping firmly on the gas so that the car leaps forward, jerking the harrow behind it with a metallic rattle. The claws dig into rutted ground, the engine revs, and it is all I can do to keep the car moving steadily toward the ring. Once I hit the sand, it isn't nearly so bad.

I drive carefully in circles and lines, breaking up the compacted footing and making the ground soft again. There is something very satisfying about it; like creating a gigantic zen garden full of elaborate lines and curves. Even the half-rotted jumps and barrels dotting the ring look a little less shabby when I'm done.

Oriel is going to love this.

He is very picky about his footing and only does his best work when the ground is exactly to his liking. He'd ridden on Olympic quality surfaces all his life before his move to Happy Acres, so it is only natural that he expects the best.

I glance at my watch and groan. Harrowing, and my encounter with Barb, have taken longer than I expected and I now only have time for a quick ride before I need to get ready for work. Oriel is not the type of horse you can rush through his routine. At twenty years old, he is a bit set in his ways. And he is very particular that I don't neglect his grooming and warm-up time.

I grab his soft, padded leather halter from my locker and trek out to the big pasture to find him.

"Come on, handsome," I call as soon as I reach the gate. He already knows I'm here, so he won't be too far away.

Sure enough, off to the right I hear his rumbling nicker and then Oriel's big head pops up from behind a shrub, his thick black forelock tangled with sticks and greenery.

This is the one thing that Happy Acres has done right. When he's not in his stall, Oriel is turned out on fifty untamed acres with a herd of other horses.

At first, I'd been terrified that he'd get injured because the pasture is full of rocks, stumps and fallen trees. Lots of sharp things to get cut on or break a leg tripping over.

Also, the other horses are a feral mix of sizes and personalities and there is zero supervision for them out there. Sometimes they'll be running, kicking, and biting each other like a herd of wild mustangs, and it seems like a miracle that nobody gets badly hurt.

But it turns out that Oriel thrives running with a herd. He's not as stiff as he used to be. He's less spooky and is generally happier. And he rules over the small band of horses like a king, putting anyone who tries to mess with him in their place with a well-aimed kick or bite.

His newfound freedom is probably the single good thing that came out of our forced move.

"What have you gotten into this time, monster?" I laugh at the assorted bits of nature clinging to him.

Snorting, he strides toward me, his head swinging with each step. He's a solid, well-muscled guy, standing over sixteen hands with a thick chest, powerful hindquarters, and legs like tree trunks.

He is all black, or at least he used to be before his muzzle and ears had turned grey a few years ago. Our old coach, Elliot, used to call Oriel's white bits his frosting, and that's exactly what it looks like: icing on a cake. Grey strands sprinkle his dark mane and tail, but they don't make him look old. Instead, he looks even more like an exotic, fairy-tale horse.

He isn't the tall, willowy type of Friesian that you see pulling carriages. He is much stockier and more compact than that. But he has a nice, sloping shoulder, an elegant neck, and a powerful, confident way of carrying himself that makes people automatically turn to look at him when he swaggers by.

I'd fallen in love with Oriel the day I walked into Capriole for my first lesson. I hadn't gotten to ride him for another two years, but I'd always hung out with him when I could, slipping him carrots whenever his owner, Pablo, wasn't looking.

Eventually, I was allowed to take a lesson on him instead of one of the school horses, and then to lease him and finally, once Pablo realized how much I loved Oriel, I was allowed to buy him. I'd had to promise three things; that I would always take excellent care of him, that I'd never sell him, and that he would spend his days at Capriole Farm forever.

I'd already broken one of those promises, but I didn't intend to break the others.

My phone pings just as I clip Oriel into the cross-ties. And a little jolt of nervous energy shoots through me as I glance down at it. Only a few people send me messages these days. Most of my friends dropped me a year ago, shortly after the first scandal broke out. My best friend Zara had hung on a little longer, but eventually she'd disappeared, too. Now, the only one left is Zack. Kind of.

Do you forgive me for what I said last night? You make me so angry sometimes and then I lose my temper.

My fingers dig into the plastic phone case and I take a deep breath. I know Zack was probably just drunk when he'd sent those horrible messages, but it had still hurt. A lot. Last night, I'd been certain that I never wanted to speak to him again. So why is it such a painful relief to hear from him now?

I keep forgetting that you're not like the other girls. Don't be mad at me. I can't stop thinking about you. It kills me that we can't be together in real life.

A little more of my resolve weakens and I let out a sigh. The fact that Zack and I are in any sort of relationship, even a slightly toxic online one, is crazy. He's so out of my league that it's not even funny. We might as well be from different solar systems.

Come on, Sidney, I just wanted some pictures and videos to keep me going until we can be together. You're making a big deal out of nothing.

My fingers tighten on the phone again. Right there is the reason for the fight we'd had last night. Those damn videos. I know that some people have no problem firing off a few naked pictures and videos of themselves online, but it's not my thing. Even if it *was* my thing, this last year has made me extra wary of anything involving the media. Our family had been dragged through the mud by both the mainstream news and gossip sites. I couldn't risk giving them more ammunition. What if those photos accidentally leaked out? I'd tried to explain this to Zack, but he'd been livid when I'd said no.

It's a big deal to me, I type finally. *What you said to me last night was awful.*

I know. I was angry and I said some stupid things. It won't happen again. Forgive me? I'm working on a new song just for you.

Despite myself, I melt a little more. Zack writes the most beautiful poetry and music. He says that I'm his muse and that I inspire him.

Okay. I hesitate, wondering if I should say anything else to smooth this over. Maybe I had overreacted a little bit last night. *Talk to you tonight?*

Before I can see his response, Oriel abruptly nudges my arm, hard, and the phone tumbles to the ground, the case cracking loudly against the concrete.

"Whoa, buddy, that was a little unnecessary." I retrieve my phone and brush bits of hay and dust off the screen. "Wasn't I paying enough attention to you?"

Oriel snorts and bobs his nose, eyeing up the curry comb in my brush bag. Or maybe he smells the carrots hidden in there.

"Fine, you're right." There's no answer from Zack anyway, so I shove the phone in my pocket and turn my focus to my horse.

Oriel loves being groomed more than anything, and he sticks his head high in the air and leans into me as I move the brush in circles down his long neck.

He wriggles his upper lip, eyes half-closed in bliss as I work my way down to his shoulders and along his wide back.

The barn is, thankfully, empty. The place is usually packed with small children and young teenagers running around. Especially during the holidays. But today it is strangely silent.

Happy Acres attracts two types of people. Boarders like me who don't have the money to move somewhere better. And the children of neglectful parents.

During the holidays and after school, this place is basically a free daycare. Parents drop their kids off in the morning and then pick them up again at night, not having a clue what their children are up to while they run around completely unsupervised all day.

It's not like Barb is going to care if one of them accidentally breaks a leg or dies or something. Barely any of the kids wear helmets when they ride and some don't even wear *shoes* in the summer, let alone boots. They're allowed to roam around in a feral pack doing whatever they like.

As loud and annoying as they are, though, it's a good thing that they hang around because they are usually the ones doing all the feeding, filling water buckets, and turning out the horses. I am skeptical that Barb would remember to do any of these things if the kids weren't around.

When Oriel is clean and I fix his polo wraps in place, I pull a matching red saddle pad from my locker and smooth it onto his broad back, admiring the way it contrasts with his dark coat.

At Capriole, Pablo only permitted us to use white or black pads and polos whenever we schooled. So now, even though I can barely afford them, I like to pick out something pretty every few months to dress Oriel up. Sometimes it's the little things that keep you going when the rest of your life sucks.

"Don't you look handsome," I say, standing back to admire him once his saddle and bridle are in place. I snap a quick photo out of habit, not that I have anywhere to post it now. I'd had to shut all my social media down after the thing with my parents blew up. "Come on, buddy, we'd better get to work."

Oriel needs a slow warm-up at the beginning of each ride. At least fifteen minutes of walk on a loose rein while he stretches, then some relaxed trotting so he can poke along with his nose out, snorting and coughing and clearing his lungs. Then some easy lateral moves. Which is followed by a light canter, and then finally we can get into the more difficult work.

His grey-tipped ears prick when he sees the freshly dragged ring. He snorts in excitement, his neck curling into a tight arch, and he bears down on the bit impatiently. He knows fresh footing is good for galloping.

"Easy, friend," I say, smoothing his mane against his neck. "Pace yourself or you'll get hurt. You're not the young war-horse you think you are, and I can't afford to get the chiropractor out for you. Again."

I drop my feet out of the stirrups, letting my legs stretch down as Oriel settles into a powerful march. Gradually, I feel the weight sink evenly into my seat bones and my muscles relax. It's a good thing that Oriel needs the extra walk time, because it usually takes about that long for all the pent-up anxiety to drain out of me. My heart rate slows, my breathing deepens and I can feel my muscles unwinding one by one.

I haven't always been such a tense person. But, since the scandals broke so publicly last year, it's like I'm walking on eggshells all the time now.

My parents' lawsuits had gained a lot of nasty media attention, especially from that tabloid show, True Dirt. And my siblings and I had been caught in the cross-fire.

Nobody really blamed *us*, of course; it's not like my ten-year-old brother had anything to do with my parents' financial decisions, but that still didn't stop complete strangers, as well as people we had considered friends, from making the most awful comments online. And sometimes screaming accusations in our faces.

We'd had media vans camped outside for weeks, plus people peering in the windows and digging through our garbage. It was like my parents had been serial killers or something, not just involved in fraud.

The whole thing had been awful, and even though we'd long since been abandoned for juicier, more current, news stories, the situation had left me with a healthy dose of paranoia and anxiety.

Once I'm in the saddle, that all fades away. I forget about all the scary things that can go wrong. I think it's one of the few times I'm truly at peace anymore.

Oriel cuts his walk routine short on his own. He can't resist the lure of the freshly dragged ring, and he springs up into his ground-eating trot. It's all uphill, like a powerful wave rolling across the ocean, suctioning me to the saddle as he steam-rolls across the ring.

Oriel has never been an easy ride. His engine is always revving, the power always building. I could hardly sit his trot when I'd first started riding him and I'd had to learn how to accept his forward energy, to shape it and build it rather than shutting it down when it felt out of control.

"Good boy, go on," I say, barely shifting my weight before he plunges into a ground-shaking canter. That first stride always feels like he's left the earth completely, his shoulders rise up and up before he launches, and each great bound feels impossibly huge. I can't help but grin.

The world narrows down to just him and I, like we've been transported to another place where only the two of us exist.

I'm so focused on him that I don't notice the people standing by the gate at first. But when I do, it takes everything I have not to fall out of the saddle.

The first person is Valentine, one of the kids who spends practically every waking minute at the barn. She is usually underfoot, asking questions and following me like a shadow, so I'm surprised that it's taken this long for her to appear today.

But the second person... *No, it can't be.* It's like seeing a ghost. *Why has she tracked me down after all this time?*

Oriel's canter falters for a second, and I turn my focus back on him. My mouth has gone dry and I feel wobbly and cold all over.

The woman watches me with a small smile as she leans on the half-rotted gate.

Wearing breeches and boots like mine, her glossy hair pulled back in a high ponytail, is my old coach, Elliot.

CHAPTER 3

ALICE

From down the hill, our head coach Darla's angry bellows drift in through my open bedroom window, which is impressive considering that the indoor arena is not anywhere close to the house.

I can't make out the exact words, but I can imagine them.

More leg. Don't sit there like a useless lump. A monkey could ride better than you.

I sigh, fidgeting with the edge of the blanket. Even though Darla is probably a certified psychopath, I still really miss our lessons. They'd been a big part of my life and she'd helped me become the amazing rider I am...that I was.

"Oh, screw it, I'm going down there."

Who cared if I was technically grounded? I wasn't going to spend the rest of my life being locked in the house. And what would my dad punish me with if I broke my grounding rule? The ponies were the only thing I'd cared about, so there is literally nothing left anyone can take away from me.

I creep to the door, listening carefully to make sure there isn't anyone lurking nearby, before slipping into the hall.

I trail one hand outward to touch the polished log walls, orienting myself. I haven't told anyone yet, but this part of the house has become a nightmare for me. My depth perception is terrible now and the hallway lighting is the wrong mixture of bright spots and shadows, so I can hardly see anything at all.

The worst part is when I get close to the top of the stairs. There is always this precarious moment right near the edge where I can't see where the hall ends and the stairs begin. It's like walking out into a blurry void, and the fear of falling has nearly overwhelmed me more than once.

I keep this a secret though, because if I even hint to anyone that I'm afraid then they'll make me use one of those white canes for blind people or force me to give up my spacious bedroom upstairs for a smaller one on the first floor. Nope, never going to happen.

I shuffle forward, blinking, reaching out to feel for the handrail that I know is somewhere on the right.

"Two more inches that way," a quiet voice says and I leap backward, nearly jumping out of my skin, the image of myself crashing down those stairs imprinted on my brain.

"Trin, don't do that," I gasp, clutching my chest. "I hate when people sneak up on me."

"Sorry, I thought you heard me." Her small hand closes over mine and she places my fingers on the polished wooden railing before I can object. "It's right there. Are you sneaking out to the barn?"

"Maybe. Are you going to tell on me?"

"No, but you'd better hurry. Mom is in her office and Mrs. Pitts is scrubbing out the pantry, so the coast is clear. Want to come watch my lesson with Elliot?"

I bite back my sarcastic response to her innocent use of the word *watch,* because I am extra cautious about how easy it is to hurt her feelings. Which is the last thing I want to do.

I used to hate my stepsister Triniti. Or almost-stepsister since my dad's wedding isn't until June. But she has become one of my favourite people over the last year. I get along better with her than I do with my actual sisters. She might be half my age, but she is smart, funny, and as dedicated to horses as I was at her age. I really wish she wasn't going away to boarding school this winter. It's true she'll come home on some weekends, but it's still going to be lonely during the week. There is a part of me that wants to beg her not to go, but this school has a huge equestrian program and Trin is so excited that she gets to take her pony, Pearl, with her. How can I stand in the way of that?

"Yeah, I'll come watch your lesson."

Trin latches onto my free hand and takes the stairs with me one step at a time. I hate people helping me normally, but it doesn't bother me so much with Trin. Maybe because she doesn't make a big deal over things. With my dad and Tiffani there's always all this worry, sadness, and *disappointment* whenever they're around me. But Trin is just her natural self without all their drama.

The air outside is fresh and I feel a delicious sense of freedom as we sneak out of the house. Two weeks grounded, cooped up inside that stifling mansion, is almost more than I can stand.

"Want to drive?" Trin says as we reach the golf cart.

I'm tempted, but I shake my head. There will be too many witnesses around this time of day. Sneaking out while being grounded is one thing, but getting caught driving the golf cart again might be the thing that puts my dad over the edge and has us selling the farm and moving to a condo or something.

"No, it's all you."

She hums to herself happily as she fires the cart to life and we cruise down the hill toward the stable.

We can hear Darla yelling at some unlucky rider as soon as

we park in front of the barn. It seems to be her only tone of voice these days. And, as much as I hate to admit it, I'm sure we've lost some clients because of her.

Three Sisters actually has two stables on the property. Barn A, which is the posh one where the upper-level, wealthier boarders stay. And Barn B, which houses the beginners and the riders who either don't have the money, or the talent, to be truly competitive in the show ring.

Barn B is nice enough, of course, but Barn A is high class, with an indoor arena and a coach who knows how to win at all costs.

We've always had a long waitlist of people begging to board at Barn A, but this summer something happened that shifted things slightly. Oliver Kingsley, one of our most popular boarders, had made the unheard-of decision to move both his horses down the hill to Barn B.

It had been hot gossip at first but his defection had started a sort of chain reaction.

Oliver isn't the most brilliant rider, but he is friendly and well-liked by everyone and he's Josh Prescott's stepbrother, so that makes him automatically desirable. It didn't take too long before some of the younger boarders asked to move to Barn B, too. And then some of the older ones. Little by little, our clients have been slipping away.

"I'm so glad I don't ride with her anymore," Trin whispers as Darla bellows again. "Elliot and Anna are so much nicer."

"Yeah," I say with a sigh. "They're nice, but they don't produce results like Darla does."

The thing is that Darla is not *always* mean. When you're her star pupil, like I had been, she can heap on the praise and act like you're the best rider in the world. When everything is going her way, she can even be quite pleasant. She introduced me to top riders I might not have met otherwise and always kept an eye out for ponies and riding opportunities that would further my career.

Unlike my sisters, I've always preferred project ponies rather than ones that were already fully made. And Darla had found me top quality prospects that I could develop.

I'd assumed Darla was my friend as well as my coach. But the second my riding career came to a crashing halt; she basically dumped me overnight. She only visited me in the hospital once and even then, it was like she could hardly stand to look at me. Now she acts like I don't exist at all. Something I'm trying to pretend doesn't hurt like hell.

"Do you want to help me get Pearl ready, or wait outside here?" Trin asks carefully. She is probably the only one who knows how hard being in this barn is for me now.

"I'll come in with you," I say firmly. This is *my* family's stable, after all. It was built with my parents' money. And I don't intend to feel awkward and out of place in it.

The shadows close in as soon as we step inside, and I falter for a second, waiting for my eyes to adjust.

Trin subtly bumps her elbow against mine and I lean into her slightly, allowing her to lead me toward Pearl's stall without making it too obvious.

When my eyes adapt as well as they're going to, the barn looks like a shadowy version of its old self. I can't see colour in here but I can see outlines and contrasts. Enough that I can avoid bumping into anything and stay out of people's way.

Trin bustles around, getting her grooming supplies and chattering to her pony excitedly while I stand there, trying to feel like I still fit in.

My own ponies are all gone from Barn A. Even though Jiggs hasn't sold yet, he's been demoted to the new overflow paddocks behind the barn to make room for paying customers. I guess it makes sense since he's not in full work, and because it's easier for me to see things when I'm outside instead of in the dark barn. But it still feels like I've been kicked out.

I've lived and breathed this stable since I was a kid. I know every inch of it. I hate that I feel like a stranger here now.

"Hey, Alice, I didn't expect to see you here so soon." It's Ben, our barn manager, and I can hear the amused note in his voice. He obviously knows about the grounding and that the barn is supposed to be off-limits to me, but, luckily, he's also nearly always on my side.

"Are you going to rat me out?"

"I might look the other way." He laughs, leaning against the stall door next to me. "Jiggs is out on pasture, but I can bring him in to his paddock if you'd like a visit."

"No," I say quickly, "that's okay." The last time I'd snuck out to visit Jiggs it hadn't gone so well. He'd paced frantically around his paddock and avoided me completely. He wouldn't let me pet him and he didn't even want a carrot. It had been awful and even though I know that he's a horse and not a person, I can't help but think that he blames me for the accident somehow, and for abandoning him when we'd used to spend every single day together.

"All right," Ben says, "but since you're here, there's something I want to run past you."

"What?" My guard is instantly up. Since the surgery, everyone has been so full of well-meaning advice that I can hardly stand it.

"Your dad mentioned he was looking for a tutor for you. Elliot knows this girl who might be perfect, an old student of hers." He holds up his hand to stop me before I can argue. "She has a Friesian."

"Oh." My protest dies instantly because Ben has touched on one of my secrets. Something that I had spilled to him by accident one day when we'd been rehabbing my old pony Checkers together. I am a secret fan of Friesian horses. You know, the tall black ones with the flowing manes and tails and the high knee action that makes them look like they're always moving uphill.

I pride myself on being a practical, unsentimental sort of person, but I do have a few hidden weaknesses.

For example, sometimes, in the middle of the night when there are absolutely no witnesses, I use my tablet to watch horse movies. Or at least I *used* to before I went blind. Not documentaries or training videos. I mean the sappy, full of drama, completely unrealistic type that make you cry at least five times per movie.

I think I have literally seen every horse movie made, even going way back to the films that were in technicolour and the ancient ones in black and white.

One of my favourite retro films is a movie from the nineteen eighties called *Ladyhawke*. It's a fantasy and one of the main characters rides a Friesian named Goliath that I fell instantly in love with.

Anyway, since then I have secretly followed a bunch of Friesian breeders and riders online. I might be borderline obsessed, honestly, but that is something that only Ben and Trin know about.

"That's interesting," I say, keeping my voice as indifferent as I can make it. Ben knows me, though, and isn't fooled.

"Elliot thinks there's a slight chance his owner might do a part lease on him too. It wouldn't hurt to ask."

A tiny spark of hope flares in me before I squash it ruthlessly. I am not about to let anyone manipulate me into getting a tutor. Bribing me with a Friesian is low.

"Sorry, not interested," I say, even though I have to force the words out. "But thanks."

"All right." Ben sighs, but doesn't push it any further. He knows how stubborn I am once I set my mind on something.

At the other end of the barn, the arena door opens with a familiar, gentle thud, followed by the slow clopping of hooves coming down the aisle. Which means that Darla's lesson is over. For a second, I hold my breath, wondering if this time she'll stop and say hello, to laugh and joke with me like old times.

But, nope, I hear her boots banging up the stairs to the loft where the viewing area and the snacks are located. My heart constricts, and I put a hand to my chest, as if I can physically push back the hurt lodged there. Darla had been one of my mom's good friends growing up. That's why she'd gotten a job at Three Sisters in the first place. Having her here had always felt like part of Mom was around too. Now that feeling is all but gone.

"Hey, Alice."

I hadn't even heard the big horse stop in front of me and a prickly heat climbs up my neck when I realize who the rider is.

"Oh, hey, Josh," I say, stumbling a little over his name. And although I can't make out his perfect features anymore, I know every one of them by heart.

Tall, dark-haired, with brown, solemn eyes that study everything with a deep, intelligent gaze that pierces through me every time he looks my way. I know exactly why my sister Clara had been obsessed with him when she'd lived here. Although she'd never gotten him to fall under her spell like most guys do.

Josh rarely laughs or smiles, but when he does, it is like the sun opening on a cloudy day. And best of all, he is a brilliant rider who loves his horse, Hectic Electric, more than anything. They have this bond that all the other riders envy.

My attraction to him is completely one-sided. Josh has always been nice to me in a big-brother type of way. He just sees me as Clara's little sister, a kid who rides ponies. My brain knows that, of course. I'm not stupid enough to think he'd ever be interested in someone my age, but my heart is a complete traitor and lately I find myself sort of turning to mush whenever he's around.

"Um." I realize that I'm standing there, frozen like a statue. "Good ride?"

"Heck was great. Darla was.... Well, she was Darla."

I nod, not quite knowing what to say. Despite everything that's happened, I still feel disloyal talking behind Darla's back. I know not everyone appreciates her teaching style but she does know how to get results.

"Well, I should get this guy cooled out. It's nice to see you out and about, Alice. We need to get you riding again."

I fumble for some sort of intelligible answer as the horse clops past us down the aisle and heads outside. But the moment is gone.

"Alice, are you all right?" Trin asks from the nearby grooming stall where she's fussing over Pearl. "You have a funny look on your face."

"I'm fine," I snap, heat stinging my cheeks. "You concentrate on getting Pearl ready or you'll be late for your lesson with Anna."

I force myself not to glance in the direction Josh has gone. He is just another good thing I'm not going to have in my life. I should be used to disappointment by now.

CHAPTER 4

SIDNEY

"*S*idney!" Val shrieks, jumping up and down. "There's a lady here to see you. A *dressage* lady."

"I see that, Val. Thanks." My voice sounds high-pitched and wobbly, almost like I'm about to cry.

"Hello, Sidney." Elliot's smile is warm and familiar, and for a second, it's like no time at all has passed. "It's good to see you."

It's been over a year since I've seen her, or anyone from Capriole. And it's like being visited by a ghost. So many buried memories struggle to the surface, some good, but others I'd do anything to forget.

"Um, hi?" My voice is so small that it's barely audible. She doesn't *look* angry. She seems exactly like her old, smiling self. Like there's nothing at all odd about her showing up here out of the blue after all this time.

Maybe she's here to bring me back to Capriole, I think suddenly. *Maybe Pablo wants me and Oriel to come home. He's willing to forgive me. He's...*

"Pablo sold the farm," Elliot says quietly, studying my face. "He already moved back to Spain. He sold the horses."

"What?" All the air whooshes out of me at once. "He's gone? Without saying goodbye?"

"It was sudden." Her expression is sympathetic. "He felt it was time to make a change. He asked me to tell you in person, though. And to make sure you and Oriel are doing all right."

Crushing disappointment settles on my shoulders and that small bit of hope I've always clung to in the back of my mind shrivels and dies. There is no going back to Capriole Farms now. That dream is over.

"Oh." I bite my lip and look down at Oriel's glossy mane. "Are you working for the new owners, then?"

"No, they don't have horses. They're using the place to host events and weddings, I think. I haven't been at Capriole in a while though, Sidney. I left shortly after you did."

"You did?" This is news to me. Elliot had always been such a big part of Capriole that I couldn't imagine it without her. "Because of me?"

"No." She shakes her head. "It was time for a change for me too. I travel to people's farms to give private lessons and I also coach at Three Sisters a few days a week. Have you heard of it?"

"No." I absently scratch Oriel's withers, struggling to process all of this.

"My brother Ben works there. You remember Ben?"

I nod. Elliot and her brother had practically grown up riding at Capriole and, by the time I came along, Pablo had depended on them for everything.

Capriole had been a busy facility. Not only did Pablo breed and sell world-class Friesians, like Oriel, he also had a dressage lesson program that had a waitlist a mile long. I'd had to beg for nearly a year before he'd agree to take me on. He'd given classical dressage clinics all over the world and had even trained his horses for the movies occasionally. Without Ben and Elliot to keep things running, Capriole wouldn't have been able to function at all.

"Three Sisters is focused on hunter-jumpers mainly," Elliot goes on, "although I have quite a few dressage clients there now too. It's a fantastic place; top care with lots of pasture for the horses, an indoor, and they have an amazing system of trails."

"Sounds nice," I say wistfully, although anything seems nice compared to Happy Acres.

"You should come for a tour. We could have a coffee and catch up."

"Um, sure, that would be great," I lie. It sounds more like it would be an awkward and painful reminder of all the things I don't have anymore.

"I could come too," Val pipes up, looking back and forth between us eagerly. "I've heard of Three Sisters. It's fancy. And I love dressage. Are you a real coach? Barb doesn't let other coaches come here so Sidney has been teaching me…"

"I haven't," I interrupt quickly. "I'm not allowed to give lessons. I've just been giving her some tips."

"She's helping Diva and me to get to the Olympics," Val adds confidently, beaming widely at both of us.

"Something like that," I say, because who am I to crush a child's impractical dreams? "Val, can you let Elliot and me have a few minutes to talk in private?"

"I guess so." Her expression falls, and she scuffs the toe of her rubber boot into the dirt. "But I'd rather hang out here with you."

"Maybe next time." Elliot looks at her kindly. "Sidney and I have a lot to catch up on."

"All right," Val huffs, her shoulders sagging as she drags her way toward the barn as slowly as possible, glancing back at us mournfully over her shoulder every few steps.

"Are you really okay?" Elliot asks, the second the girl is out of earshot. She looks up at me solemnly. "I heard about your parents on the news…"

"Yes, our family is fine," I say quickly. "The media makes everything seem more of a big deal than it is. People have lawsuits and go bankrupt all the time. It's part of doing business."

"Hmmm. I meant you specifically, Sidney. I was surprised to hear that you're not going to university this year. I know how important that was to you."

Outrage and embarrassment surge in my chest. What is it with horse people knowing everything about your business? Who had I accidentally shared that tidbit of gossip with and how had it gotten back to Elliot? The vet? The farrier?

Of course, going to university was important to me. I'd only been dreaming about it since I was a kid. I loved to read; my room at home was packed so tightly with bookshelves that there was barely room for my bed. Not just because I could get swept up in a good story, but also because I loved the words themselves, their sounds, their shapes, and their origins.

Languages were like living things to me, and I longed to explore them. I was the person who translated old books into English for fun in my spare time. And I'd always imagined myself someday immersed in those giant, ancient libraries in Europe, being able to study to my heart's content.

But it's not in the cards this year. Even though my nanna had set aside an education fund for me, I still had Oriel to consider. I couldn't exactly go off to Europe now. I had to pay for his board and his feed, and take care of him every day. Even going to a local university would be hard if I had to work full time as well. And, while I knew that lots of people juggled jobs and school, my nerves weren't up to it right now. The stress would probably kill me.

"I'm not trying to pry," Elliot says quickly. "I came here today to check on you, and on Oriel. I knew you must be going through a tough time and I wanted to make sure that you know that there are people in your corner."

"Oh." I feel my cheeks get hot and a lump form in my throat.

For a second, I want to pour out the whole sordid story to her. Our family embarrassed so publicly, my friends abandoning me when things were at their worst. My conflicting thoughts about Zack. But I don't. I nod, biting my lip.

"Sidney, I've been worried about you ever since you left Capriole so suddenly. I sent you messages last year, but I never heard back."

"I know." I look away, clenching my teeth. The way Oriel and I had left Capriole Farms was so mortifying that I can hardly think about it now, even over a year later, without feeling sick.

I'd been away visiting my gloomy nanna in Calgary when it had all gone down. I didn't know anything about what was happening until it was too late. And Oriel had already been dumped unceremoniously at Happy Acres.

Nanna is my grandmother on my father's side, and she's ultra strict and religious. Which is weird, because my dad is the complete opposite. She doesn't believe in technology, so she'd confiscated my cell phone and tablet the second I'd arrived at her condo so that we could spend *quality* time together. There hadn't been much quality, though. She spent nearly the whole time badmouthing my parents and telling me how my family was going to hell if we didn't change our ways. And when she wasn't doing that, she was watching British soap operas nonstop. The entire week had been awful.

But I didn't realize how awful until I'd reached the airport to fly home and had discovered dozens of angry messages from Pablo. That's how I learned that a bunch of crazy things had happened in that short week I'd been away.

My parents' many shady business deals had finally caught up with them. A lot of their assets had been seized, including things like my dad's luxury car collection and some of our household furniture. And my parents had moved Oriel out of his home, away from everything he'd known, and deposited him at Happy

Acres, where the board was cheap enough that I could pay for it myself.

When I'd found out, I'd gone completely ballistic.

"I don't understand what the problem is," my mom had said blankly when I'd confronted her in hysterics. "You get to keep the horse, don't you? That last barn was outrageously expensive and you wouldn't believe the things that awful man, Pablo, said when he called me. He was *shouting*. You'd think we'd committed a crime by moving our own horse to another barn."

Imagining the scene made me burn with shame every time I thought of it. Pablo had bred Oriel, he was part of their family, and he'd only been sold to me with the understanding that he'd live his life out there at Capriole.

It wasn't until later that I learned the full horror of the situation. The five months of bounced board cheques that we still owed Pablo, and the fact that the trailer had showed up and carted Oriel away while everyone was at a show. Nobody even knew where he had gone at first or if he had been stolen.

My parents had been completely oblivious, of course.

"Just think of all the hours you spent at that barn working for that man for free, Sidney. Really, he should pay *us* instead of being so concerned over a few months of late board money. An attitude of gratitude would have gotten him a little further in life than being a stable owner, that's for sure."

"Sidney, are you all right?" Elliot is looking up at me with concern.

"What?" I shake my head to clear it of the old painful memories. "Yes, sorry."

Oriel has drifted right up against the gate and Elliot rubs his face gently, watching me out of the corner of her eye.

"This guy looks good," she says quietly. "You've been keeping him in decent shape. How are his feet doing?"

"Er." I glance down at his slightly too-long hooves and bite my lip. "I booked the farrier for next week. We tried to stretch his shoeing cycle out a little, but his hooves grow too fast."

"I remember that about him. Do you still have his gel pads on?"

"Of course," I say, not admitting that we tried him without the protective hoof pads for a few weeks, but he'd been much too sore without them and we'd had to put them back on. Which was unfortunate because they cost me seventy dollars extra, on top of the cost of his regular shoes, every time the farrier comes. "He's my horse, Elliot. I know how to take care of him."

"I know you do," she says quickly. "You're right. I should stop snooping. I've just been worrying about you. Are you working right now?"

"I work nights at a restaurant," I say stiffly.

"Hmm, not what I pictured you doing."

"Well, I like it. Look, it was nice seeing you, but I need to finish my ride."

"Okay, I won't keep you. I only wanted to let you know that I'm still here if you need me, Sidney. Here. Take my card. I have a new coaching website you should check out. And I'm happy to give you a couple of lessons on the house if you'd like. For old times' sake."

"Thanks." I take the card from her and stuff it in my jacket pocket without looking at it. I miss taking riding lessons. I've always loved to learn and improve myself. But even if I *could* afford lessons now, Barb is too territorial to let outside coaches teach at Happy Acres.

Oriel reaches out with his nose and nudges the fence next to the gate, causing one of the rotten boards to tumble free and hit the ground with a thud.

I cringe with embarrassment. Stuff like that happens all the time here because the entire place is falling apart. But why did it have to happen in front of Elliot?

"This place needs a good overhaul, doesn't it?" Elliot laughs, pulling the board off to the side to sit with the others piled in a heap nearby. "I remember it back when it was one of the fanciest barns around."

"You do?" I say in surprise. I can't imagine Happy Acres looking anything other than decrepit.

"Yep, I went to a couple of clinics here back in the day. One of the old owners' daughters is a coach at Three Sisters now. Darla."

"You mean Barb's sister? I didn't know she lived nearby."

"Yep. I don't think they get along very well. Darla is a successful coach in the area. Her students win quite a bit."

"Huh," I say thoughtfully, wondering if Darla is as awful as Barb.

"It's kind of sad to see this place falling apart, though. Pretty soon there won't be much left to salvage. It's almost not safe for the horses." She looks dubiously at the rotten fence and shakes her head.

"It's fine," I say quickly. "It's not fancy, but there's a huge pasture and a herd of horses that Oriel loves. He's happy here." That last part comes out sounding defensive, but I can't help it. If only she knew how hard I work to make sure Oriel is taken care of.

"Oh, I can see that he's happy." She looks at me kindly. "The question is, are *you* happy?"

I stare at her, not knowing how to answer that. Of course, I'm not *happy*. Except for Oriel, the rest of my life is a sinking ship. I'm barely staying afloat.

My silence must be answer enough because she nods like I've confirmed something and clears her throat.

"So, I know this is a bit of a long shot, but I might know of a job that could solve a few of your problems."

"What kind of job?" I ask cautiously.

"Well, it's complicated. The owner of the barn where I teach has a daughter who could really use a friend right now. She's lost most of her vision and her dad is looking for a companion, a sort of tutor, to spend some time with her this winter, so she's not alone all day. And it would be nice if it's someone who is horsey."

"She's blind?" I feel a flicker of interest. "Is she in a program like at Pablo's?"

Pablo's little sister back in Spain had been born blind and had loved riding, so he always had a soft spot for helping visually challenged riders. Every year he'd run a short program to connect people with vision loss with horses. And some of those riders had stayed on as his students.

Elliot makes a face. "Alice is temperamental and isn't the best at taking advice from anyone. When she was fresh out of the hospital, she rode without permission and crashed a jump badly. So, her dad put all her ponies up for sale."

"Wow, that seems harsh."

"Well, I can't say that I blame him entirely. Those were some high-octane ponies, and she wasn't willing to slow down and change the way she rides. She was in danger of breaking her neck if she continued like that. Not that she cared. Her dad wasn't willing to take the risk."

"Fair enough. Why me, though? I'm not that great with kids. And you helped with Pablo's program more than I did. Why can't you help her?"

"She's not my biggest fan, honestly." Elliot laughs and shakes her head. "And she hates dressage with a passion. I'm the last person she wants helping her."

"Okay, but you think I can do something?"

"Well, you and Oriel. Ben told me she has a thing for Friesians, so I thought of you right away. Maybe you'd consider doing a part-lease on him down the road?"

"No," I say quickly, laying a protective hand on his neck. "No way. Never. Besides, he'd be too much horse for her."

"She's an excellent rider," Elliot presses on. "And he's powerful but he's also steady and sensible. And they'd probably pay you very well for a lease. It might help you out with money, so you didn't have to struggle so much."

"I'm not struggling," I say quickly. "Oriel and I are doing fine."

To her credit, Elliot doesn't argue.

"Could you do me the world's biggest favour and just come see the stables?" she begs. "No pressure. We can have a visit and a tour of the farm. We could go right now if you like."

"I have to work tonight," I say, a little reluctantly, because now I sort of want to see this place that she loves so much. And it wouldn't hurt for me to have a backup plan if they end up cutting my hours at the restaurant like they are always threatening to do. "Would tomorrow work?"

"That would be great. I teach there in the morning, but I can come get you around lunch time. You could get a feel for the place, anyway."

"All right. I'll do it."

"It's good to see you, Sidney," she says, reaching out suddenly to squeeze my kneecap. "I'm glad to see that you and Oriel are doing well."

She lets go abruptly and turns away. "See you tomorrow."

I stare after her, feeling a whole mixture of emotions. Pity for the blind girl who lost her ponies, horror at the thought of ever letting anyone else ride Oriel, and a desperate longing for Elliot to come back and sweep me away to the way life used to be.

CHAPTER 5

ALICE

"Come on, Alice, we're going to be late," Trin calls, halting Pearl on the driveway.

My dad had hung around the house all morning so it had been a bit of a challenge to sneak out this time, but it's worth it. I want to spend as much time with Trin as possible before she and Pearl head off to boarding school. Even if it means suffering through her boring dressage lesson with Elliot.

"Okay, okay, I'm coming."

Pearl nickers to me as soon as I get close. Despite being much too quiet and well-behaved for my tastes, she is a nice, fancy pony. She's the colour of buttermilk, with huge dark eyes and long lashes. She has cute little hooves and a fluffy mane and tail. A perfect kid's pony.

I reach out and pat her shoulder affectionately, glad that she's taking care of Trin. The one good thing about having a well-trained pony, instead of a project, is that you can relax and enjoy yourself instead of having to work so hard.

Here in the bright sunshine, my vision is much better and I almost feel normal. If I tilt my head and move my eyes in a sweeping motion, I can see the wide driveway and the grass, the fences, and the sky. The colours are diluted, a little like water colours or pale stained glass. I can see Pearl's head bobbing along beside me and the shapes of the horses who are grazing closest to the fence.

The sun is on my face and the birds are calling overhead. Pearl snorts contentedly beside me, and I sigh with happiness. For a second, I feel like everything will be okay after all, because this is where I belong.

That is, until we reach the ring.

"Hey, Alice. We heard you were grounded. We heard about the ponies. Can you really not ride at all? Your dad is so mean. Sorry, sorry, sorry."

Voices surround me on all sides and I'm suddenly in the middle of a flock of little girls on ponies.

"You didn't tell me it was a group lesson," I mutter, reaching out to clutch the fence in front of me. I feel like they're crowding too close, that one of these stupid children is going to run me over with their fat, useless ponies and crush me to death.

I have never, *ever* in my life been afraid around horses, so the fact that I feel even a spark of anxiety now has me going straight from fear into rage. Which is an emotion I'm much more comfortable with.

"All right, girls, into the ring," Elliot's voice rings out, her tone firmer than usual.

As soon as they're gone, I exhale slowly, gripping the wooden top rail until my fingers ache.

It was a mistake to come down here. I should have stayed in the house.

I don't know how long I stand there, frozen, but gradually I notice the sounds in the ring again; Elliot calling out instructions, the thud of hooves on sand, the huffing of the kids trying to catch their breath and their laughter.

I hadn't believed it when the doctors told me that some of my senses would get better to compensate for my sight loss, but it's kind of true. I mean, it's far from having super powers or anything, but I can hear many more detailed sounds than I had in the past. Or maybe I'm paying more attention now. My sense of smell is better too and sometimes I can sort of *feel* when people are near me or looking at me. It's weird and interesting, but not interesting enough to make up for me going blind. Nothing will make up for that.

"Hey, Alice," Elliot says suddenly, looming up in front of me. I hadn't even realized she'd moved to my end of the ring. "I spoke to your dad last night."

Oh, here it comes, I think in frustration. *Another sales pitch.*

"Don't bother. I'm not looking for a tutor, Elliot," I say, my simmering anger ratcheting up another notch. The whole reason that I stayed home from school this year is so that I didn't have to deal with people.

"Well, one of my old students could use a job." Elliot goes on as if I hadn't spoken. "She's had a rough year and is taking time off before going to university. She's nice, smart, and might be a good match for you."

"She sounds boring," I snap, just to be annoying, and because this conversation is making me uncomfortable.

I'm not sure why people think I'm interested in any sort of learning. I'd never planned to attend university like my sisters, because my life goal was to ride on the Olympic team and have a career with horses.

The only reason I'd put up with school at all was because of my special extracurricular activities. My dad doesn't have a clue about any of this, of course, but I'm proud to say that I had single-handedly run my entire school through a mixture of blackmail, intimidation, and bribery. And I'd had an entire underground network for buying and selling contraband, fixing failing grades, and dealing with problem students. I'd commanded my inner circle like a general leading an army. Even the teachers were afraid of us. It had been brilliant while it lasted, but I'm not stupid enough to think that life wouldn't be drastically different if I went back. Now that I have a fatal flaw, a weakness, those people would eat me alive. I'd be a bottom-feeder like all the other losers. No thanks.

"She's really nice," Elliot says. "And Oriel was an upper-level dressage horse in his time. Of course, he's older now so needs to slow down a bit."

"Oh, I get it," I say, gritting my teeth. "He's old and washed up so he'd be perfect for pathetic, blind me, right?"

Elliot takes a breath and lets it out slowly through her nose. "You know that's not what I'm saying. He's a brilliant horse. He's a Friesian."

She turns toward me expectantly, but I keep my expression indifferent. Obviously, Ben had spilled my secret to her, but I won't give her the satisfaction of seeing me react.

"Sorry, a what?" I say, sounding as disinterested as possible.

"You know, a Friesian. The old trainer I worked for used to breed them, so when Ben mentioned you liked the breed, I thought maybe I could see about arranging a half-lease on Oriel if you were interested."

"Oh, *those* things." I turn my head as a pony trots by, listening to the familiar thud-whoosh of the sand under its hooves. "I guess I might have liked them when I was a kid or something. Before I got into jumpers. I don't remember."

All lies. But I can't have annoying Elliot, of all people, knowing my weak spots.

"Oh," she says, sounding disappointed. "Darn it. I thought it would be perfect. Still, she might work out as a tutor. Your dad said..."

"He says a lot of things," I interrupt. "Look, I know you think you're helping, but I don't need your charity. I can handle this myself."

She's silent for a moment and I hold my breath, half-hoping that she'll start arguing with me. These days I can always use a good fight to cheer me up.

"All right, well, you let me know if you change your mind," she says. "I have to get back to my lesson. See you around, Alice."

And then she's gone and all that combative rage swirling inside me has nowhere to go. I stand there, simmering for a second before it all drains out of me, leaving me feeling limp. And a bit stupid for losing what might have been a good opportunity.

I should have just agreed to meet the dumb horse, I think with a sigh. *Why do I always have to fight about everything? At least the Friesian would be something different and interesting to think about.*

Part of me wants to call Elliot back and apologize, and to ask her nicely to introduce me to this girl and her horse. But the other part of me knows I'll never do that. It's too much like giving in. Like losing.

And I never lose.

Or at least I never used to.

CHAPTER 6

SIDNEY

I drive as fast as I dare toward home, wanting nothing more than a nice hot shower before I head to work.

But, less than two minutes into my drive, the car begins to ring.

"Darling!" my mom's voice blares through the car speakers, making me jerk sideways, the car wheel slipping through my fingers. Swearing, I fumble with the volume and get myself back in my lane.

"Mom, tone it down. I nearly drove off the road. I'm on my way home now."

"Well, that's what I'm calling about, sweetheart. I just had another unpleasant phone call with the dealership. There's been a bit of a misunderstanding about your car lease, and they are being completely unreasonable."

"What do you mean? I gave you the lease money last week. Didn't you pay them?"

"Oh, I'm sure it's a minor accounting error of some sort. It will take your father a few days to sort it out. So, it's best that you don't come home right away. I mean, *you* can come home, of course, but not the car. It's safer if you just leave it a few blocks away and then walk."

"Right." I sigh heavily, glancing at my saddle in the back seat. I'd gotten in the habit of bringing it home with me every day after I'd caught some of the barn kids climbing all over it. Now I will have to carry it all the way home. "Um, okay."

"Only for a week or so until things calm down," she says reassuringly. "Hurry home. We're having a family meeting. I made pasta for dinner."

"Okay, but I have to work..." The line disconnects with a sharp click, leaving me seething with frustration.

My parents are Nora and Ned Jones, the real-estate royal couple, and self-improvement gurus, whose hundred-watt grins have been plastered across every bus, park bench, and billboard in the city at one point or another. They were the top realtor team in our area for six years running and had sold fancy houses to a lot of famous people over the years. And they also ran all these expensive workshops and seminars that teach people how to get rich quickly.

Our family had once enjoyed the type of low-key local fame that got us free dinners at fancy restaurants and low-interest loans on our luxury cars. Now we probably couldn't even get a reservation in *any* restaurant even if we begged.

The collapse of their empire had started over a year ago with the Evergreen Towers scandal.

Evergreen Towers was a massive upscale condo project that a lot of wealthy people had bought into. The fancier corner units cost well over a million dollars.

Unfortunately, the building began crumbling as soon as people moved in. The roof leaked, the pipes inside corroded and snapped, the elevators broke down and the fire department had to rescue people. On and on until finally the city declared it was not fit to live in at all and everyone had to move out.

During the investigation, they uncovered that a lot of the building hadn't been built to code and most of the inspections should never have passed. Words like bribery, falsified documents, and fraud started getting thrown around.

My parents immediately folded the development company they co-owned and declared bankruptcy. Their rented offices emptied overnight and Ned and Nora went on a month-long trip to the Caribbean until the dust settled.

There was no money left to give back to the people who had bought condo units. And, although some residents had been rich enough that they'd recover, a fair number of owners had lost their retirement savings and were left badly struggling.

And the worst part, the awful part, was that one senior, a man in his nineties named Tom, had jumped from his fifth-floor balcony rather than face homelessness. And he had left a note blaming both my parents specifically.

The media went nuts. There was a criminal investigation and multiple lawsuits were launched. And it didn't take long for angry people to start digging into my parents' *other* companies, looking for more sketchy things. And, unfortunately, for us anyway, they found lots. Unpaid loans, fraud, tax evasion, money laundering and embezzlement.

The complicated legal battle would probably stretch out for years. So far, my parents had managed to avoid jail time, but it was always hanging over their heads.

Contrary to the garbage that's posted on the internet, especially on that online gossip show True Dirt that always has it out for us, my parents aren't completely evil.

In fact, they're the type of charismatic people that others are instantly drawn to. They're charming, funny, clever and can sell anything to anyone. As parents, they never disciplined us or made a bunch of silly rules for us to follow. They generally let us run our own lives without interfering. Sometimes, I think they forget we exist at all.

The downside is that they are both obsessed with being rich and they don't let much stand in the way of that. They are not afraid to take the huge risks that scare the pants off most people. Their lives are like roller coasters, either way up in the sky or crashing to earth. Neither of which bothers them at all; they both love the thrill.

Their crazy lifestyle has allowed my siblings and me some really nice things over the years. Fancy houses to live in, housekeepers, a revolving string of nannies, and nice cars. They'd bought me Oriel and paid for board and lessons for years, so I am hardly in a position to complain now.

I have very mixed feelings about my parents, honestly. I love them, but there is no doubt at all that they're guilty of most of the charges against them, even though they'd deny that to their last breath.

I only wish that the fallout from Evergreen Towers had affected them more, that maybe they'd be so wracked with guilt and remorse that they'd change their ways.

But, nope, my parents haven't let anything about our current disaster slow them down one bit.

Instead, my dad had written a new book, *Hustling in the Hurricane*, and they'd both thrown themselves into launching their new company, Manifest Now, which is an empowerment and financial life-coaching business that teaches people how to use their minds to get rich. Nothing keeps my parents down for long.

I find a spot by the park a few blocks away from home and hurry down the street with my saddle weighing down my arm. I now only have a little over an hour to get to work. The Shrimp Shack is ten minutes away from home, but I still have to shower and get dressed in my uniform once I've eaten. I should be able to make it there on time if nothing else slows me down.

I am in such a hurry that I almost don't notice the large For

Sale sign on our front lawn until it is practically right in front of me.

I skid to a stop, my heart sinking. I'd known this day was coming, but it still feels way too soon. Yes, our house is oversized and pretentious, but I really love it. The floors are marble and there are vaulted ceilings and enormous windows that let in the light. We have a massive kitchen, a floor-to-ceiling stone fireplace in the living room, and a huge backyard with a big indoor pool that has a fake-rock slide and a little waterfall at one end.

Before we'd moved in four years ago, Mom had hired a professional decorator to pick out all the art and furniture so the whole place looks like something out of a magazine. Or at least it used to before we had half of our things repossessed.

"Hey, what's with the sign?" I call as I push open the front door. "Nobody told me we were listing the house."

Claws clack excitedly down the marble hall toward me, accompanied by a huffing, snorting, choking noise like the sound of a freight train leaving a station.

"Slow down, Beans." I wince as he skids around the corner and gallops toward me, his hind end travelling faster than his front. He slams his round little body into my legs, his wide face splitting open into a delighted, tongue-lolling grin. "Take it easy, buddy. Catch your breath."

He is a questionably bred, geriatric French bulldog that my parents had brought home from a fundraiser when I was a kid. I think my mom thought that a cute puppy might look nice on their promotional material. But it only took a couple of weeks until they'd gotten bored with him and had handed his care over to me.

He'd started out a handsome chocolate brown colour with brindle stripes, but now he is almost completely grey and his little body has become potato-shaped and lumpy.

Even though he is old, wheezy and has horrible gas that can clear a room, he is my best friend next to Oriel.

Beans wriggles his way down the hallway after me, puffing and snorting in happiness. I head toward the kitchen, where I know the counter will be stacked with take-away cartons and wine bottles. When my mom says she's *making dinner*, what she really means is that she's ordering it from a restaurant.

"Hello, dear," Mom calls excitedly as soon as she catches sight of me. Her cheeks are flushed and her eyes sparkle unnaturally brightly. "We're having a celebration. Your father and I have thrilling news."

"Does it have anything to do with the sign on the lawn?" I ask, glancing over at my younger siblings.

Eden meets my gaze coolly and shrugs, no trace of emotion on her carefully made-up face. But my brother is hunched over his plate with his shoulders up around his ears. His face is beet-red and I can tell that he's trying not to cry.

All those years of winning pageants and acting in commercials have taught Eden to show only the emotions she wants you to see, no matter how she feels on the inside. Leo, on the other hand, is the complete opposite. Thoughts and feelings flicker across his face with zero filters. He goes through life like a defenseless baby snail without a shell, getting squashed by everything.

"Partly. But more importantly, there are fantastic things happening for Manifest Now. We'll wait for your father to share the good news. He's still in the shower, so eat your dinner and then we'll have a quick family meeting."

Great, I think grimly, putting my saddle over the back of a chair and filling my plate with the delicious-smelling pasta. *At least it can't be as bad as last time.*

The previous big family meeting was over a year ago when this whole disaster had happened. When the bank and other shady creditors had repossessed a lot of our stuff and I'd been dealing with Oriel's move to unhappy Happy Acres.

Finally, my dad comes trotting down the stairs in his bare feet, still rubbing his damp hair with a towel.

"Sorry I'm late. Nora, have you filled them in?"

"No, I was waiting for you to share the good news." She picks up her wine glass and downs it in one gulp before instantly pouring another.

I narrow my eyes at her, because despite the fake smile that never leaves her face, she looks nervous. And that's never a good sign.

"All right, team." My dad claps his hands together and fixes us with his megawatt smile, the one he uses when he's trying to sell something dubious for a lot of money. "We've had a bit of a bump in the road this year, but things are looking up. Your mother and I have secured a fantastic opportunity to launch Manifest Now to the next level. We are on our way to a new adventure in prosperity. Does anyone want to guess where this success-train is heading?"

There is complete silence while we all stare at him. I shove another forkful of pasta into my mouth.

"No? Well, I'll tell you then. We're going to Vegas!"

More silence. Just the slow scraping of Leo's fork across his plate.

Both our parents are staring at us as if they expect us to leap up and do a cheer or something.

"Vegas!" my dad says again in the same excited voice as if we hadn't heard him the first time.

"The land of sun and fun," my mother adds helpfully, "where the city never sleeps and the party never stops. While the market is dead here, real estate is booming there. And so is the self-improvement landscape. It is an ocean of opportunity ready to be sailed."

"Las Vegas is in the middle of the Mojave Desert," Leo says flatly, dropping his fork with a clatter and pushing his half-eaten food away. "There *is* no sailing."

"That's right, slugger," Dad says jovially, "it is a vast desert of opportunity. And it's about to be our new home. We move in a week."

"You already bought a house? In Las Vegas?" My mind is whirling, already clicking away, calculating the cost of shipping a horse over twenty hours away. "What about my job? And my friends?"

Not that I have any friends to miss me right now.

"Well, it's a rental." Dad clears his throat, his smile dimming slightly before brightening again. "It's a new condo in an upscale development right in the vibrant heart of downtown. It's the next rung on our golden ladder to success, Sidney. I can feel the shift in our fortunes. Our time has come."

He glides his hands through the air like he's some sort of magician finishing a trick and looks at me expectantly. There is a small part of me that wants to get caught up in their excitement, that wants to believe in them like I did when I was a little kid. I used to think that they were magic, that they could do anything. I hadn't realized until last year that what they called *being good entrepreneurs* was what other people called lying.

"I have school starting next week," Leo says in a small voice. "And astronomy lessons on the weekends. I paid for them with my own money."

"Sorry, champ." Dad ruffles Leo's hair in the way my brother hates, then gives his shoulder a hearty thump. "I'm sure there are astrology lessons in Vegas you could take. Or maybe you'll find new, more exciting things to do when we get there. Maybe something outdoors, like swimming or hiking, so you can get some colour on your skin. You're looking a little pale there, partner."

"Astronomy, not astrology," I correct him. "And Leo is allergic to the sun, remember? He gets hives."

"Right. Well, maybe that will go away with more exposure when we move to the desert. Mind over matter, son. That's all it is."

Leo pushes his glasses up his nose and carefully flattens his ruffled hair back in place. "That is not scientifically…"

"I'm moving in with Patrice then," Eden interrupts. She sits very still and upright with her hands folded on the table in front of her. Her face, looking much older than her fourteen years under the layers of makeup, is impassive, but her eyes glitter with anger.

I don't much like Eden's talent manager, Patrice. She has a fake Southern accent, manicured nails about four inches long and bleached blond hair that she keeps teased up into a shellacked halo around her head. She has two kids of her own who also act and do the pageant thing, and they'd pretty much adopted Eden into their lives back when she was still in kindergarten and starting out.

"Oh, darling, don't be silly. You belong with your own family. We're on this adventure together."

There is something insincere in my mother's voice and when she exchanges a small, triumphant look with my dad I realize, with a sudden shock, that not only are they *not* surprised at Eden's announcement but that they are relieved about it.

"No," Eden says flatly, "I have acting jobs to do this winter. I signed contracts. I need to stay here."

"Well." My dad clears his throat, struggling not to smile. "I don't think we should stand in the way of your career, Eden. I admire your hard work and dedication."

"Sure." Eden doesn't look at me or Leo. She pulls her plate toward herself and begins to eat in small, measured bites.

"I know it's overwhelming." My mom frowns over at where Leo is sitting, red-faced and blotchy, his lower lip trembling. "But change doesn't have to be bad. It's exciting. A new life. New friends. Time to shake off the old and embrace new beginnings."

"I don't want new friends," Leo says, sniffling. "I like the ones I have."

"So, what am I supposed to do?" I ask. "How do I get Oriel to Vegas? Are there even places to keep a horse there?"

They exchange another glance and then my dad turns his beaming smile on me full-force.

"Sidney, you're looking at this from all the wrong angles. This is an opportunity of a lifetime. As I always say in our Manifest Now workshops, *Sometimes, to move forward, you must shed off the dead weights that are holding you down.* Having attachments to material things is not how we get things done. You must stay mobile in this world in order to surf the thrilling wave of change. Otherwise, you'll get swept under. See?"

"Are you saying that Oriel is dead weight? You want me to sell him?" I honestly can't tell *what* he's saying half the time when he's making a sales pitch like this. It's like he's speaking a different language.

"Well, if you *wanted* to come with us, you could find him a lovely retirement home someplace." My mom waves her hands in the air like she is constructing an imaginary grassy field far, far away. "A place in the country where he can frolic around being a horse. Then you wouldn't have to work at that awful shrimp place and come home all sweaty and smelling like seafood. You could just have fun being a teenager; going to the mall and hanging out. You would have had to sell him eventually, anyway, when you go away to school."

"I am never planning to sell Oriel," I say flatly. "He's family."

From the corner of my eye, I see Eden lift her head, watching me while she eats.

"You *might* consider spending this year discovering new things outside of the horse world," my mom continues. "We could always use help with Manifest Now. You could be the head of our Youth Recruitment Team if you wanted to. You're such a pretty girl when you're cleaned up. I bet Eden could give you a few tips on how to enhance your assets. A girl your age should have loads of boyfriends trailing after her."

Eden's gaze meets mine and I see the corner of her mouth twitch.

"Sidney doesn't need real boyfriends. She has her fake internet boyfriend that she lusts over every night."

"Ugh, I do not, Eden. It's not like that."

She raises her eyebrows and her smirk gets even bigger.

"Oh, yeah, I forgot. You have a *spiritual* connection. He writes you *poetry*. He's not just using you for..."

"Girls," my father breaks in before I can snap back at her. "We're trying to have a serious family meeting here. Sidney, your mother and I understand that you are probably ready to spread your wings and fly in your own direction. We get that and we respect your choices. To tell you the truth, the condo layout is a little smaller than we'd like. We thought maybe you'd like to spend this next year living with Nanna. There are lots of horses in Alberta, from what I hear."

Mom takes another large sip of wine and my father busies himself getting a plate of food.

There is a moment of silence, only punctuated by Leo's quiet sniffles.

"Nanna's building is for seniors only," I say slowly. My mind is trying to catch up with everything that is happening, but it's not quite there yet. "And they don't allow pets. Unless you were planning to take Beans with you to Vegas?"

I glance down at Beans, who is leaning his plump body against my shins, staring up at me lovingly.

"Well," Dad clears his throat a few times and focuses on a point somewhere over my head, "here's the thing, Sidney. Beans is getting up there in age and it doesn't make sense to base our decisions on him being around much longer. Our new condo is in a vibrant urban area right in the thick of things. It has a pool and a fitness center and a splendid view of the mountains. But I'm afraid it doesn't allow pets. At his age, it would be much kinder for everyone to let him go."

And now my brain finally catches up to what they're really saying.

"So, you're telling us that you found a place in Vegas that doesn't have enough room for me, is too far from Eden's work for her to even go, and you'd like to conveniently get rid of our dog and have me sell my horse. And you're taking your allergic son to the desert when he can barely handle being in the sun. Eden's birthday is coming up in a few weeks. We were going to have a big party. We sent out the invitations, remember?"

I look over to my brother and sister for backup.

"Am I not right?" I ask them. "Is this whole thing not completely insane?"

"No more than usual." Eden shrugs. Leo sniffles.

"Now, that's just cruel." Mom's smile drops away and her eyes fill with insta-tears. Seriously, both my parents should get an Oscar for all the stellar acting they're attempting today.

She looks over at my dad helplessly. "Of course, we want what's best for everyone, but we can't let the needs of our children rule our entire future, can we? Your father and I have sacrificed a lot for you kids, but we are still young and have our whole lives to look forward to. You're welcome to come along on this adventure if you're on board to see Manifest Now transform. But I'm afraid we can't allow all these minor details like pets, birthdays and material things to hold us back any longer. We are meant for much bigger things, Sidney."

I shake my head, staring at their ridiculous, earnest expressions. For the first time, I wonder if I'm even related to these people. Maybe there's a chance I was adopted.

My hands shake as I hoist Beans protectively into my arms. There is no way anyone is putting this dog to sleep. I would defend him with my life.

"I don't see why you bothered to have children at all," I snap, my voice trembling. "If you were just going to dump them and leave them homeless when they get too inconvenient for you."

"Having children sounded like a good idea at the time." My mother sighs wistfully. "All our friends were doing it."

Dad lays a hand on her arm and smiles at me reassuringly. "Of course it was a good idea. We have very much enjoyed being positive, progressive role models for you kids to look up to. We know this might feel hard, but in time, you'll see that it's for the best. One day, you'll thank us for giving you all this opportunity."

"That's a brilliant speech, Dad," I say bitterly, turning toward the stairs. "Too bad it's complete crap. You should save it for one of your workshops."

"Sidney Jameson Jones," Mom says, her eyes flashing me a rare warning. "We don't allow that type of negative speech in this house. Let's not lose sight of the big picture here. You're looking at the individual trees and forgetting about the forest. As your father wrote in chapter six of *Hustling in the Hurricane*..."

"I have to go to work," I say quickly, trying to make my escape before she can go any further.

"Look, Sidney, we know this has caught you off guard." My dad smiles. "And you must be a little shaken up. Of course, you will not be homeless. Your mother and I will figure something out. The universe always provides if you have the right mindset."

"Uh-huh. Thanks." I hurry upstairs, my heart thumping in my chest as I try to squash down the panic that is building. I don't have much faith that my parents will spend *any* energy figuring out my housing situation. And there is no way I'm going to live with Nanna. And no way I'm giving up Beans and Oriel.

I shower and get dressed in my red Shrimp Shack uniform in record time. Then I pick up Beans again and head for the front door. I will have to take him with me wherever I go until my parents leave for Vegas. I don't trust them not to take him to the vet to have him euthanized or drop him off on a deserted country road or something if I leave him home unprotected.

How am I going to afford a place to live? How am I supposed to support him and Oriel? Desperate thoughts swirl through my head as I slip out the front door without anyone seeing me. My job at the Shrimp Shack barely covers Oriel's costs and the lease on my car. It certainly won't be enough to pay rent in this city.

"You need to go on a diet, Beans," I tell him when I finally deposit him on the front seat. My arms ache from carrying his solid bulk the two blocks to my car.

He scrambles over to the passenger side and smooshes his face up against the window, leaving nose prints on the glass.

As I look over at him, I feel an overwhelming surge of love wash over me. How could my parents even think of putting him down just because he's older? He is happy, healthy and has many more years yet to live.

"I will never let them do that to you, buddy," I say, smiling as he wags his little stump of a tail. "You and I are in this together, no matter what."

For the first time, I start seriously thinking about Elliot's earlier offer to me. I'm sure I'd make a terrible tutor, but my options are looking bleak right now.

CHAPTER 7

SIDNEY

The Shrimp Shack parking lot is packed as I navigate to the rutted, gravelled area in the back that is meant for staff.

"Right, you stay here and be good," I say, tucking my warm jacket around him.

I smooth out my uniform, take a deep breath, and head inside.

A blast of steam, noise, and chaos hits me as soon as I open the kitchen door.

"You're late," Vinny bellows even though I'm four minutes early. It's just his way, and he claps me on the back as he scurries by to show me he doesn't mean it.

As much as I dislike having to do any job that doesn't involve horses, I have come to enjoy the fast-paced life in the kitchen. Everything here is done at full speed and involves shouting, crashing pots and pans together and tossing plates around like they are indestructible.

It never gets boring. I started out in the dish pit and then moved to serving, which I'd hated, and now I'm back in the kitchen doing prep work, which is what I like to do best.

You'd think that a place called the Shrimp Shack would only serve shrimp. But they have a huge menu, mostly seafood, and Vinny and his brother Carl are both the chefs and the owners. Carl went to a posh culinary school, but Vinny is completely self-taught, so between them they've created an amazing menu that brings people in from miles around.

"You're on shrimp," Kumiko barks at me from the salad station. This is not a surprise. I'm almost always on shrimp because nobody else wants to do it. I know I should hate prepping, but I don't. It's easy, monotonous work and I'm able to let my hands do their job while my mind is listening to the surrounding chaos.

I am a fast worker so there is no pressure, no stress, no worries for me here. I know exactly what is expected of me. It's a bit like riding Oriel, actually. I get into a peaceful zone where everything unfolds exactly as it should.

My thoughts drift while my hands work and, not wanting to dwell on my own messy life, I think about Elliot's mysterious blind girl instead. The riders who worked with Pablo had all different levels of vision loss; some had been born completely blind, while others had injuries or illnesses that had taken part, or all, of their sight away.

Several of them had been aiming for spots on the Paralympic Equestrian team, so I'd gotten to know a little about the different competition categories. Riders were graded depending on how much vision loss they had, so someone who had zero vision wasn't competing against someone who could see a bit. They only offered dressage at the international level, not jumping, but I knew that there were Para riders who jumped at the local level.

"Break time, Sidney," Kumiko calls, adjusting the thick red bandanna she always wears across her forehead. "And then we need help with dishes. Greg is leaving early."

"Here, take this," Vinny adds, shoving a steaming plate of lobster and rice into my hands as he swoops by. "Table six said they didn't like the way the server set their plate down, so they sent it back. Don't worry, they didn't touch it. Eat up."

"Thanks." I hold the plate tightly in both hands as I weave my way through the chaos to the tiny break room. The smell of butter and garlic wafts up from the plate and my stomach rumbles.

There might have been a point in my life where I wouldn't have touched a stranger's rejected dinner, but that time is not tonight. I sink gratefully into one of the hard plastic chairs and hoover down the delicious food.

Ping. My phone vibrates in my pocket and I fish it out reluctantly.

Hey, sexy. I've been thinking about you all day. What are you wearing? Send me a pic.

I sigh, taking another bite of lobster while I study my phone. There was a time when any message from Zack would have thrilled me to my core, but lately all his messages kind of sound the same.

I'd first met Zack at one of Zara's famous parties. One of the last ones she'd dragged me to. He'd gone to a different high school than us, but the two of them had played in the same band for a while and had hung out. He had blond, wavy hair to his shoulders, and deep green eyes that seemed to stare directly into me.

I didn't have a clue why he'd singled me out at that party. I was a very average person, not like the squealing entourage of girls that usually followed him. In fact, when he walked in, I'd been hiding by the snack table trying to unobtrusively read an ebook I'd loaded on my phone. Parties were never my thing, but I was trying for Zara's sake.

Something had made me glance up and there was Zack. He'd

pinned me with that sultry gaze from across the room and from that instant I was mesmerized.

"You look like a girl with a soul," he'd said, which is a line from one of my favourite books.

And somehow, I found myself spending the next few hours making out with him in a shadowy corner of the kitchen. Right until his friends had interrupted and dragged him away. Up until then, I'd had exactly zero experiences kissing anyone and certainly not a guy like Zack, so the whole thing had felt like a surreal dream.

I'd assumed that it was a one-time thing, because why would someone like him pay attention to a girl like me? Especially when my family was caught up in a massive scandal? He could have any girl he wanted and being seen with me might even hurt his music career.

But a few days afterward, he'd started messaging me. And I'd been thrilled to discover what a deep, interesting guy he was inside, which is completely different from what he projects on the outside.

The first few months were so intense. We talked about all sorts of deep things and I'd often poured my heart out to him, telling him all about what was going on with my life, and my parents' lawsuits. Things I couldn't tell anyone else.

And then he'd tell me how beautiful I was, and share his poetry or the songs he was working on. We never met up in person again, although he always promised we'd be together in the not-too-distant future.

But, I'm wondering now if that's ever going to happen. Or if I even want it to.

I'm at work, I type back, *although this lobster dinner I'm eating is pretty sexy.* I take a picture of my half-empty plate and send it to him.

There is no response, so after a minute I try again.

Have you finished that song you were working on? I still want to hear the new lyrics.

Nothing.

Finally, I sigh and put my phone away. My break is over anyway and it's time to get back to work.

By the time my shift is finished, I am tired and sweaty and my hair has curled up into ringlets around my face from all the steam.

"Good work tonight," Vinny yells at me as I'm heading out the door. "See you tomorrow."

"Thanks for taking that shift for me next week," Kumiko calls over her shoulder. "You're a lifesaver."

"No problem," I say. "I can take any extra shifts you like. I can work overtime too. Whatever you need."

"That's what we like to hear." Vinny grins at me approvingly as I slip out the door into the chilly night air.

I rub my arms briskly, already missing the heat and the camaraderie of the kitchen. Now that I'm not in school anymore, I'm rarely around groups of people, unless you count the kids at the barn, and I'm starting to feel like a bit of a hermit.

Beans is passed out and snoring heavily, still burrowed under my jacket, but he wakes up with a snort as soon as I open the door, looking at me blearily in the dim light.

"It's just me, buddy," I whisper and his back end wiggles with recognition.

In my hurry to get to work this evening, I had forgotten to bring his leash, so I cautiously set him down on the grass at the edge of the parking lot so he can relieve his bladder, crossing my fingers that he doesn't try to run off.

Luckily Beans hates the cold, so the second he's done, he turns around and heads back to the car, leaping and scrambling to get up onto the seat and burrow back into my coat.

"Glad you're enjoying that jacket," I say, turning on my heated seat and cranking the heater to full blast, waiting for my shivers to stop. I'll have to find a blanket for him to use from now on.

Before I'm out of the parking lot, my display lights up with an incoming call.

Zara. I hesitate, wondering if she's pocket-dialled me by accident. Zara hasn't voluntarily spoken to me in months.

I hit the answer button on my steering wheel and the car fills with the sound of thumping music, high-pitched laughter, and loud, drunken voices.

Beans wakes up with a low woof, tilting his head to figure out where all the noise is coming from.

"Sidney, where arrrre you?" Her voice comes out loud and distorted and for a second, my heart skips a beat because it sounds like she's been injured or something. I'm suddenly picturing her hurt and lying in a ditch somewhere, needing my help. "This is the party of the year and you're missing outttt."

I inhale a deep breath. Not being murdered then, just very drunk. Same old Zara.

Close to the phone, a loud chant starts up and I can imagine some sodden person chugging beer from a funnel held upright by a dozen football players. I had been to a couple of college parties with Zara's new crowd, and I have witnessed things I wish I could forget.

"Uh, hey, Zara." I can't believe I'm having a conversation with her, even a drunken one after all this time. "Sounds like a good party."

"Fantasssstic. You should be here, Sids. Zack is here, and he wants to know why you're not."

"Zack is there?"

"Yes, and you're making him so sad. He's totally into you, you know. He told me he'd make it public if he could. If things were different. It's just his career..." Zara's voice drops for a second, and in the background, I hear muffled laughter.

"Did he?" My hope and skepticism are warring with one another, and I can't tell which one is winning.

"Oh, absolutely. He told me he thinks you are soul mates or something."

I hold my breath, pushing back the sudden desperate longing that I feel. Not for Zack exactly, but to belong to *someone*. To be wanted. To be connected to the world and not an outcast. To be surrounded by a crowd of people again and to not be lonely.

"Earth to Sidney. Are you still there? Are you coming to this party or what?"

"Uh, yeah, I'm still here." I glance across at Beans, wondering if he'd be okay sleeping in the car for longer if I popped in to the party for a few minutes. Then I remember I am still in my uniform, and that I most definitely reek like shrimp.

"I could maybe be there in an hour," I say, glancing at the clock. I have to be at the barn early if I want to ride tomorrow before I go see Three Sisters with Elliot.

"Aww, but Zack is here *now*. Don't make him hook up with some slutty groupie, Sidney. It's you he wants."

There is more snorting laughter in the background, as if she's surrounded by a crowd of people listening in on our conversation, and I'm suddenly alert and on guard. A shiver of cold runs down my spine and I reach over to turn the heat even higher.

"Right, well, he knows where to find me," I say carefully. "Maybe I'll see him around. Have fun at your party."

"No, wait." Zara rushes the words out. "Don't hang up, Sidney. Sorry, I'm a little drunk. I've missed you. We need to hang out."

"I've missed you too," I say, but suddenly the music turns up and all I can hear is people laughing and singing some song all together at the top of their lungs.

"Zara, I'd love to…" The line disconnects abruptly, leaving me in echoing silence.

Don't think about it, I tell myself firmly, struggling not to feel hollowed out all over again by the loss of her. Zara had been my best friend once, and she'd left a giant fissure in my world when she'd abandoned me. *Think about Oriel, or visiting that stable tomorrow with Elliot, or about the German translation you're working on. Think about anything but this.*

My internal pep talk almost works. At least my hands stop shaking by the time I park a few blocks away from my house and start the long walk home. But there's not much I can do about the heavy feeling of loneliness that settles over me again.

CHAPTER 8

ALICE

I almost always dream about horses. It's been that way since I was a little kid. And, oddly enough, my dream brain doesn't care that I'm nearly blind now. The images I see when my eyes are closed are as clear as day and in vibrant colour.

Usually, I'm jumping some epic course, or flying along the beach with the wind in my hair.

But this dream is different. Mom is in it for one thing, wearing a long white dress that she would have never worn in real life. We're both on horses, Mom on Jiggs and me on an unfamiliar chestnut with pricked ears and a wild mane. We're riding side by side on a steep trail that curves steadily up a mountain.

"Oh, Alice, here you are," she says happily, grinning. "Just in time for the race."

"Race? What race? Where?"

The path ahead of us is rocky and growing narrower by the second; to one side the mountain rises straight up, towering above us. And on the other side is a straight drop hundreds of feet down.

"Come on, Alice. Don't be a coward. We're going to be late."

And before I can stop her, Mom has banged her heels against Jiggs' side, making him leap forward into a full gallop.

"Wait, you'll hurt him." All I can think of is both of them slipping and getting tossed off the mountain into the abyss below.

Mom doesn't look back but I can hear her laughing.

"There's no glory without risk, Alice. Second place just means you're the first loser." She kicks Jiggs again and the two of them fly around the corner, out of sight.

I wake up gasping and am surprised to find that my cheeks are wet with tears.

"Stupid dream," I mutter, rubbing furiously at my face. Mom's words still echo in my ear.

The thing is that dream-Mom wasn't just a figment of my imagination. That's pretty much what she'd been like. Beautiful, wild, reckless, and always flying off on some adventure. There wasn't a single thing that scared her and she expected her daughters to be fearless too.

I know it's wrong to think anything bad about people who have died. You have to tell everyone that they were perfect and only ever talk about their good qualities. But some of my memories of Mom aren't that fantastic.

She'd had a temper and had often slapped us when we irritated her. She heaped praise on us when we won ribbons and trophies but then shamed us when we lost. We weren't allowed to be scared or unsure; we always had to be bold risk-takers, even when we didn't want to be.

I'd just assumed that all parents were like that, until Tiffani came to live with us. The unconditional love and support she showers on Trin has been a bit of an eye opener.

I don't ever plan to have kids, but if I *do* end up with them, I hope that I treat them like Tiffani treats her daughter; at least they'd know they were loved.

From downstairs, the faint smell of bacon and toast wafts up through the floor vents and for a second, I'm sorry that I've missed breakfast again. Mrs. Pitts has a rule that she will only serve us breakfast from seven until nine and after that we're on our own.

I reach over and hit the top of my clock.

Ten, fifteen, a.m., the robotic voice says serenely.

"Perfect."

I roll slowly out of bed, feeling like I'm fifty years old or something. I am stiff and sore all over even though all I do now is lie around on my bed all day. I used to ride from dawn until dusk when I wasn't in school, but now I have nothing.

I could have gone to the city with Trin and her mom on a shopping trip. They'd invited me last night; Trin had practically begged me to go, but they'd planned a sort of girls-day-out with lunch and pedicures and that's way too much family time for me. I can last about five minutes in Tiffani's company before I start saying sarcastic things that inevitably hurt her feelings. I don't have the energy for that drama today.

The lingering smells from the kitchen are tempting, but I turn toward the front door, preferring to sneak out and avoid an encounter with Mrs. Pitts if I can possibly....

"Good morning, Alice."

"Gah!" I jump sideways, banging my elbow sharply against the wall.

"I saved you some breakfast," she says in her creaky voice. "I'll heat it up for you."

I open my mouth to argue, but my stomach rumbles and in the end I follow her resignedly to the kitchen.

Mrs. Pitts, or Pitty as Clara always called her, has worked for our family since Mom died. She cooks, takes care of the kitchen, and does some light cleaning. She also oversees the army of housekeepers that arrive one day a week to scrub the rest of the house from top to bottom.

How she'd lasted in those early days when Clara was at her worst is beyond me, but somehow, she'd stuck it out. She and Clara had openly hated each other, and it had been an all-out war sometimes when my sister was home from boarding school.

Pitty and Isabelle are good friends, and she loves Trin, but with me she is...distant.

Okay, I haven't exactly made her life easy over the years, either. I'd been Clara's sidekick, after all, and we'd pulled some mean pranks, so I can't blame Pitty for not being overly warm.

Until the surgery, I hadn't cared at all how she felt about me. I mean, she was just another one of Dad's employees, not anyone important.

But, afterward, something shifted in me. And I feel *uneasy* around her. She always seems to be lurking in the shadows and popping out of nowhere when I least expect it. Sometimes I imagine that she's watching me, like a cat watches a mouse.

What if she's been waiting all these years to get revenge on me for being such a brat? She could easily poison my food or push me down the stairs and nobody would even know.

I rub my arms, following her into the kitchen.

"Sit," she orders, as if I'm a prisoner in for interrogation. With anyone else, I would have snapped back or said something scathing, but now I sink into my chair without a word.

"Coffee with cream and sugar," she announces, setting a mug roughly down in front of me. "Careful, it's hot."

"Um, thanks," I say in surprise. My dad and Tiffani are not thrilled about my coffee addiction, so they rarely make it for me. I wrap both hands around the warm mug and then take a tentative sip. It tastes normal, delicious even, but then some poisons are undetectable by taste.

"Breakfast." She drops the plate in front of me with a clatter. "It would have been better fresh."

"No, this is good," I mumble, hungrily shoving two strips of bacon into my mouth. "Everyone stares at me like I'm some sort of freak when I come down for meals."

I pause, with a piece of toast halfway to my mouth, surprised that I've finally admitted that to anyone, especially Pitty.

In those first few weeks after the surgery, I'd knocked over, run into and smashed a lot of things by accident. Okay, sometimes on purpose, but mostly by accident. For a while there, everyone had constantly hovered around me, handing me utensils, cutting up my food and watching me like a hawk. It had been maddening. So, lately, I'd started eating snacks in my room just to have some peace.

There is a long, disapproving silence from Pitty and I take a giant bite of toast so I can get this uncomfortable meal over with.

"You parents are out of the house on work days by nine thirty," she says in her dry, no-nonsense, voice. "You be down here by nine forty-five, no later mind you, and I'll make you breakfast."

I pause mid-chew. "Really? Why?"

"Because nobody in this house is going to go hungry on my watch. Take it or leave it, Alice."

"I'll take it," I say quickly.

Finally full, I hum a little under my breath as I make my way to the front door and pull on my heavier coat and paddock boots.

By the time I get outside, clouds have covered the sun, and the temperature has dropped.

I can still make out the driveway well enough in this light but my range of vision recedes the darker it gets, so I can't see the pastures beyond the fence line or anything mort than ten or so feet ahead of me.

Hooves crunch on the gravel and I see dark blobs headed toward me, riders on horseback obviously, but I can't tell who they are until they get closer.

"Hi, Alice," Mia calls out cheerfully. "We're going on a trail ride to see the foal next door."

"Great," I mutter under my breath. It's not that I don't like Mia; she's Josh's cousin, after all, and an excellent rider. But she must be one of the most annoyingly cheerful people I've ever met.

She and her dark mare, Nim, had showed up suddenly at Three Sisters last year and I'd heard rumours that Mia had come to live at Josh's and Oliver's house under mysterious circumstances.

She is the complete opposite of moody Josh, but I much prefer his personality to hers. Give me quiet and thoughtful over bubbly nonstop talking any day.

"You could come with us if you like," Josh adds. "We could go back and tack up one of the school ponies."

For a second, I'm even tempted to accept his offer, but in the end I shake my head.

"Not today, but thanks."

"You can always ride Nim too," Mia adds. "I don't mind."

"Uh, great." I plaster on a smile and edge past them. "I'll keep that in mind. See you guys around."

It's a relief to escape without having to explain to yet another well-meaning person that I don't want to ride their boring horse. Nim is like my sister Isabelle's horse Shamus; obedient and boring. No fun at all.

I skim around past the front of the barn, heading right to the paddocks at the back.

Luckily, neither of the two ponies I have left are out in the fields today, and Checkers nickers low under his breath the second he sees me.

"Here, piglet," I call softly, sticking my hands between the fence boards so that Checkers can lip the tiny bits of carrots I'd cut up for him off my palms. He's not allowed to have a lot of treats because he's prone to laminitis, but small amounts are okay once in a while.

"No, that's it for you, don't be greedy."

He uses his little teeth to gently snag my coat sleeve and give it an experimental tug before turning back to his hay net.

"Here, Jiggs," I say quietly, moving to lean on his gate. "I brought you some too."

I hold my breath, waiting, straining my ears to hear what he's doing. His paddock is more shadowed than the one that Checkers lives in, so it's harder to make him out.

He's silent for a moment and then he lets out a loud snort and I see his shape come striding out of his shelter. He doesn't move toward me confidently like Checkers had. Instead, he lets out another alarmed snort and breaks into a slow trot, circling the perimeter of his small paddock but avoiding the gate, the spot where I'm standing, completely.

"It's okay," I croon, pushing aside my rising frustration, "it's just me. I'm bringing you a nice treat. There's nothing to be scared of."

But he obviously doesn't believe me because, after a few more anxious trot-circles, he charges back into his shelter and then stays there.

I call a few more times and then finally toss the carrots onto the ground at my feet in frustration.

"Fine," I snap. "Don't have any treats. See if I care. Stupid pony. You deserve to get sold."

I don't really mean that and I blow out a deep breath, irritated with myself that I lost my temper. I make it a personal rule to never take out my anger on the ponies.

"He's having a tough time, isn't he?"

I whip around with a startled yelp.

"Ben?"

"The one and only. Sorry to sneak up on you. I thought you heard me."

"Why does everyone keep saying that? It's not like I've developed supersonic hearing overnight or something. Maybe people should stop lurking around so much."

He laughs and instantly I feel bad for snapping at him. Ben has been one of my few allies in this world for a long time and he's great at taking care of the horses. Ever since Clara had made up stories about him and nearly gotten him fired, I took extra care with how I treated him. I don't want him thinking that I'm anything like my sister.

"Sorry," I say quickly. "I'm not in the best mood."

"No worries. Is that because of Jiggs?"

I shrug. "Partly. I don't know why he hates me so much now. I feel stupid saying that he blames me for the accident because I don't suppose a horse's brain works like that, but, honestly, that's what it feels like."

His jacket rustles as he nods. "His entire world has turned upside down too, you know. He's already an anxious guy, but you had him in full program where he got to expend a lot of that energy through work. And he had structure and a set schedule to depend on. All that's gone now."

I mull that over for a minute. "But he's never acted like he hated me before. I mean, he could be hard to halter sometimes, but he never avoided me or didn't let me touch him."

"He was in a stall almost all the time, Alice. He only got turned out for a few hours a few times a week and then was brought back into his stall for dinner. It was his routine. Being in a big paddock where he has a choice about whether to interact with people is a whole different story. This is probably how he would have been all along if he'd had a say in it."

I shake my head. "No way. I've handled this pony for nearly two years. I'm pretty sure I would have noticed if he didn't want me to touch him."

"Okay," Ben says mildly, and I can't tell if he's agreeing with me or not.

I grit my teeth in irritation and glare toward Jiggs, who is now a palomino-coloured blob in the far corner of his paddock.

What Ben said is completely ridiculous, of course. I mean, sure, Jiggs had paced his stall when he was anxious. And you had to go up to him quietly when it was time to halter him or he'd whirl around and pin himself against the back of his stall. Not everyone could handle him. I was always the one who caught, groomed, and rode him, and it was usually Ben who turned him out.

"How is Kira catching him to ride?" I ask suddenly. Kira, another rider from Barn B, has been schooling for me until he sells.

"She brings Oliver to help her when I'm not around. If they are both in the paddock, then he will go hide in his shelter and let her halter him."

"Wow." I bite my lip, feeling angry and a little embarrassed. "We should put him back in the barn. Being out here isn't doing him any good. Nobody will buy him if he acts like a freak all the time."

"You *could* put him back in the barn," Ben says quietly. "But that would just be masking the symptoms, wouldn't it? Not fixing things."

"So?" I say sharply. "At least I could pet him and brush him if he were in a stall. He couldn't avoid me then."

"True. It's easier to force them to do what you want when they're locked up."

I glance over at him in irritation. "That's not what I meant. I just want him to act like a normal pony."

"Sure, I can see that. But you have to decide if that's what is best for *him*. You're his caretaker, you're the only advocate he has, Alice. That responsibility goes a lot deeper than brushing and riding him."

"I know that," I snap. "I've always treated him well. He's had the best of everything."

Ben doesn't say anything and I grip the top bar of the gate in both hands until my fingers hurt. How dare Ben accuse me of ignoring Jiggs' feelings? I'd worked hard every day to make that pony perform his best. To be a winner.

He was never truly happy, a tiny voice says inside of me. *He did what you told him to do because you were smarter than him, but he never really enjoyed it, did he?*

I exhale slowly and then turn to Ben.

"All right, what would you do if you were me?"

"If it were my pony, then I'd want him to *like* to be in my space, to seek me out and voluntarily spend time with me. I'd want to be the human he felt completely safe with."

For some reason, I think of that time I'd caught Josh playing in the ring with Heck. We're technically not supposed to free-lunge in the indoor because it can wreck the footing, but Josh was jogging around the perimeter with Heck following loose behind him. When he stopped, then Heck would stop and when he turned, the horse would instantly follow. It was like they'd been doing a dance.

I'd never done anything like that with my ponies, not even with Checkers when I'd been a little kid.

"Okay, fine," I say a tad grumpily, "let's say you're right. How do I *make* him want to be with me?"

Ben laughs again and I raise my head sharply, wondering if he's making fun of me. Not being able to read people's expressions now is the worst. So much of human communication is about body language and subtle facial movements and not about words at all.

"I think it's less about *making* things happen and more about inviting things to happen. You want a partnership, right? Not a dictatorship."

I frown and scuff my boot into the soft ground near the gate. "I don't let my ponies walk all over me. They need to know who is the boss or they'll take advantage. That's how people get hurt."

"Hmm, interesting," he says. "Do you really think any of the horses that live here would hurt you on purpose if you weren't strict with them? Would they attack you?"

"Well," I pause, considering, and then shake my head. "No, I guess not. Not most of them, anyway. Not on purpose."

"Right. Most horses I've worked with are kind and good-hearted. Jiggs, especially, doesn't have a mean bone in his body. You can afford to let your guard down and be his friend, Alice."

I wrinkle my nose a little in distaste and sigh. I have always prided myself on being a great horse person. Kind, firm, practical, and not sentimental. I give my ponies the best care money can buy. But I have never considered any of my ponies to be my *friends*. They were athletes who were there to do a job, to win and to be sold for a profit, and that was all.

But obviously this isn't working for Jiggs right now since nobody will buy him. And I don't have anything else to do with my time anyway, so I don't have anything to lose.

"All right," I say finally. "What exactly do you want me to do?"

And that is how I find myself seated in a lawn chair in the middle of Jiggs' paddock with a blanket over my knees and a handful of carrots in my lap.

Ben has gone off to do chores and here I am; alone, cold, and bored, facing a pony who still wants nothing to do with me. I've already been here for what feels like an eternity and so far, no magical bonding between me and Jiggs has happened.

"This was such a dumb idea," I say out loud.

Jiggs snorts and throws his head up dramatically, like I've set off fireworks or something.

"You know, you're a pretty stupid pony," I tell him casually. "I mean, you're pretty and you're a talented jumper, but I'm not sure there's much up there rattling around in your brain. Look at Checkers, you don't see him acting like that."

Jiggs snorts again, but this time it's quieter and is followed by the sound of him munching his hay.

"Look, I'm sorry about the accident. I shouldn't have tried to jump you when I couldn't see properly. It sucks that you got hurt and your friends got sold off. I take full blame for all that."

I idly lift a carrot off my lap and take a bite, wishing that I'd packed some proper snacks along.

At the sound of me crunching, Checkers nickers greedily from his own paddock and Jiggs comes back out of his shelter. I can feel him standing there, staring at me.

I can't make out his expression, but I see that he's facing me straight on with his head raised. I take another loud, crunching bite and swallow.

"Doesn't that sound delicious, Jiggs?" I coax. "You know, you could have some too if you wanted. All you'd have to do is come over here and let me pet you."

He stays where he is, still staring, and finally I give up and throw the top of the carrot in his general direction, which causes him to wheel around and trot off in an animated lap around his paddock.

I want to give up and go back to the house where it's warm. But the truth is that I'll have nothing to do if I go back inside. At least out here I have some sort of project, even if it's a stupid, pointless one. I can stick it out long enough to prove to Ben that he's wrong about Jiggs.

Still, it is incredibly boring sitting here, waiting. I like to get things done, to take action, to *make* things happen. Not sit here like a lump.

Sighing, I pull out my new, oversized phone and give it a shake to wake it up.

This brick is what the occupational therapists had my dad replace my sleek, foldable phone with. It has all sorts of accessibility apps and features that I haven't bothered to even open yet.

They'd tried to show me how to use it in the hospital, but I hadn't been interested. The large screen is huge, and when I touch it, it blows up the part of the screen near my finger to enormous proportions. So, each icon can be nearly the same size as the screen. Even using my damaged peripheral vision, I can see well enough to pull up my texts, even though I have to read them slowly, letter by giant letter.

I scroll slowly through my old messages. So many people had sent me well wishes when I'd first gone into the hospital, but those had all dried up by now. People had moved on with their lives without me.

I stop on one from Darla, the one she'd sent me after I'd cleaned up at my last show. *Amazing job out there as usual. I'm proud of you.*

My eyes sting from unshed tears and I rub at them furiously with my sleeve. This is literally the last text Darla ever sent me. Not long after that, I'd been hospitalized, and she'd started treating me like I had a contagious disease or something.

"I really don't get it," I mutter to myself. "How can she be praising me one minute and then pretending that I don't exist the next? It's not like I did anything wrong."

Something warm and soft touches the back of my hand and I flinch away instinctively before I can stop myself.

Hooves thud on the ground behind me and then stop a few feet away.

I freeze, holding my breath for a minute, but he doesn't come any closer.

"It's okay," I say softly. "I didn't mean to scare you."

There is a quiet snort a few inches from my elbow.

I carefully pick up a carrot and hold it flat against the armrest of the chair, sticking it out sideways so Jiggs can reach it if he likes.

Another small snort, and then a tentative nudge on my shoulder.

"Hey, buddy," I murmur. "Look at you being so brave. That's a good pony. Good job, Jiggs."

I don't move and I don't try to touch him. I have the feeling that if I even breathe wrong that he'll take off again.

Gradually, he inches closer. He whuffles his soft breath into my hair, running his nose across my jacket and up my arm. When he reaches the carrot, he hesitates as if he's not sure if it's a trap or not. And then he takes the whole thing right out of my hand in one bite and trots back to his shelter to crunch it up in peace.

I laugh out loud, surprised at him. That's the most personality I've seen Jiggs display the whole time I've owned him. He's usually a bundle of nerves.

I pick another carrot up and hold it in the same way, and it doesn't take long for him to inch his way back, looking for more snacks.

We do this a couple more times, until my small stack of carrots is gone, and still I haven't reached out to touch him.

He doesn't leave entirely when the snacks are gone, though. Instead, he moves a few feet away and stands there, as if he's napping, with his head half-lowered and one hind leg propped up.

This time I hear Ben's boots on the path next to the paddocks.

"Well," he says softly. "Looks like you've made some progress."

"Not much." I shrug, but I can't help the smile that tugs at the corner of my mouth either.

"You know, if he doesn't sell tomorrow, then you'll have to keep working with him. It would be fun to watch his attitude improve."

"Wait, what? Sell to who?"

"Didn't your dad tell you that Darla lined up potential buyers? I thought you knew."

His voice is loaded with sympathy, and the sound of it makes my stomach heave. If there is one thing I can't stand, it's people's pity.

"Of course I knew," I snap. "I...thought it was a different day, that's all."

I get up abruptly, tangling my legs in the blanket for a moment and nearly dropping my phone.

"Maybe he won't sell," Ben says quietly. "Maybe you'll have more time."

"It doesn't matter."

Even if it did matter, there's nothing I can do about it.

CHAPTER 9

SIDNEY

*A*fter a long, sleepless night, I stumble out of bed at the crack of dawn and head blearily to the kitchen for some coffee.

The house is completely silent except for the sound of Bean's claws clicking on the tiles behind me.

I had stayed up late into the night, filled with worry about my future prospects. Rent in this city is out of control and finding a place that I can afford and that will also allow a dog is terrifying. I can't believe that my parents have given me a week's notice to find a new place. Maybe I can ask them to put me up in a hotel short-term or something.

I had also done a little investigating into Three Sisters Farm. The pictures on the website are incredibly beautiful and I can see why Elliot thinks so much of it. I even found some pictures and videos of Alice competing on a string of flashy ponies.

She is a good rider, I have to give it to her, but in every single photo she has this grim expression on her face. And yes, I know that people who are concentrating hard aren't usually smiling, but Alice looks the same whether she's on the ground or in the saddle. Hard and driven. Not somebody you'd want to spend a lot of time tutoring.

I let Beans out into the backyard and then pad to the coffee machine, slipping a Keurig pod into the top and waiting impatiently for it to brew.

The kitchen is a mess. Nobody bothered to toss out the empty takeout containers from last night's dinner, and dirty cups and cutlery are still piled on the counter next to the dishwasher.

Which is typical for our family. I don't know how our revolving series of housekeepers and nannies had put up with it, honestly. Nobody here knows, or cares, how to clean up after themselves.

I toss the trays full of congealed food into the trash and then load the dishwasher and wipe the counters with a damp paper towel before letting Beans back in and carrying my sloshing coffee cup back to my room.

I don't really want to run into any of my family today. I'm still angry with my parents and I feel guilty about Leo. He'd been so upset during our family meeting and I'd been too concerned with my own disaster of a life to be much of a comfort to him.

I sip my coffee while I slowly get dressed, thinking about my impending visit with Elliot. I don't have a choice about getting a second job anymore; I *need* one. But I'm not sure that anyone would hire me to be a tutor. Sure, I'm smart and I love school, but I don't have any real credentials.

Still, it won't hurt to just go *see* the place.

Beans bounces excitedly down the hall as I grab his leash and a blanket for him to curl up with in the car. I have to go to Happy Acres before I meet with Elliot, and Barb doesn't allow dogs at the barn. Not that Beans will mind staying in the car. He's the type of guy who can nap anywhere.

I scoop my saddle up onto my other arm, grab my house keys, and fumble my way out the front door.

The sun is out, but the air is chilly as we walk the two blocks to where I had to park the car last night. It's a perfect fall day; crisp air and a beautiful blue sky overhead.

When I get to the barn, it is practically empty. Only two of the younger teenagers are here, cleaning stalls with the radio blaring some sort of techno K-pop.

There is no sign of the usual pack of feral barn kids. But school starts up next week, so they have probably all been dragged off to get haircuts and new clothes so they can at least pretend to be civilized.

Somebody has already turned Oriel out in the field. He's standing with his face planted inside a massive round hay bale, a circle of other horses flanking him from a respectful distance.

They have learned, mostly the hard way, that he is king of this pasture and not to be messed with.

He looks up with a rumbling nicker when he sees me. After pinning his ears and shaking his head at his neighbours in warning, he comes striding over, ears pricked and eyes bright.

Despite all the trouble weighing on my shoulders right now, I sigh happily as I watch him move toward me. This is why I work so hard to keep Oriel. These small, precious moments when everything feels perfect and it's him and me against the world.

"Hey friend," I whisper as he gets closer. "Let's get you cleaned up and we'll go for a ride."

I've already set his brush kit and tack outside by the hitching post so we can take advantage of the good weather. The inside of the barn is dark, moldy, and falling apart, so I usually try to spend as little time in there as possible.

Even though I don't like Happy Acres, I love these early mornings all to myself where I can lose myself in my grooming routine.

I hum quietly as I brush out his thick mane and then loop it up in a long running-braid that lies neatly against his neck.

"There, look how handsome you are."

He nickers in agreement and turns to sniff at my pockets, knowing that compliments often come with treats.

"All right, just one, though." I give him a small chunk of the gourmet cookies that he loves, laughing as he flicks his nose up and down while he chews.

The ring still looks decent from where I'd raked it the day before. Only a few hoof prints mar the smooth surface.

I swing up from the mounting block and let Oriel stride along, his head bobbing in time to his footfalls.

Time disappears when I'm riding, and we are halfway through our workout when the gate swings open with a squealing of hinges.

"Hi, Sidney!" Val calls, her voice high-pitched with excitement. "I came to ride with you!"

"Oh, great," I mutter under my breath, trying to keep my focus on my own ride.

Val is a nice kid, if you like kids. She's about ten years old, although she's small for her age, and completely obsessed with horses. But she never shuts up. And she follows me everywhere asking endless questions or blabbing on about her day or about every little random thought that enters her head.

Also, watching her handle the poor little mare she leases from Barb is complete torture sometimes.

Don't look, focus on Oriel. We do a series of large triangles across the ring, an exercise that helps him to rock back on his haunches and use his hocks properly, carefully avoiding the rusting barrels and half-rotted jumps that litter the ring.

Happy Acres isn't a jumper barn, or a western barn or anything specific, but the ring has a few old jumps and some inconveniently placed barrels in random spots around the ring. Everyone learns to navigate around them.

I do some leg-yields, Oriel's favourites, and some shoulder-in. We drop to a walk and ride a few squares, then add some turns on the haunches before trotting again.

Val is watching me from her spot a few feet from the mounting block where the bay pinto mare, Diva, is refusing to budge. The mare's eyes roll in protest as she plants her front feet, refusing to go anywhere near the mounting block.

I don't blame the horse at all. She's wearing stiff, ancient tack that doesn't fit her properly, her feet are overgrown and she looks bony and uncomfortable all over. Which is typical of Barb's handful of school horses.

I remember when Diva had first arrived at Happy Acres, and she'd been a much different horse. Not just in looks, but in temperament, too. A year in Barb's care has transformed a happy, willing horse into a sullen, angry animal who wants to do as little work as possible.

She'd been beautiful once. I keep hoping someone will buy her and fix her up again. Pablo had taken in a few project horses over the years, gotten them massage, chiropractic treatments and put them on a good feeding program. It had been amazing to see how differently they'd looked and acted once they weren't in pain anymore.

"Oriel looks so good, Sidney," Val calls as I pass. "Do you think I could ride him today? Just one time?"

"Nope," I say firmly. "It's against Barb's rules. Sorry."

This is kind of a lie, since Barb couldn't care less about what I do with Oriel. But I'd learned early on to set firm boundaries with these kids and stick to them. Not much scares them except Barb, so I used her as an excuse whenever I needed to tell them they couldn't ride my horse, use my tack, or borrow my things.

Oriel flicks his inside ear back at me, sensing my lack of concentration, and then breaks into a disjointed canter. He has always been the type to take advantage if his rider's mind wanders. He doesn't buck or bolt, but he will randomly switch speed or direction if you give him the opportunity.

"Sorry, boy," I whisper, reaching down to pet his neck as I bring him back down to a trot. "It's a bit of a train wreck over there. Hard not to watch."

"Sidney," Val calls excitedly, "I want to show you something..." She breaks off as she clambers up onto the mounting block. "We've been working on the things in that book you gave me."

"I'm busy schooling, Val..."

"No problem, I'll be quick, I swear. I want to show you..." She yelps as Diva makes a sudden dive toward the gate. "I read that book you gave me three times and I've been trying some things. I want to see if I have the shoulder-in right. Please?"

Oh, for heaven's sake. Sighing, I transition back down to a walk and then draw Oriel to a halt a few feet away.

"You know I'm not supposed to give you lessons." I latch on to the first excuse that comes to mind. "Barb said that if she caught me helping again..."

"You're not giving lessons if I'm not paying you," Val insists quickly. "You're giving me free advice because that's what friends do for each other. We are friends, aren't we?"

She looks up at me so hopefully that I plaster on a feeble smile.

"Um, sure we are, Val. But Barb..."

"Oh, she won't care. She can't stop us from talking, can she?"

Knowing Barb, she'd probably try. She doesn't want any other coaches on the property except herself, but she also despises teaching. Perfect traits for an instructor to have.

"All right," I say finally. "You have ten minutes. Warm her up properly first."

"She doesn't need a warmup. She's fine." Val scrambles on board and gives the mare a little kick to get her moving. Diva's head shoots up, her back hollow, so she looks inverted like an unhappy camel.

"I won't help you unless you're gentle with her, Val," I warn. "That saddle doesn't fit her properly. She can't relax if she's uncomfortable."

"But I got her a new saddle pad that's supposed to help. I saved up my birthday money for it. Do you like it?"

"The colour is very nice," I say diplomatically. "But it's making the problem worse. Your saddle is tilting backward right into her..."

"I just want to show you what we've been practicing." Val nudges the mare firmly again and Diva breaks into a reluctant, choppy trot, her eyes tight and suspicious.

I sigh heavily and glance back toward the barn to make sure Barb is nowhere in sight.

"Fine, but you need to ride her properly if you want me to help."

Luckily for me, Diva is out of shape. And even though Val spends hours in the saddle, she isn't used to using her core when she rides, so it really doesn't take much to tire them out. Especially after I have Val pull the mare's saddle off and ride with only the pad.

It's not my first choice, especially when Diva is obviously sore, but the saddle fits her so badly that it's the lesser of two evils.

"That was so much fun," Val giggles as she finishes her last attempt to post bareback at the trot. "Thanks for helping me, Sidney, I always learn so much from you."

"Well, you have a natural seat, Val. But you need to stop kicking her and pulling on her mouth. That's not much of a partnership. You don't see any top riders doing that, do you?"

I don't bother to soften my words. The kid has that instinctual grace that comes from spending hundreds of hours in the saddle, but she also has very little empathy or understanding for her horse.

Val looks up suddenly, her face paling as Barb's little car

shoots down the driveway from the house, careening around the bend and sliding to a stop behind the barn.

Crap, what bad timing.

"Do you think she saw us?" Val jumps down from Diva's back and ducks behind the mare's shoulder, although it is much too late for hiding.

"I hope not. We'd better go, though. I still have to clean Oriel's stall before Elliot picks me up."

"The dressage lady? Are you going to go see that farm now?"

I nod, still thinking about what Barb will do if she had noticed us in the ring. She's threatened to kick me out so many times that this might be her final straw.

There is no sign of Barb at all when Val and I get back to the barn, which is probably good news. Barb usually likes to confront you in a good dramatic blow-up, so her staying in her office most likely means that she was too hung over to notice us in the ring at all.

Elliot shows up right as I'm putting Oriel back out in the pasture. Val is bouncing along eagerly beside her like a golden retriever puppy.

"Are you a real coach? Have you ridden a Lipizzan? Did you ever go to the Olympics? Can I go with you guys today if I promise to be quiet?" Val hovers at Elliot's elbow, peppering her with endless questions.

"Yes, yes, no and I'm sorry, but not today," Elliot says good-naturedly. She doesn't seem to find Val as irritating as I do.

"Hey, I'm almost done. I just have to clean Oriel's stall quickly."

"Don't worry, I can clean his stall for you," Val pipes up. "It's only fair since you gave me a lesson."

I flinch, looking around warily to see if Barb is lurking nearby.

"Don't say that too loud," I warn. "Are you sure you don't mind doing my stall?"

"Nope. My mom isn't picking me up until dinner anyway, so I have lots of time. I like cleaning stalls."

"All right, well, thanks. I owe you one. I'll see you later."

"Have fun at Three Sisters. Maybe next time I can come with you." She gives us both one more hopeful look and then trudges off.

"Aw, I kind of wish we could bring her along," Elliot says, laughing. "She reminds me of myself when I was a kid."

"I really doubt you were that annoying."

"Oh no, I was. I never stopped asking questions from dawn until dusk. It drove Pablo crazy. But that's why he eventually gave me so many horses to ride. Mostly to shut me up."

I laugh, shaking my head as we head toward Elliot's car. I take a slight detour to lock my saddle in my car and scoop Beans up.

"Hey, look at this guy," Elliot says fondly. "I haven't seen him in a while."

"I hope you're okay that he comes with us. Things are a little complicated at home right now, so I have to keep him with me."

"Oh sure, this car has seen its share of dog hair, hay, and muddy boots. He won't hurt anything."

"Thanks." I settle Beans between us and buckle up, wondering whether I should tell her about my changed circumstances or not. I don't want her to feel like she *has* to give me a job out of pity or something.

The drive with Elliot almost feels like old times. We'd driven to so many horse shows with Ben and Pablo and a revolving crowd of other riders that I'd probably spent more hours with them than I did with my own family.

Back then, Capriole Farms had basically *been* my family.

And I'd forgotten how easy Elliot is to talk to, which makes me wonder now why I'd never reached out to her again over this last year. Why I'd never answered her texts or phone calls.

"We're going in the back way so you can see Barn B first," Elliot says as she maneuvers us up an alarmingly steep driveway that leads straight through a swath of old-growth forest.

I stare out the window at the massive moss-covered trees towering over us. You rarely saw trees this big so close to the city; it is a wonder the area hadn't been logged for the valuable timber by now.

"Are you ready for this?" Elliot says to me with a grin.

We crest the last rise and suddenly the entire farm is laid out before us.

"Oh wow," I say, staring at the lush, green fields full of horses. The pastures are huge and bordered by neat white fences. I can easily envision Oriel grazing in a place like this.

"Impressive, isn't it? It's one of my favourite places to teach. The horses are really happy here, or at least most of them are."

I turn to look at her, wondering about that last cryptic statement, but she pulls up to the sprawling barn and hops out, beckoning me to follow her.

"You'd better bring Beans," she says over her shoulder. "It's too hot to leave him in the car."

I look up at the sky where the sun has been crowded out by thick grey clouds. It is definitely not too hot out, but I scoop the little dog up anyway, deciding not to argue.

Beans strains at the end of his leash the second he's set on the ground, snorting and wheezing as he pulls after Elliot into the large barn.

The stable is hushed and serene when we go inside, and I'm surprised at the silence. Other than the last couple of days, Happy Acres is usually full of kids galloping around or sprawled in the aisle eating junk food, blaring music, and generally being loud and annoying.

Even Capriole always had a radio going. Although Pablo had insisted on either a classical music station or jazz so it wasn't exactly a treat.

"Why is it so quiet?" I ask in confusion.

"Oh." Elliot laughs. "Almost everyone from Barn B is at a show down island. It's the last fun show of the season, so nearly the whole barn went. Here, I'll give you a quick tour."

"Are you sure they won't mind us poking around?" I say, feeling a little out of place, like we're trespassing or something.

"No." She blinks at me in surprise. "Of course not."

Every single stall is empty of horses, but they are all clean and piled high with fresh bedding, thick enough for a horse to lie down comfortably in. Hay nets, bulging with green hay, hang ready and waiting for the residents to come back.

I trail after Elliot as she shows me the tack room and the feed room and we take a quick peek into the office, which is a much different place from Barb's.

"Wow, it's so well organized," I say, eyeing the complicated lesson and training schedule that is neatly laid out on a giant white board. There are no piles of unpaid invoices lying around, no ash trays and no smelly Barb day-drinking at her desk.

"Yep, Anna runs a tight ship here. Come on, I'll show you the rings and then we'll go up the hill."

There are two rings near the barn, a large one scattered with colourful jumps and a smaller one clearly meant for dressage.

The place isn't completely deserted after all. A rider pilots a fresh-looking palomino pony around the upper end of the dressage ring and a boy leans against the fence, his elbows propped on the top rail as he watches her ride.

"Looking good, Kira," Elliot calls out as the girl canters by.

The pony rolls an eye at us and then suddenly shies and whirls around snorting, his gaze fixed on Beans who is innocently wheezing at a tuft of grass at the edge of the ring.

"Sorry." I reel the dog in a little closer. "He's kind of a heavy breather. Beans, stop that."

I tug on his leash to pull him back further from the ring.

"Oh, don't worry about this guy." The girl, Kira, shakes her head and rolls her eyes. "Jiggs worries about everything. I don't know how he survives life, honestly."

She reaches down to give the pony's rigid neck a reassuring scratch.

"Hopefully he sells soon and she won't have to keep riding him." The boy pushes himself off the rail and turns to us with an easy smile. "He's a maniac."

It is impossible not to smile back at him. He is tall, lean and maybe a year or so younger than me, wearing a T-shirt with a burning robot on it.

"Hey, that's not fair," Kira protests. "And if you'll remember, Flicker was a bit of a handful when we started with him, too. This guy needs more time."

"That's what you say about all of them," he says affectionately, clearly teasing her.

"Kira, Oliver, this is Sidney," Elliot interrupts. "She is an old student of mine. I'm giving her a tour of the farm today and hopefully I can convince her to take a job with us here."

"Oh, do you want to be a groom?" Kira asks, looking at me with interest. "I heard Margo took that internship in Portugal and they need to fill her spot. Or are you applying to be Darla's teaching assistant?"

"No, no," Elliot says quickly before I can answer. "I hope to have her work partly as a groom for Anna and partly as a tutor for Alice. But we'll see how it plays out. Today is just a tour."

"Ugh, Alice." Kira makes a face. "Good luck with that. I swear she gets worse every day."

"Come on, she's not always so bad," Oliver protests. "Plus, being forced to sell all your ponies would make anyone cranky."

"Alice has been scary as long as I've known her," Kira says firmly. "Long before she lost her vision, or her ponies. I think the only thing she truly likes is this guy here." She reaches down and pats Jiggs' shoulder, which makes him shiver and prance sideways a few steps.

"Any interest in him yet?" Elliot asks, eyeing the pony with a frown.

"No." Kira shakes her head. "Someone was supposed to come try him today, but they backed out last minute. He's a hard sell, honestly. He's too much for most kids to handle and too small for most adults. Not many people ride as well as Alice."

"You ride him well," I say, and it's the truth. She sits in the saddle like she's glued there and doesn't seem to mind his prancing and spooking.

"Kira makes it look easy." Oliver shakes his head. "She's one of the best riders at Three Sisters. That pony is mental."

"I'm adequate," Kira says, shrugging off the compliment. "And Jiggs is not crazy. Honestly, if he were my pony, I'd give him six months off to trail ride or something. I think his mind is kind of fried. He is an amazing jumper, but he needs to be finessed the whole time you're riding him. Alice has the knack, and the interest, for managing him. Most people find him exhausting."

"He's borderline dangerous," Oliver adds.

"So, Alice isn't allowed to ride him at all?" I ask slowly. Elliot had told me that the girl could still see a bit, that she hadn't lost her vision completely. So, I didn't get the part about why she wasn't allowed to ride.

"Not Jiggs. He's way too hot and unpredictable," Kira says emphatically.

"Alice needs a quieter horse now, but there's no telling her..." Elliot breaks off abruptly.

"Oh, what a sweet dog," a voice behind me says, and I turn to see two of the last people I'd ever expected to run into here. Mia, one of the popular girls from my old school, and my ex-best friend, Zara, who is staring at me with wide eyes like I'm a ghost who has been conjured up in front of her. A lanky, dark-haired boy with what looks like a permanent scowl on his face trails behind them.

"Sidney?" Zara squeaks. "What are you doing here?"

A few expressions skitter across her face until she plasters them over with a polite smile. Anger, sadness, and strangely enough, a glimmer of fear. I don't understand it.

"I'm just visiting." I gulp, studying her familiar face longingly. I haven't seen her in person for months. Heck, I haven't even heard her voice on the phone until her recent drunken phone call. Losing my best friend had been the worst part about last year's disaster, and the pain that I've been doing my best to squash down comes roaring to life.

"Hey, Sidney." Mia beams her winning cheerleader smile at me, crouching down on the cold grass to pet a wriggling Beans.

"Hi." I force as much enthusiasm as I can muster. Mia has never actually done anything *mean* to me, but I still don't like her. I can't help but blame her and her popular crowd for stealing Zara away.

"We haven't seen you all summer," Mia goes on enthusiastically, as if she's somehow surprised that we haven't been attending the same parties. The ones that I don't get invited to. "This is my cousin, Josh."

"Hello." His voice is stiff and his gaze stays fixed on my face as if I'm a slightly offensive puzzle to solve.

"Why are you all down here slumming at Barn B?" Oliver asks coldly. All the previous warmth in his expression is gone, and he's staring at the other guy with an almost hostile expression.

"Dad asked me to see if you wanted a ride home since your car is in the shop," Josh says, tearing his piercing gaze away from me. "And you weren't answering my texts. So, I'm reluctantly fulfilling my family obligations, stepbrother."

"Right," Oliver mutters. "Well, I'm going to Kira's place for dinner, so don't bother."

They glare at each other in simmering silence, like two bulls trying to decide whether to charge.

But I'm distracted from their argument when I realize that Zara has sidled up next to me.

"Um, do you ride here, Zara?" I gulp nervously. I don't even know how to have a basic conversation with her now. It's like standing next to a stranger.

"Oh, no. I've outgrown playing with ponies." Zara rolls her eyes dismissively. "Mia and Josh still do the horse thing. I'm meeting them here so we can go to a show tonight. We're headed back to their house to have pre-concert drinks and get ready. Everyone who's anyone is going."

"That's great," I say, trying to muster up any traces of enthusiasm. Zara has always loved music and singing. She'd dragged me to countless concerts and festivals over the years.

"So, how are things with your parents? The last episode of True Dirt was brutal. Did you watch it? They really have it in for you, don't they?"

"Uh…" I hesitate, feeling a hot flush creep up my neck.

"Wait, you're not Ned and Nora Jones' daughter, are you?" Josh says sharply, fixing his accusing gaze on me as if he's finally figured me out.

"Um, yep. Guilty." I wince at my bad choice of words.

"Hmm." He crosses his arms over his chest. "And you're planning to work here at Three Sisters? With Alice?"

"Sidney is only visiting for today," Elliot says quickly. "We haven't really talked about a job yet."

"Well, enjoy your visit," Josh mutters darkly, shaking his head like I've already committed some shameful crime. "We'd better head out. See you around, Kira. Oliver."

"Bye, everyone," Mia calls cheerfully, skipping after her sullen cousin without a backward glance.

Zara hesitates, staring at me with a look I can't interpret. "It's good to see you, Sidney. It's been a long time."

"Yeah." I hope I don't start to cry or something ridiculous. "It has."

"Look, you and I should catch up. We should go for coffee one day."

"That would be amazing. I'd love that." My heart leaps in my chest at the thought of rekindling our friendship. Maybe if we started hanging out again, we could find our way back to the way things used to be. "When are you free? I work nights, but I can be available almost any day. You could come to the barn and see Oriel even. Or we could..."

I break off, realizing that I'm desperately babbling and that Zara is edging away.

"Oh, we'll figure it out," she says breezily. "I'll call you sometime and see where I can fit you in."

"Oh, okay," I say to her retreating back. "Great."

I swallow hard as I watch her catch up with Mia and Josh, leaning in to whisper something that makes them both laugh.

"Come on, Sidney," Elliot says quietly. "Let's finish our tour. You still have the whole upper barn to see."

"Right, sure." I swallow hard, trying to push aside all the anxious thoughts that seeing Zara and Mia again have stirred up. Automatically, I trail behind Elliot, but the day has lost some of its shine and I suddenly feel tired and sad. Even if I get a job here, I'm going to have to run into Mia and Josh nonstop. Or other people like them. People who have no problems judging me and condemning me for something my parents did. I'm not sure any job is worth that.

CHAPTER 10

ALICE

I walk down the hill to the barn, already feeling grumpy. The people who were supposed to try Jiggs today backed out at the last minute and I can't decide whether to be angry or relieved. I'm happy that he gets to stay at the barn a little longer, of course, but I'm also annoyed that these people think they're better than my brilliant pony.

We feel the pony is not right for our daughter at this time, the message had said. *We reviewed the videos again with our coach and have decided to purchase a more thoroughly schooled pony who can keep our Lucy in the winner's circle. We know you'll understand.*

What a bunch of crap. I know who their daughter is, and she rides like a sack of potatoes. She couldn't pilot Jiggs around a course to save her life. He is an impeccably schooled pony, if you know how to ride.

"Alice?"

A car door slams and I tilt my head until I can make out Josh's figure standing next to that annoying girl, Zara's, car. She's been hanging out a lot in the last few weeks, trailing after Mia and Josh like an annoying, yappy puppy. I can't stand her and her stupid, high-pitched hyena laugh.

"Oh, hey." I feel a little trill of excitement just being in Josh's presence, which is both mortifying and irritating. I really don't want to be *that* girl.

"Hi." His boots crunch across the gravel as he comes to stand beside me. "I was hoping to run into you. Do you know the girl that Elliot brought here today? Sidney?"

"No. Why?"

"Rumour is that Elliot wants her to be your tutor or something. But I think it's a bad idea. Her family is trouble, Alice. You should stay far away from her."

"Really?" I feel a flicker of interest. I know that most people, when they're told that someone is bad, or a situation is dangerous, might take good advice and avoid trouble at all costs. But I am not that person. "What's so bad about her?"

"Do you know who Ned and Nora Jones are?"

I shake my head. "Never heard of them. Are they serial killers or something? Gangsters?"

"No, but they've been on the news a lot this year. Real estate fraud, embezzlement, and a few other things. A lot of people in town invested money in their shady business dealings and lost everything. One man even committed suicide. They're con artists. Even Zara's grandmother lost a fortune."

"Oh." I shrug, disappointed. I couldn't care less about Zara's grandmother or fraud. "I don't watch the news. Are they this girl's parents or something?"

"Yes, and I heard the whole family is trouble. Zara was telling me all about it. That show, True Dirt, did a bunch of episodes on them. One of the kids is a professional *actress,* too."

He says the word distastefully, like acting itself is a crime. I like Josh, way too much for my own good, but sometimes he acts like a fussy, suspicious old man who was born a hundred years ago. He is the exact opposite of his easy-going stepbrother, Oliver, or bubbly Mia.

"Hmm, sounds interesting."

"Alice." He draws out my name disapprovingly. "I'm just saying it's best if you don't get involved with her."

I stare at him thoughtfully, my irritation at being bossed around warring with being pleased that he's concerned about me.

"Fine, I'll think about it. Thanks."

"I'm only looking out for you. I'd hate for someone to take advantage when you're vulnerable."

Vulnerable? Okay, now I'm annoyed, but before I come up with a snappy response, Zara bangs on the car horn, making us both jump.

"Come on, Josh. We're going to be late," she shrills out the window.

"Sorry, I have to go. See you around, Alice." His boots crunch back to the car, the door slams and Zara peels out of the parking lot in a spray of gravel.

I glare after the car, irritated that Zara is still circling around Josh like a hungry jackal. As if he'd ever be interested in someone like her. She is shallow, annoying, and she doesn't even ride. And if my older sister Clara hadn't been able to snag Josh, then someone like Zara certainly doesn't stand a chance.

Not that he'd ever be interested in you either, I remind myself firmly. Still, he deserves so much better than Zara.

"Alice?" I turn at Elliot's familiar voice and tilt my head slightly so I can see her approaching. The day is overcast, so most everything is in grey shadow, but I can make out two blurred figures.

There is a weird sound as they get closer, a snuffling-snorting-wheezing type of noise that sounds like a dying accordion.

"What is *that?*" I take a step back. The noise is coming from the direction of the ground and it's the kind of slavering, choking sound that a Tasmanian devil might make.

"Sorry," the girl with Elliot says, "it's my dog. I know he sounds a bit like a gremlin."

"We don't let dogs here," I snap. "Barn rules. Darla hates dogs. Why didn't you leave him at home?"

"Sorry," she says again, "home is a little complicated right now, and I didn't want to leave him behind."

"Oh?" I prick my ears with interest, sensing some potentially juicy gossip. You never know what small bit of information will be useful to you in the future. "Why couldn't you leave him?"

"Um…" She hesitates, and Elliot clears her throat.

"Sidney's here to see about a possible grooming job," she says. "And also…"

"No," I snap. "Don't even say it. Talk to Anna about the groom thing, but I definitely do not want a tutor. No offense, Sidney."

"Are you sure, Alice?" Elliot asks. "Your dad said…"

"Yeah, I know what he said. The answer is still no."

I turn to Sidney, who has taken a few steps backward, and struggle to calm my anger. It's not her fault, after all. "You have the Friesian that everyone has been going on about, right?"

"Um, yes, I do. His name is Oriel." Her voice has a tremor in it and I can't tell if she's nervous, sad, or angry. Not being able to read people's expressions or their body language anymore is so annoying. It's like I'm missing crucial pieces of a puzzle.

Oriel. Something clicks in my head as I realize I might actually know who this horse is. "Was he from Pablo Garcia's barn?"

"Yes." She sounds surprised. "Pablo was my trainer for years. He bred a lot of great horses, including Oriel."

"I've seen his website before. That farm looks amazing. He trained some horses for the movies too, right?"

"Yes, he did. Capriole was an incredible farm. I miss riding there so much."

Her voice dips at the end and I tilt my head, trying to figure her out. Why doesn't she ride there anymore if she liked it so much? What is so bad about her home that she can't leave her dog there for a few hours? If there is one thing I can't resist, it's a mystery.

"I'd like to meet your horse," I find myself saying. "I'd like to ride him. I've never ridden a Friesian before."

There is a long pause and I wait impatiently for her to answer.

"You can definitely meet him," Sidney says slowly. "But I don't let other people ride him. He's special and I..."

Instantly, a wave of dark anger washes over me and I hang on to it, letting it build to cover my embarrassment. Who does this girl think she is to say *no* to me when I asked politely? I could out-ride her any day of the week. She would be *lucky* to have me ride her horse. Nobody says no to me and gets away with it.

"Well, I don't think there's a job for you here then," I say in my frostiest voice. "Not as my tutor, and not with Anna. Josh said your parents are criminals, anyway. We have a reputation to uphold here. You'd better leave now."

I turn to march triumphantly toward the barn, hearing her sharp intake of breath and Elliot's hurried apologies. A tiny part of me feels bad, but it's not as strong as the part of me that takes satisfaction in hurting her feelings after she'd hurt *mine.*

You lost your chance to meet the horse, the reasonable, not-evil, part of me says. *If you'd just been polite for two minutes, she might have let you meet him. And if you played your cards right, you might have been able to ride him later, once she trusted you. But you blew it. Exactly like you always do.*

My shoulders slump, like a heavy weight is pushing down on me. My conscience is right. I always do this. It's like I have this compulsion to sabotage every chance I have at happiness. I'm such a....

And that's when something hits me. Literally. Some sort of dense, flailing object hits me in the back of the knees and sends me sprawling onto the grass.

Before I can push myself up, I am being assaulted by a snorting, wheezing beast that leaps up and licks my face with a warm, slobbery tongue.

"Gross, get off me," I squeal, keeping him back with one hand and wiping the disgusting saliva off my face with the other. But instead of backing off, the animal crawls into my lap, turns around in a clumsy circle and then flops down with a final wheeze.

"Um, excuse me," I call, "can you come get your revolting dog?"

"I'm so sorry." Sidney crouches beside me and starts brushing dirt and grass off my jacket. "He pulled the leash right out of my hand. I can't believe he knocked you over. Come here, Beans. Leave her alone."

The dog doesn't move. In fact, he burrows into my open jacket and curls up, like he's about to have a long nap there, completely ignoring his owner.

"Beans," I say slowly, tentatively reaching out to run my fingers over his short, silky coat. The solid feel of him isn't totally unpleasant. In fact, it's kind of comforting. "That's a weird name. What is he?"

"He's a French bulldog."

"Are they all so fat and lumpy?"

"No," she snaps, suddenly defensive, "he's old. But he's a great dog. Sorry that he knocked you over. We should go now. Beans, come here."

He suddenly goes limp in my lap and begins to snore loudly as if he'd instantly fallen asleep.

"Is he faking?" I ask, starting to laugh.

"Probably," she says glumly. "He obviously thinks you're a comfortable place to nap."

"I've never had a dog," I say, giving him a pat. "My older sister hates pets. She'd have a fit if there was a cat or dog in the house, so we could never have them."

"Really? Does she have allergies or something?"

"No." I shrug. "But she always gets her way."

"That's terrible."

I nod, tracing the little guy's silky ears and trying to remember what French bulldogs looked like. Right now, he feels like a potato with legs and a smooshed-in face.

I find my body relaxing against his. *Maybe I can get a dog of my own now that Clara isn't living at home.* I don't know why I didn't think of this earlier. Everyone else in the house likes pets. And Trin would be so excited to have a dog. It's not like Clara can punish me from halfway across the world. Can she?

"If you came to work here, would you bring this guy?" I ask suddenly.

"Beans goes everywhere with me," Sidney says slowly, "so I guess so. But it doesn't sound like there's a job for me here. Since I'm from a criminal family and everything."

"Yeah." I sigh and rub a hand across my aching eyes. "So, here's the thing, Sidney. Everyone at Three Sisters accepts that I'm a jerk who says mean stuff. I do it to everyone, so don't worry. It's kind of my brand. You'll have to be okay with that if you come to work here."

"Um," she says, but I hold up my hand to cut her off. My mind has made one of its abrupt switches and now, suddenly, I want this girl with an interesting past, an interesting dog and one of Pablo Garcia's fancy horses here.

"Look, my dad is going to force a tutor on me eventually," I say, "so it might as well be someone I don't completely hate. If I let my *dad* pick a tutor, then he's going to find some moldy old school-teacher-lady who tries to boss me around."

She snorts out a laugh, and I'm surprised to find myself smiling back at her.

"We normally don't let grooms bring their horses here, but if you were my tutor, it would be a different story. The barns are full, but there are paddocks with shelters available if you like. That's where I keep Jiggs and my old pony Checkers. You'd only have to spend a couple hours a day with me since I hate school, anyway. So, it isn't like you'd need to do much classwork or anything. You could just pretend to do the tutoring thing for all I care. Whatever keeps my dad off my back."

I pause, waiting for her to answer, but she says nothing.

Boots scuff on the gravel and I turn to see Elliot heading toward us from wherever she's been hiding.

"How are you doing here, girls?" she asks cautiously.

"We're fine." I glare at her, wrapping my arms a little more tightly around the fat dog in my lap. "We're having a private discussion about the tutor position. You don't need to be involved."

"Alice offered me a job," Sidney says quietly. "And a place to board Oriel."

"Hmmm, that's great." Elliot's voice has a doubtful note in it, and I narrow my eyes at her, hoping she's not about to interfere. Isn't this why she brought Sidney here in the first place? "We should probably discuss this with your father first, Alice."

"Why?" I snap. "It's my life, so it's my decision. End of story. Sidney, do you want the job or not?"

"I do," she says slowly, not sounding convinced. "I need to find a second job. And I know Oriel would love it here, but..."

"Of course he would. It's the best barn on the whole island. Ben can pick him up in one of our trailers. I can show you his paddock right now if you like."

"This is moving fast," she says. "I need to think..."

"Why would you need to *think* about anything?" I demand, closing in for the kill. "I'm offering you a dream opportunity here, but you have to decide right now if you want to take it."

"Alice," Elliot warns. "Stop bullying her. Your dad..."

"Time to decide, Sidney," I say, ignoring annoying-Elliot completely. "Tick-tock."

"Fine," Sidney says suddenly, just like I'd guessed she would. Desperate people are so predictable. "But I want to do a month trial first to see if we're a good match. And only if your dad is okay with it. Oh, and I'm not agreeing to lease Oriel to you either."

I grit my teeth for a second because I hadn't expected her to add that last part. But then I nod. I can force myself to be patient for now.

"Deal. And this dog comes with you."

"Deal," she gulps, suddenly sounding uncertain again. "But shouldn't we sign a contract or something?"

"Fine, whatever." I shrug. "I'm sure Elliot will call my dad the second my back is turned, so you two can work the details out with him."

I lift the dog up so Sidney can take him and then rise to my feet. My jeans are damp from the wet ground, which would normally annoy me, but right now I don't care.

"See you later, tutor." I stride away to the house, pleased with how my afternoon has turned out. Hopefully, my dad will hire her without doing any sort of background check. I'm pretty sure he'd feel the same as Josh if he knew that her family was wrapped up in some scandal.

I hum under my breath as I walk up the hill, pondering on how I can make the situation work best to my advantage. The first step, after getting her officially hired, will be to make her trust me enough to ride that horse. I'll need to apply just the right amount of pressure.

And if I really like Oriel then I'm sure my dad will buy him for me if I ask. Sidney has a strong aura of desperation around her. If her family is going through all this legal stuff, then she probably needs money. If we throw her enough cash, then I'm sure she'll part with her horse, eventually. Heck, maybe she'll even sell me the dog too if I use enough leverage.

I smile to myself, doing a little skip on the gravel.

I'll just have to find the perfect way to convince Sidney that my vision for the future is best for everyone.

CHAPTER 11

SIDNEY

*W*ell, that was hands-down the weirdest encounter I've ever had.

I hold Beans tightly against my chest, watching Alice walk away.

I don't trust her one bit, but right now she's given me an opportunity to unravel part of this mess my life is in. And for that I'm cautiously grateful.

"I have to make some phone calls," Elliot says, wandering across the lawn toward the small group of ornamental trees out front.

I'm guessing that she wants some privacy so I let Beans pull me through the large front doors into the immaculate barn.

Immediately a sense of calm settles over me, which is the exact opposite of what I feel walking into the barn at Happy Acres. This place feels peaceful, like a sanctuary.

Someone is sweeping far down the aisle, the broom moving in steady, rasping strokes across the concrete floor. The sound mixes with the rhythmic crunching of the horses eating their hay and the occasional hoof stomp. It all sounds so familiar and homey, so much like Capriole had, that I feel like I already belong here.

Most of the stalls are empty but there are a handful of horses still left inside. All are wearing spotlessly clean quilted stable blankets with the Three Sisters logo embroidered on them. Some even have hoods that go right up their necks and over their heads so that only their ears, eyes and the tips of their noses are exposed.

They all look posh, glossy, and fully clipped without a hair out of place. Each mane is neatly pulled and not a single horse has a speck of shavings or dirt on them. They all look beautiful. And expensive.

"Hi ponies," I say softly, pausing at each occupied stall in admiration.

A few look up with interest as I walk by, most are too absorbed in eating to notice me, but there are a small handful who pin their ears at me as soon as I look at them. One big chestnut dives to the back of his stall and stands there, with his hind end pointed toward me defensively, his eyes rolling unhappily as if I'm about to do something horrible to him.

Oh, poor guy, I think, moving quickly past him. *Why is he so unhappy? This place seems perfect.*

"When I say forward, I mean forward!"

I jolt as a voice bellows from down the aisle, so loud that it feels like the shouter is only standing a few feet away. For the first time I notice that there is an indoor arena attached to the long row of stalls, down at the very end. Hooves thud rhythmically against the footing and I see a glimpse of horses flashing by through the gap above the door.

"Sidney?"

The sweeper has worked his way down the aisle and I realize that he's not a stranger.

"Ben!" I smile at him in delight. Ben had ridden at Pablo's too, like his sister Elliot, and he'd always been kind and friendly to me. He'd left a couple of years before I had, heading to Europe to be a working student, and I hadn't seen him in all that time.

"Good to see you, kid." He pulls me into a quick hug and then steps back to untangle himself from Beans' leash and give the little dog an affectionate scratch behind the ears. "I see Beans is still trucking along. How is that horse of yours doing?"

"He's good. Really good. Did you know Elliot's trying to get me a job here?"

"I do." He laughs. "I might have been the one to put her up to it. I thought you and Oriel might be just the ticket to cheer up my little friend Alice."

I raise my eyebrows. "Does she know you call her your little friend?"

"Oh, you met her, did you?" He shakes his head, still laughing. "She's a feisty one, that's for sure. But she does have a good heart, especially where her horses are concerned. She had a rough start in life."

I look around the fancy barn, raising my eyebrows. "It doesn't look very rough around here."

"True. Very few things in life are what they seem on the surface, though."

I nod slowly, thinking of my own family falling apart inside our fancy designer home. Until the scandal had happened, it had looked like we had the whole world at our fingertips. But things on the inside had been crumbling for a long time.

"Have you completely lost your mind? That was pathetic!"

I jolt again as another loud bellow comes thundering down the aisle. It is a voice that is eerily familiar and suddenly I realize that the instructor must be Barb's sister. They sound nearly identical.

"Is that who I'd be working for?" I whisper, my heart sinking.

"No, no. We'd have you working with Anna in Barn B. It's a

much different atmosphere down there. I manage this barn but that's our head coach, Darla." He drops his voice to a whisper too. "She's a yeller."

"Yeah, I guessed." I wonder how a peaceful person like Ben can stand working with someone like that. Barb is bad but this lady sounds even worse.

"It's all sorted," Elliot says, striding into the barn, her face all smiles. "Anna can use you part time down at Barn B during the day. I assured her you knew all about standard show prep and that you're a top-notch braider."

I nod, hoping I haven't lost my skills.

"You'll have an interview with Mr. Carlisle and his fiancée Tiffani tomorrow around noon. You are free, aren't you?"

"Sure, I can come after I ride and take care of Oriel."

"Perfect. Would you like me to pick you up again?"

It's tempting. But I don't want to depend on her too much. She's already done a lot for me in the last couple of days.

"No." I shake my head. "I can handle this one on my own. Do I go to that big house up the hill?"

"That's right. They're very nice people, so I don't think you'll have any trouble at all. Call me when you're done and Ben can figure out bringing Oriel over if that's what you want to do."

"After the trial period," I say firmly, "just in case things don't work out here. I've already paid board for this month anyway."

Elliot shares a look with Ben and then nods.

"Don't worry about Alice too much. She is unpredictable and will probably change her mind at least twice about having a tutor, but she doesn't call the shots on who gets hired and fired, no matter what she tells you. We won't leave you stranded."

I let out a relieved breath.

"Thank you both so much for finding me this opportunity," I say sincerely. "I don't know why you're helping me after all this time but I appreciate it."

"We're helping you because you're a good person." Elliot

smiles. "And because you've been dealt a few bad hands in life that you didn't deserve. I've never felt comfortable with the way you left Capriole. And I honestly wish I'd done more to get you and Oriel back."

The afternoon light is fading when Elliot drops me off at Happy Acres. I check on Oriel one more time, glad to see that he has hay in front of him and that Val had kept her promise and cleaned his stall. She'd even put in extra shavings, which is something I do myself that always drives Barb crazy.

Then I get in my car and head for home.

CHAPTER 12

SIDNEY

The restaurant is booked for a fancy private party that night and, luckily, I'm run nearly off my feet trying to keep up so I don't have much time to dwell on all my personal worries.

"Good work tonight," Vinny says, slapping me on the back at the end of my shift and pushing a hundred-dollar bill into my hands. "Go treat yourself to something nice."

"Thanks." I cram the money into my pocket, already bookmarking it for Oriel's upcoming farrier appointment.

All the lights are blazing when I get home, even though it's after midnight, but I don't think too much about it at first. Nobody in our house does basic things like shut off the lights and television when they leave a room.

I kick my shoes off and then walk down the hall, switching lights off and closing the refrigerator door that someone has left ajar. As I turn to head to my room, I nearly trip over the pile of luggage sitting right in the middle of the hall.

"What is all this?" I ask out loud, even though it's obvious what it is.

"Oh, Sidney, you're just in time." Mom clicks toward me from the back of the house in a towering pair of heels. She's wearing a grey skirt and blazer and her makeup is flawless even though it's the middle of the night. She looks as if she's ready to teach a seminar. "We had to speed our timeline up a little, so we're flying out tonight. We'll call you as soon as we arrive and get settled in."

"What?" I stare at her in astonishment. "You're leaving *now*? I thought we had a week to figure stuff out. Are you kicking me out tonight?" My panic kicks into overdrive.

"Oh, Sidney, don't be so dramatic. Of course we're not kicking you out tonight. Your father came up with a brilliant solution. Since the housing market is slow right now, it could take months for the house to sell. You can just stay here until it does. The real estate agent will call whenever she needs to do a showing, so just make sure to keep the place clean. Bye, darling. We'll meet up for Christmas once Manifest Now kicks off in Vegas."

"Wait," I say as she shoves a key into my hand and gives me an air-kiss about a foot from my cheek. "Where's Leo? Aren't you taking him?"

She pauses, blinking at me. "Damn it, I knew I was forgetting something." She whirls around and clicks back down the hall. "Leo! You better have packed your things like I asked you. The taxi is here and we need to leave right now. Your father expected us at the airport ten minutes ago."

"Well, at least we have a place to live, Beans," I whisper, hoisting him up away from the luggage he's sniffing. "For a little while anyway."

There is no sign of Eden anywhere. And when I head down the hall to look for her, I discover that while I'd been at work, her room had been cleaned out and stripped of nearly everything. Only her bed has been left behind. She's even taken her curtains.

I pull out my phone and send her a quick text to make sure she's okay, even though it's well past midnight and I don't think she'll appreciate any disruption to her beauty sleep.

I stare at the screen for a second, hoping for a response, and then stuff my phone into my pocket with a sigh.

I shouldn't worry about her. Eden always lands on her feet. She's tough as nails and has probably been dying to leave this family behind since she was a toddler. Leo, on the other hand....

"Leo, we talked about this," I hear my mother saying in the hall. "We can have the rest of your things shipped out later. Let's not have a scene. The taxi is waiting and we don't want to miss our flight."

"I'm not going," Leo says stubbornly, catching sight of me. "I'm staying with Sidney. She'll take care of me."

My mother stares at me, her eyes widening as if she's seriously considering it. "Oh, well, maybe that's..."

"Mom, no," I protest, "I can't keep him. I'm practically homeless myself. I have one, maybe two, full-time jobs and Oriel to take care of. What am I supposed to do with him when I'm working all day and night?"

The words are out of my mouth before I can soften them. I'd meant to sound convincing and practical, not cruel. But the injured look on Leo's face stops me cold.

His lower lip trembles as he turns away and shuffles down the hall, his overflowing backpack weighing down one shoulder. He opens the front door and trudges outside, leaving the door hanging open behind him.

"Yes, I suppose that would be too much to ask of you," my mom says, huffing out a deep breath, "he's not self-reliant like you and your sister are. We're a little at a loss of what to do with him, honestly. We thought perhaps boarding school, but the fees are so outrageous. I mean, he barely eats anything, so why would board be so expensive?"

I'm hardly listening to her as I watch Leo climb woodenly into the waiting taxi, pulling his backpack in across his lap.

"Mom, he was really looking forward to taking astronomy classes this year after school. If I find a program out there and send you the links, can you make sure he gets signed up? I'm worried…"

"Oh, what a wonderful idea. You're always so thoughtful, Sidney. Send them to me and we'll see what we can do. Help me with this luggage, please. Your father has sent me three messages already, and he's not too happy that we're late."

Sighing, I help her haul the multiple suitcases down the hall toward the stony-faced taxi driver.

"What about the rest of Leo's stuff?" I ask. "He only has a backpack with him. Does he even have enough clothes?"

"Oh, I'm sure we'll sort it all out when we get there. Lots of love, darling. Remember not to let any strangers inside. And you should probably park your car down the block from now on just to be safe. The dealership is being completely unreasonable. We won't be using them again; I can tell you that. We'll see you at Christmas, darling. Or Easter at the latest."

Then she's gone, leaving only a cloud of perfume in her wake.

The taxi squeals off down the road and suddenly I'm alone, except for Beans and the gnawing feeling of guilt churning inside of me. I hope Leo isn't badly hurt by what I'd said. I hope that he makes friends and learns to love Vegas.

I chew at my bottom lip, wondering if I should have kept him here after all. Maybe we could have figured something out if I'd had more time to think it through.

"Well, I guess it's too late now, Beans," I say, looking down into his lolling doggy grin. He honestly doesn't care what is happening as long as I'm somewhere nearby. "Let's go see if they left us any food in the house."

CHAPTER 13

ALICE

The morning after my meeting with Beans and Sidney, I wake up feeling like a bit of the usual gloom has lifted off my shoulders.

I potter around my room, listening to music and tidying up a little. I'm feeling pretty good until there is a pounding knock at my bedroom door.

"Alice, we need to talk," my dad calls, rattling the door handle. "This silent treatment isn't helping anyone."

Muttering under my breath, I shut off my music and march to the door. I haven't been giving him the silent treatment. It's not like I'm five years old and pouting. I simply haven't been interested in talking to him or being in the same room with him. There's a big difference.

"Hello, Father. How can I help you?" I unlock the door and swing it wide open, smiling up at him with all teeth bared. I use my most sugary fake-polite voice, the one I use on teachers when I particularly hate them.

"Alice, stop that," he says gruffly. "Look, I know you're grieving, but this has gone far enough. You can't shut everyone out forever. We want to help you."

"Oh, right. Everything you've done lately has been very helpful for my mental well-being, thanks, Father. Do you need anything else or can I go back to listening to my music in peace?"

"No, we need to talk."

"If it's about the tutor, I've already solved it. I'm surprised Elliot hasn't called you about her already."

"She did call me," he says, clearing his throat. "But I wanted to speak to you first. About the tutor and about, well, I think it's time for you to see a counsellor. You need to talk about your feelings."

"Gross, no. Why would I want to do that?"

"Because you're struggling with some big life changes here. And it must seem overwhelming. The doctors suggested..."

"No way. Look, you can make me go to a counsellor's office if you like but I won't talk to her. I'll sit there and stare at whatever high-priced shrink you pick out and I won't say a word. Just like Clara did when you forced her into therapy."

"Alice, you are *not* Clara," he says sharply. "I know you love your sister and that you've always looked up to her. But you must realize that she doesn't always make rational, healthy choices. Talking to a counsellor isn't a punishment. It's supposed to help you."

"It won't."

"Look, Alice, I'm trying my best to help you through an awful situation, but I'm honestly floundering here. I'm sorry about selling the ponies, even though I still think it was the safest decision. I don't want to see my daughter killed or paralyzed, on top of the vision issues. I want you to be happy. Despite living in this place and being surrounded by horses, I don't think you've been happy for a long time."

I open my mouth to argue and then hesitate. I love Three

Sisters, and of course, I enjoy my ponies. I love riding, showing, winning. Making a goal and crushing it. But happy? I'm not sure I even know what that means.

I sit down on my bed with a sigh. "I want my old life back, Dad. Everything is awful and different and I hate it. I don't want a tutor, but this girl that Elliot fished up from who-knows-where is not completely awful. So, I think we should give her a chance."

There is a long silence. "I've set up an interview with her today. But if you like her, then I'd say it's just a formality."

"She'll be bringing her dog to work with her," I add, "and her horse will board here too. We're doing a month-long trial. It's already organized."

"Alice," he groans in exasperation. "I don't like you making these decisions without consulting me."

"Oh, really?" My heart stutters as that familiar rage spurts through me like I've switched on a hot water tap. The shift in my mood happens so fast that it's almost scary, even to me. "You don't like how it feels when someone makes huge decisions about your life without even asking you? When they sell the things that mean the most to you and break your heart?"

I hadn't meant to say that last part. It sounds too much like I'm weak and hurting when all I want him to see is how angry I am. He can't do something like sell my ponies and expect me to ever forgive him.

"Alice." He takes a step toward me, but I hold up both hands to keep him away.

"I don't want your pity, Dad. And we can't go back to being friends like we were before. Those days are over."

He's silent for so long that I start to feel uncomfortable. I wonder if he's going to answer at all.

"I'll interview Sidney after lunch. And if she works out, then I'll agree to let her bring her dog and horse here. But I want you to know that I've already made an appointment for you to see a counsellor this morning. All the doctors recommended you see someone, and this is now non-negotiable."

"No way," I say, suddenly panicky. The last thing I need is someone trying to ferret out all my secrets and mess with my head. "The doctors are wrong. I'll sort things out myself. I like to do things my own way."

"That's what your mother always said about you." There is a faint trace of amusement in his voice. "She'd say, Alice is stubborn, let her figure things out by herself. She always admired that in you, Alice. I know that she'd be so proud of you if she were here right now."

I freeze at those words and don't hear anything else he says after that. I just stare at him blankly until I realize that at some point, he's left the room and isn't in front of me at all anymore. Those words have stuck ice shards in my chest, hitting all the painful parts of me in one stab.

If Mom were here. Yeah, well, it's because of *me* that she isn't here. The doctors had warned her not to have another baby. She'd lasted seven more years after I was born, but her decline had been steady and inevitable. Everyone knew it was my fault, although only Clara said it out loud, whispering it furiously to me on each anniversary of Mom's death.

"It's because you're rotten, Alice," she would hiss at me, grabbing my arms so hard that the bruises would take a week to fade. "You're toxic and that's why she died."

Even though I know now that that's not scientifically possible, the guilt has become a permanent part of me, a heavy weight that I can never shake. *Rotten to the core.*

Sure, Mom had been proud of me sometimes, but it had always been conditional. When I won things, when I brought home ribbons, or impressed her in some way. But I certainly wasn't a consolation prize for her dying. I'm sure she regretted her decision to have me. And I bet the rest of my family did too.

CHAPTER 14

ALICE

*D*espite zoning out during my dad's lecture, I'm pretty sure I never agreed to let annoying-Tiffani drive me to the office of a high-priced counsellor. But, somehow here I am, in Tiffani's tiny sports car threading through the crowded streets of downtown Victoria.

To be fair, Tiffani doesn't seem any more thrilled about this than I do. My dad had a meeting to go to, so I'd been dumped on her last minute. She has barely said a word to me the entire drive.

"Well, here we are," she says finally, as we pull into the underground parking garage. "It's on the second floor. I'll walk you up."

I am completely capable of finding the second-floor office myself, but she's probably afraid that I'll bolt out the back door or something. Which is not a bad idea.

I drag my feet across the cement floor, thankful for the bright overhead lights that at least let me know if I'm going to bump into anything. The last thing I want is Tiffani's manicured claws on my arm while she tries to *guide* me.

The ride on the elevator is completely silent, and I wonder what Tiffani is thinking. We've never been the best of friends, although we'd declared a truce for my dad's sake last year.

My sister Clara had all-out hated Tiffani and had tried to make her life, and Trin's life, as miserable as possible when they'd first moved into our house. And, I'm not proud of this, but I'd helped Clara out with her pranks and schemes a lot in the beginning. Partly because it had been fun and partly because saying no to Clara was always risky.

Tiffani had tried to be so nice to me, especially after my time in the hospital, but her kindness felt claustrophobic, like she was smothering me, and it only made me angry.

This is the first time we've been alone since the surgery, I realize, as the elevator crawls slowly upward.

Tiffani stares moodily at the closed doors, lost in her own thoughts. The silence presses in on me and I shift around uncomfortably. How can it possibly take this long to go up two floors?

Just as I open my mouth to say something, anything, to break up that oppressive silence, the elevator jolts to a stop and the doors open onto a short hallway with only one door at the end.

"Here we go," Tiffani says. "I think you're going to like Donna. She has an excellent reputation and has written quite a few books. She's the counsellor that Kira's dad recommended, and apparently Kira adores her."

"Great," I mutter. I don't really know Kira well, even though she's been riding Jiggs for me. She barely says a word when I'm around so it's hard to tell what she's thinking. She is a brilliant rider though, and I'd even heard that she'd been invited to intern at John Riddle's fancy Olympic-level barn when she graduates. Which makes me extremely jealous because he is one of my favourite riders and I could have probably interned with him too in a few years if the tumour thing hadn't happened.

The waiting room isn't what I'd expected at all. I thought it would be all white and sterile, like in the hospital, but it's more like stepping into a comfortable living room.

"This is nice." Tiffani looks around appreciatively. "Let's sit down and wait."

She must be distracted because she reaches out and puts an arm around my shoulders, all ready to lead me over to the bank of plush chairs by the window like I'm a child.

I jerk away, glaring at her and rubbing my arm to get rid of the feeling of her hand on it.

"Don't touch me."

She inhales sharply and turns away abruptly, finding her seat without looking at me or saying another word.

After a second, I trail after her, plopping down in a chair a few seats away from hers and tapping my boots anxiously against the floor.

I glance over to where Tiffani is staring out the window to the water below and feel a stab of guilt. I know I'm unnecessarily mean to Tiffani sometimes. Well, most of the time, if I'm being honest, but I just can't help it.

I don't mind that she's marrying my dad. I can see that they make each other happy and I think he deserves that in his life. But it's easier if she and I live separate lives and not get too close.

"Alice?"

I look up, then tilt my head to the side to see the outline of a gray-haired woman watching me from an open doorway.

"Yes, this is Alice," Tiffani says nervously, springing to her feet. "You must be Donna. Thanks so much for fitting us in on such short notice. Do you want us to both come in? I'm not sure how this works and I…"

"I think Alice and I can handle this from here," Donna says. "You're welcome to either wait here or downstairs in the coffee shop. They make an incredible lemon loaf. We'll be done in an hour. Alice?"

She makes a sweeping motion toward her office.

"Well, if you're sure," Tiffani says hastily, already backing toward the main office door. "Then I'll leave you to it."

She practically bolts out of the lobby, obviously relieved not to have to spend another minute with me.

Donna's office has the same comfortable feeling to it as the waiting room. One entire wall is a huge window that overlooks the Gorge Waterway and I walk over to it. I can't see the details, of course, but I can see the blue of the water and hear the hum of the cars down below.

Now that I'm here I can't imagine staying mute the whole time like I'd threatened. I'm not sure how Clara managed it for all the months Dad had forced her to attend counselling.

"So, Alice, what brings you here today? What goals can I help you with?" Donna sits down in a chair near the window and I can feel her gaze fixed on me.

"My dad forced me to be here," I say flatly. "I don't need any help. This is the last place I want to be."

"Oh, well, in that case you'd best be on your way." Donna pops up again. "I don't see anyone against their will. I only help people who want to help themselves."

She moves to the door and opens it with a sharp click. "The coffee shop is right downstairs. Can you find it yourself or would you like me to call your stepmother back to help you?"

I stare at her in shock, wondering what on earth is happening. "You're kicking me out?"

She tilts her head and I wish I could make out her expression. "I thought you didn't want to be here. Look, Alice. I help people who are stuck. Who are at a crossroads in life."

"Yeah? *My* crossroads are solid prison walls with no way out."

"Well, Alice, my specialty is in knowing how to break walls. But you're the one who must do the work. I just hand you the tools. So, how would you like us to proceed today?"

I turn back toward the window, thinking hard. This is not at all how I pictured this session going. I'd thought she'd want to talk about *feelings* and things, not try to help me solve actual real-life issues.

Still, I'm not ready to give in quite yet.

"You think you can give me my old life back?" I snap, reaching for my familiar anger. "You can make me a show jumper again? Get me to the Olympics? Can you unsell my ponies? Can you fix my vision?"

"I can't give your sight back, unfortunately," she says briskly, shutting the door again and moving back toward her desk. "That's out of my hands. But let's look at the other things. Are there no visually challenged riders out there?"

"Not show jumpers. Only stupid dressage."

"Are you certain about that?"

"Yes. Well, no." I frown. Come to think about it, I hadn't done any actual research on that. I'd just assumed. "The doctors told my dad I could never jump again."

"I see. Is there a *medical* reason for you not jumping?" she asks curiously. "Will it cause more damage to your vision?"

"Um." I tap my fingers on the edge of my chair, thinking hard. "I'm not sure."

"Well, I'd investigate that first if I were you. You can't decide what's possible without all the pertinent information. Now, let's see what a quick Google search gets us."

She taps away at her keyboard while I fidget in my chair, feeling foolish. Why hadn't I asked the doctors or my dad any of these questions? I wasn't normally the type of person to let other people dictate what I did with my life.

"Ah-ha, here it is. You're right that there isn't any show jumping at the Paralympics *yet*, but there are low vision and blind people who jump horses. There are a few websites to look at. I'm surprised you haven't already..."

"How was I supposed to do that when I can't see the damn computer?" I say sharply. "Nobody in my family wants me to jump or succeed in riding anymore. They want me to sit around and be boring and safe."

I break off, heat stinging my cheeks. Even to my ears I sound pathetic and whiny.

"Is that so? Your father mentioned that he'd set up a school room for you full of adaptive technology. He said you refused to go near it. Is that not correct?"

"Oh, I suppose," I grumble, "but I hate that stuff. I don't want to have to learn all these dumb new things. I want life to go back to what it was like before."

Donna doesn't say anything but I can feel her studying me as I struggle to get my emotions under control.

"I understand that this is difficult, Alice. But, the reality of your situation is that you must be your own advocate from now on. The unfortunate truth is that while there are many resources out there for people who experience vision loss, they are hard to find unless you dig. You will have all sorts of people telling you that your dreams are unrealistic and impossible and that you should just give up. So, you're going to have to learn to stand up and fight for yourself, understand?"

I let out a deep breath and nod. "All right, I understand. I'm good at fighting. Did you really see articles about blind show jumpers?"

"I did, and I will send you a list of links to follow up on. Now I'd love to hear more about this farm of yours. Kira has told me a lot about Three Sisters so I feel like I know parts of it already."

I am not usually a talker. I much prefer to sit back and let other people spill their secrets while I listen. But then nobody has really cared enough to ask me about my life before either.

Suddenly I can't stop the words from pouring out. I tell Donna about Three Sisters and the horses that live at Barn A. And the way the sun used to look coming up over the mountains in the morning and how I used to love to get to the barn first thing, long before the other boarders and riders got there, so I could work my ponies by myself in the stillness of dawn.

Then I tell her all about Jiggs. About what a mess he was when I got him and how I turned him into a top pony. And about how conflicted I am that he hasn't sold yet, even though he's the best pony in the barn.

"Have you told your father that you'd like to keep working him?" Donna asks curiously.

"No." I shake my head. "My dad will never let me keep him now; he's made that clear. Besides, it isn't practical to keep Jiggs if I'm not allowed to jump him. He's too expensive to sit around getting fat. His talent is being wasted and his financial value is going down. I'll outgrow him soon and he'll need to be sold anyway so there's no point in getting too attached."

I stop, embarrassed that I was rambling on.

"I see," Donna says, but I can't tell if she agrees with me or not. "And how does your stepmom feel about all of this?"

I blink at her, thrown off by the question. "Um, I have no idea. And she's not my stepmom, not yet anyway. She's just Dad's fiancée."

"Oh, sorry, you mentioned your stepsister earlier so I assumed."

I shrug, turning toward the window again. "Right. I do call Trin that. She's already like a sister to me. I don't hate Tiffani or anything. Not really. She tries too hard, you know?"

Donna doesn't say anything and for the first time I ask myself *why* I don't like Tiffani so much. She's always so nice and I can barely stand to be in the same room with her.

"Sometimes it feels like she's trying to be my mom," I say finally. "And I already had a mother. I don't need another one."

And I practically killed the first one, I think, but don't say.

"Fair enough." Donna nods and then pushes her chair back. "Well, we're out of time today, Alice. It's been wonderful meeting you. I look forward to hearing how your research goes this week."

"That's it?" I'm shocked that the session is over. It feels like I've been here for ten minutes, not an hour, and I have so many other things to tell her. "Can't I stay longer?"

"I'm afraid not. I have another client coming in a few minutes. But I'll see you in our next session. Will you be able to make it downstairs by yourself?"

I want to convince her to let me stay, to offer her more money even, but I have the feeling that Donna is not the sort of person to be swayed by bribery.

"Yes, I'll be fine, thank you." I force myself to be polite because I'm positive that she'll dump me as a client if I'm rude to her.

As I walk out of the office into the waiting room, I feel like my usual anger has been lifted off of me.

There is no sign of Tiffani in the waiting room or in the hallway, so I head to the elevator and ride it down to the next floor. Luckily, there are only three buttons to choose from, so picking the right one is simple.

When the elevator door opens, I hesitate. This is the first time I've ever been left alone in public. What if I can't find the coffee shop? What if I get lost, fall in a sewer hole, or walk into traffic? Anything could happen.

I stand there, frozen for a long minute, and then I force myself to take a deep breath and step out of the elevator.

I'm not on the street. I'm in a large, bright lobby and right across from me is an enormous sign that says Coffee on it. The letters are so big that even I can make them out.

I take another deep breath, step across the hall, and push open the glass door. A bell overhead chimes, and I'm hit by a waft of warm air and the smell of fresh baking.

I stop just inside the door, inhaling deeply. The gentle swell of voices, the sound of cutlery scraping plates, the whirring of the specialty coffee machine, all meld together into a comforting sort of hum that reminds me of happier days.

The lighting is tricky, though. Sun is slanting through the window across from me, making light and shadow mix together in weird ways. I stand still and turn my head slowly until I figure out the basic layout of the shop.

All the people look the same at first—smudged streaks of colour and shadow—but, by some miracle, I finally make out Tiffani's familiar outline in the far corner by the window.

Getting to her is another matter, because I can see obstacles, like tables and people, when they're further back, but up close they disappear. I need to move slowly and use my peripheral vision to make my way along.

I feel a swell of triumph when I finally reach her table. *I did that on my own. I survived.*

She looks up as I approach and lets out a surprised squeak. "Alice, you're done already? I must have lost track of time. You should have called me to get you instead of coming down by yourself. You could have…"

"It's fine." I shrug, struggling not to be irritated by all her fussing. I want to hold on to my good feelings. "I'm not totally incompetent."

"No, of course not, but…"

"I want some of that lemon loaf Donna was talking about. And a hot chocolate." I say it quickly, trying to change the subject. But my words come snapping out like an order. Like I'm a spoiled toddler demanding snacks.

There's a long, hard silence.

"Sure, Alice. Whatever you like." She sets down the book she'd been reading and climbs slowly to her feet, and you can tell that she'd rather tell me to get my own damn lemon loaf, but she doesn't. She just marches up to the cashier and gives them my order.

I stare blankly out the window, biting my lip, and wondering why all my interactions with people are so prickly and awkward all the time. The whole restaurant is full of people laughing and chatting easily; their conversations seem so effortless, so full of joy.

I don't remember the last time I sat with friends and let my guard down like that. I wouldn't even know where to begin.

"There you go." Tiffani sets my things abruptly in front of me, dropping the plate a little harder than necessary, and then takes her seat again. She picks up her book without another word.

"Thank you," I say stiffly, taking a huge bite of the lemon bread. Donna was right, it is delicious.

After a few minutes, the peaceful sounds of the coffee shop lull me into a state of relaxation again. I sip my hot chocolate, thinking about my counselling session.

"Donna was really nice," I say. "I liked talking to her."

Tiffani looks up from her book with a little jolt, as if she'd forgotten that I was there.

"You did?" She sounds skeptical.

"Yeah, it wasn't what I expected. I mean, she was helpful. She gave me some ideas to work on. And some things to research."

"Oh, what sort of things?"

"Like if it's dangerous for me to jump again. If it's the doctors who said that or just something Dad made up because he wants to control me."

She inhales sharply before letting her breath out again in a slow stream, like she's in yoga class or something.

"Your father made nothing up, Alice," she says firmly. "And he's not trying to control you or wreck your life. He cares about you deeply and is having a tough time with this. We all are, not that you've noticed. Of course he's worried about you riding, but the jumping scares him most of all. He doesn't want to see you get hurt."

She breaks off abruptly, wrapping both hands around her coffee cup like it's anchoring her to the table.

"So, you're saying there's no medical reason I can't jump?" I ask, skipping over the other uncomfortable things she's said.

"I think this is a discussion you should have with your dad, Alice."

"Just tell me."

"I'm not a doctor. But as far as I know, there is no medical reason for you not to jump. Other than you might smash into something and hurt yourself and the horse you're riding, of course. Although that doesn't seem to matter to you these days."

"That's not true," I snap. "I would never hurt the horses on purpose."

"No? What do you call jumping Jiggs when your father explicitly told you not to? That pony could have been badly injured and I don't think you even considered that before you impulsively did whatever you wanted, no matter what the consequences."

I grit my teeth, anger swirling inside of me. But, in this case, she's right. That day was a mistake.

"You need to earn your father's trust again, Alice. If you want to someday jump again, then prove to him you can stick with flat work on a calm horse until you know your limitations. Your vision loss doesn't have to be a life sentence away from horses. I told you all this in the hospital, but you didn't want to listen. I found these amazing programs where…"

"Those aren't for professional riders, though," I interrupt, my temper igniting again. "Those programs are for losers who can't do anything else but plod around in circles. I'm better than that."

There is a long, tense silence and I can feel her disapproving stare burning into me.

"Wow, Alice. Is that really what you think?" she says quietly, her voice so loaded with disappointment that I instinctively flinch away. "You believe that you're better than the riders who are out there, doing the work, living their dreams despite being dealt some horrible life circumstances? Who push forward rather than sulking in their rooms, blaming everyone else for the bad hand they were dealt?"

"I don't sulk," I say hotly, "and I *am* better than that. Do you know how many championships I've won?"

"We'd better go," Tiffani says suddenly, rising to her feet and stuffing her book roughly into her oversized purse. "I'm done with this conversation, and I think we both have better places to be right now."

She turns her back on me and marches toward the door, not looking back to make sure I'm following her.

I trail after her slowly, wondering how that conversation had deteriorated so fast. One thing she said had stuck with me, though. If I did some boring dressage and won some classes, maybe that would be enough for my dad to loosen my leash a little and let me jump again.

And who better to win some ribbons with than one of Pablo Garcia's former upper-level dressage horses? The judges would lose their minds when I rode into the ring. I was already a great rider, so conquering the dressage world should be a piece of cake, right?

Now, all I had to do was convince Sidney.

CHAPTER 15

SIDNEY

*W*ith the help of my GPS, I'm able to find Three Sisters again on my own without too much trouble.

I park in front of the fancy, oversized house and take deep breaths to calm my nerves.

"This is no big deal, Beans," I say as he peers excitedly out the car window, his little stump of a tail wagging. "If the interview goes badly, then it wasn't meant to be and we'll find something else. Something better."

He woofs and gives a happy wriggle, staring across the lawn toward the woods to where a few rabbits are hopping around.

"You stay here and be good. I'll be right back."

The house looks even more imposing when I step out of the car. I'm used to fancy mansions, but this towering monstrosity takes up half the hillside and is completely covered with enormous glass windows. It's like some modern architect's version of what a futuristic log home should look like. It's not exactly cozy.

I straighten my shoulders and walk the long path to the front steps and huge double doors. Taking a deep breath and straightening my shoulders firmly, I press the doorbell. Chimes ring deep in the house and eventually I hear footsteps heading my way.

I half expect it to be an ancient butler or something, but instead, a tired-looking, dark-haired man no older than my dad opens the door.

"You must be Sidney," he says kindly, stepping forward and holding out his hand for me to shake. He doesn't look a lot like Alice, but I can see a tiny resemblance there around his eyes. He gives my hand a firm squeeze, pumping it up and down a few times like he's testing it. "I'm Neil Carlisle. And this is my fiancée, Tiffani."

The woman behind him is all curves, with wavy blond hair and a wide smile.

"Hello," she says warmly, reaching out to pull me into a tight hug. "We're so excited to meet you, Sidney. Elliot and Ben have both spoken so highly of you. And the fact that Alice asked for you specifically is a miracle. Please come in."

I let her usher me into the huge front hallway where I hesitate, trying to get my bearings. Everything, from the floors, to the walls, to the massive ceiling beams overhead, is made from polished, honey-coloured logs. It's hard to tell where the floor ends and the walls begin and the effect is a little disorienting. Like being trapped inside a massive tree.

"Come down the hall to our office," Mr. Carlisle says, waving us to go ahead of him. "We have some refreshments waiting."

I swallow nervously because, now that I want the job, I can't help but think that these people are going to find me lacking somehow. That they've found out who my parents are and will judge me for that. Or realize that I'm not qualified to do what they're asking. I mean, yes, I'm good at school and great with horses, but I know nothing about tutoring difficult teenagers who might not be able to see a book well enough to read.

"Please, sit down," Tiffani says, showing me to an overstuffed brown leather chair. "I hope you don't mind tea. Do you take it with lemon?"

"Cream and sugar, please," I say, wondering if it's a test of some sort. Do successful applicants prefer lemon? "Thank you."

"There you are." She sets a solid mug on the table near my elbow and then adds a plate of cookies a few seconds later. "I hope you don't have any allergies, Sidney. I forgot to ask."

"No, this is great, thank you."

"We're so glad you offered to be Alice's tutor. She's taken a shine to you."

I stare at her and I'm sure my expression must show how skeptical I am about that, because Tiffani laughs ruefully and sinks down into the chair across from me.

"I will not pretend that Alice isn't difficult, Sidney. Especially now when things are so challenging for her. We're hoping to find something positive for her to focus on to help her transition into her new life. Some sort of goal other than winning at horse shows."

I swallow hard, wondering if she's hinting that *I'm* the one who's supposed to come up with this miraculous new goal. As if there is anything big enough to take away the hurt of losing your sight and your ponies.

"It really is a shame." Mr. Carlisle stirs cream and sugar into his own tea and takes a cookie. "She's a bright, talented girl, and she's always had her heart set on being on the Olympic equestrian team someday. This summer has been extremely difficult for her. For all of us, really."

I nod and take a quick sip of tea to calm my nerves.

"This tutoring business is a little complicated," Alice's dad goes on. "She has never been much for school, honestly. Horses have been her whole life since she was a toddler. My late wife encouraged it, maybe too much. Alice has always had a heavy competition schedule, and it didn't leave room for much else."

He runs a hand through his hair, leaving a messy wave behind.

"We don't want Alice to fall behind too far in her school work and miss out on any future opportunities," Tiffani says. "She has her whole life ahead of her. And she's quite smart, even though she isn't a fan of her studies."

"It's been hard on her to have Clara and Isabelle as her older sisters," Mr. Carlisle adds. "They're both brilliant, you see. And Clara was always the one to steal the spotlight." He shoots a quick, almost guilty, look at his fiancée and sighs. "Alice has been mostly left to her own devices over the years. Sometimes I feel like I don't even know her."

I sit there awkwardly, feeling like I'm intruding on private, family business that I don't want, or need, to know about. I'm pretty sure Alice would not appreciate them telling me this stuff about her.

"She has a forceful personality," Tiffani continues, "and she has been adamant that she doesn't want help from a companion or a tutor. So, when she said she wanted to work with you, we had to meet you, even though you don't exactly come with the same level of accreditation as the other applicants."

"Sorry?" I stare at her blankly.

"What Tiffani means is that the people who applied are care aides or retired school teachers. They look good on paper, but we're not sure that any of them will work for Alice. We'd like to try you out for a month if that's all right with you. It would only be a few hours a day to start. But Ben assures me they can find enough work for you in the barns to make it a full-time position. Is that something you're interested in?"

"Yes," I say quickly. "I'm interested. But would there be a place here for Oriel? Alice mentioned my horse could come here if things work out."

"The Friesian," Tiffani says to her fiancé, raising her eyebrows and nodding.

"Oh right. Yes, I think we can manage it. She's grounded from riding right now but, if she takes a shine to him, then we'd love if you'd consider letting her ride him in the future. It would be a step toward getting her back in the saddle."

My heart sinks and I swear internally. Am I desperate enough to even consider leasing out Oriel, yet? Has it come to this? I can find another job...

"No pressure," Tiffani says quickly, her kind eyes studying my face. "You just think on that one and decide later once you and Alice get to know each other. I can tell you she's a nice rider, and she genuinely loves her ponies. She comes across as rough with people, but never with the horses."

"Okay, I'll think about that." I look down at the brown tapestry rug on the floor at my feet.

"Excellent," Alice's dad says. "So Elliot tells us you are quite the scholar, Sidney, and that you have goals to study abroad. What are you planning to focus on when you go to school?"

The question catches me off guard and I hesitate. I always hate when people ask me this because the true answer never seems to satisfy them.

"World literature mostly. And I'd love to take some philosophy courses and study history and languages. I don't have a specific degree in mind. I love learning for its own sake."

Mr. Carlisle blinks at me twice, frowning. "That, ah, sounds enjoyable." He clears his throat, drumming his fingers on the table in front of him. "But what exactly would the career path be there? Do you want to be a writer? A teacher?"

"No, nothing specific. I am planning to get my English degree first and then see."

"Well, that's admirable, I suppose. Still, it's best to pick something that can earn you a good income. It's never too early to plan your financial future. And an English degree..."

"I'm sure Sidney will figure it all out," Tiffani interrupts, patting his arm gently. "Elliot says you speak a few different languages, dear."

"Um, yes. English, of course, French, Spanish, German, and a bit of Mandarin."

"Ah, now that's handy," Alice's dad says, looking slightly less worried about my future financial prospects. "A very useful skill to have. And how do your parents feel about your career path?"

I pause, not sure how to answer that. I can't tell him that my parents don't have a clue what my interests are, other than horses. They have never shown up for parent-teacher meetings or have any idea which universities I've applied for.

"They're happy with whatever I choose," I say finally, which is close to the truth.

"Well, if you're free, then I'd like you to start work tomorrow." Mr. Carlisle rises smoothly to his feet. "Anna would like you to go to Barn B first so you can meet the other girls. Then afterward you can come here and have a proper tour of the house and see Alice's school room. So far, she has refused to step foot in it, but hopefully you can change her mind on that."

"Thank you for coming," Tiffani says and then suddenly pulls me into another tight hug, squashing me against her chest. "I'm crossing my fingers that this is what Alice needs to make her happy. Heaven knows it's not me that does it for her."

"She'll come around," Mr. Carlisle says, picking up Tiffani's hand and giving it a gentle squeeze. "She needs time. I know there's a happy girl in there somewhere."

"I hope so." She leans against him for a second and then pulls away. "Anyway, we've kept you long enough, Sidney. Come tomorrow and we'll get started."

I walk away from the house, feeling a little dazed. I'm glad that I have the job and a potential spot for Oriel, but I'm actually not sure what my job description is supposed to be or how much I'm getting paid. These are probably questions I should have asked before agreeing to work for these strange people.

But when I see Beans' eager face waiting for me at the car, I know that I've made the right decision. He can come to work with me now, and it will be a safe place for Oriel, so I don't have to worry so much about him under Barb's sketchy care at Happy Acres.

Halfway up the driveway, once I'm out of sight of the house, I pull over to text Elliot the good news and to check if either my brother or sister have responded to the many messages I'd sent them.

They haven't, but Elliot sends me back a smiley face right away and about ten congratulatory thumbs-up symbols in a row.

Her enthusiasm comes across loud and clear, making me smile, and when I glance up, I'm startled to see that there is a rider on a tall bay horse watching me from the woods nearby. The forest is too dim for me to see his face, but there is something annoyingly familiar about the set of his shoulders and the arrogant tilt of his head. Mia's spoiled cousin, Josh.

Beans woofs low under his breath and I reach out to give him a pat.

"Good boy," I mutter quietly, putting the car back in gear and stepping, a little too hard, on the pedal. The tires spin in the gravel for a second, kicking up a small spray of rocks, as I speed down the rest of the driveway.

I feel heat creeping up my neck and into my face. I hope that irritating boy isn't going to make things difficult for me at Three Sisters. I really don't need any more trouble in my life.

Walking into my empty, echoing house feels strange at first. I've never been completely alone in it for more than a day or so. In the past, even when my parents were off travelling, we usually had nannies or housekeepers around for company.

I'm not sure how long I'll get to stay here until it sells, but for right now, it's all mine.

"The first thing we're going to do is clean this place up, Beans," I tell him as he trots over to his feed bowl.

I fill the dishwasher and wipe down the counters, tossing away more take-away containers. Then I vacuum the floor with the stick-vac hanging on the wall and give the whole thing a quick mop afterwards.

I'm not a huge fan of housekeeping, but I do like living in a clean place. My room is always neatly organized, even if the rest of the house is not. Working in Pablo's barn had given me an appreciation for clean spaces. Although, I would much prefer to be cleaning stalls rather than a kitchen any day.

"Now, what should we make us for lunch, Beans?"

There is thankfully still food left in the fridge and the freezer, so at least I won't starve for a while. Ordering takeout is going to be off limits from now on. I need to focus on saving as much money as possible just in case the house suddenly sells and I'm left homeless.

I pull out a frozen lasagna, read the instructions and set the oven to pre-heat. Then I search through my parents' liquor cabinet and find myself a bottle of wine. I'm not much of a drinker. But it just seems appropriate to toast my freedom right now, and to celebrate landing the job at Three Sisters.

My phone rings right as I take my first sip and I grab for it eagerly, thinking it might be my sister or brother at last. Or Zack, who has been strangely silent these last few days.

But, to my surprise, it's Zara. Again.

After a long hesitation, I hit the button.

"Hey, Sidney? Are you there?" At least she sounds sober now.

"Hey Zara." I try to sound casual. "What's up?"

"I want to apologize to you for calling you from that party. I was drunk and, anyway, I'm sorry. That was rude."

"It's…it's okay, Zara. It was good to hear from you."

There's a heavy silence and then a sigh.

"Look, I've been a jerk. I want us to catch up and hang out again."

I tap my finger against my wineglass, trying to tell if she's being genuine or not. She sounds sincere, and once I would have trusted her without question, but now I'm not so sure. She's been so weird this year.

"Okay, well, I'd like that," I say slowly. "I'm not sure why we stopped being friends, honestly. You said you didn't blame me for what happened with my parents but..."

"We never stopped being friends," she says quickly. "I've just been busy. It's nothing personal."

I stare at the phone, not sure how to respond. Her avoiding me like the plague sure felt personal to me. "Zara, I know you hate talking about what happened to your grandmother's condo. But we should probably..."

"No, I don't want to talk about *that*," she snaps, practically snarling. "It's old business, Sidney. I already told you I don't blame you for what your psycho parents did."

"I know, but..."

"Seriously, drop it." She takes a deep breath. "Look, that's not why I called. Seeing you at Three Sisters the other day made me realize how much I've missed hanging out with you. Can't we do that again, like old times?"

"Of course we can," I say with relief. "Zara, I've missed you so much too. There's been so much crazy stuff going on here and I've had no one to talk to except for Zack and he's so complicated..."

"Oh, I know. It's a good thing he's hot." She laughs, sounding like the old funny, sarcastic Zara I'd grown up with. "He really has a thing for you, though. You're not an obvious choice for a couple, but it works in a weird way. We need to figure out a way to get you two together properly."

"Yeah, I'm not sure that's ever going to happen."

"Of course it will. Now, tell me all about what's been happening with you. I want all the details."

Talking to Zara again after all this time is such a relief that, for the next hour, I pour everything out. About my mixed feelings over Zack, about crazy Happy Acres, about my parents' taking Leo to Vegas and leaving me and Eden behind. About Three Sisters and how I'll be homeless the second the house sells.

"Don't worry," Zara promises me. "We'll figure it all out together."

"We will?"

"Of course. Now, there you are, sitting all alone in an empty house with no supervision. I think this calls for a gathering."

"You mean like a party?" I say skeptically. "I don't think that's a good..."

"No, an informal gathering between friends," she interrupts. "Something to cheer you up. We'll get a few of our old gang to come. And Zack."

That stops me.

"You really think he'd come *here?*" I chew nervously on my lower lip, my mind turning over the idea. "Even with all the lawsuit stuff still going on?"

"Sidney, I can literally hear you overthinking things." She laughs. "This is not that complicated. We haven't done anything fun together in a long time and I miss that. I miss you. We used to be each other's person, remember? We were a team."

"Yeah," I gulp. "I remember."

"So, what's there to worry about then? It will be like old times."

That vision is almost too much to resist and she must feel my willpower faltering because she goes in for the kill.

"Look, I'll arrange everything so you don't have to stress. We'll invite a few select people over, we'll have a few drinks, swim in the pool. We can even have everyone out by midnight if you like, and then I can stay over and help you clean up. Just like we always used to do. Remember when your cook taught us how to make crepes that summer? I think we ate them for three meals a day for weeks."

"Yeah," I laugh. "I can still make a mean strawberry crepe."

"Well, it's decided then. Saturday night."

I hesitate and then give in. I'm young, after all, and my parents are hundreds of miles away. Maybe it is time for me to do something a little wild and crazy.

"Sure, okay. As long as it doesn't get out of hand."

"Of course not. Don't worry. I've got everything under control."

CHAPTER 16

SIDNEY

I'm up at the crack of dawn on my first day of work at Three Sisters. The plan is that I'll do the morning shift and meet everyone in Barn B. Anna and most of the students won't be back from the horse show until late tomorrow, so it will be some of the other barn staff showing me around.

Then I'm supposed to go spend an hour with Alice before I head back to Happy Acres to take care of Oriel. If I'm lucky, there will be just enough time to ride him before I head to my shift at the Shrimp Shack tonight. The timing will be tight, but if I'm organized, I should be able to manage it.

Even though there's nothing to be scared about, I can't help but be a little nervous about the day ahead of me. What if the girls in Barn B don't like me? What if they tell Anna not to hire me after all because I'm incompetent? What if I can't even do hunter braids after a lifetime of dressage braids?

Or what if Alice is awful, or she's changed her mind again?

What if Three Sisters turns out to be a terrible place and I don't want to bring Oriel there at all?

My stomach is flip-flopping as Beans and I roll up the narrow, wooded driveway to Barn B.

I pull up in front of the barn, turning the engine off right as a willowy blond girl in a blue polo shirt leads a cute buckskin pony out the front door.

"Hi," she calls, waving as soon as I get out of the car. "You must be Sidney. Welcome to Three Sisters."

"Thanks," I say, feeling immediately more at ease. She has a kind smile and her blue eyes crinkle at the edges like she's used to laughing.

"I'm Lena, and this handsome guy is Butterscotch. I'm taking him up to the ring to give him a quick lunge if you'd like to come along."

"Sure." I fall into step beside her, already certain that I'm going to like her. She has an easy way about her as she leads the pony, one arm draped casually over his neck like they're old friends.

"Butterscotch here had a month off after an injury, so he's slowly getting back into work. Do you know how to lunge?"

"Yes." I nod. "Of course."

"You'd be surprised how many people don't. Here, you take him. The lunge whip is there. Just stick to walk and trot and make sure to switch up directions every couple of minutes."

She pushes the lunge line into my hands and opens the gate to the ring.

So, I guess this is my first test, I think, sending the pony out to the end of the line with a small flick of the whip. He's a good-natured guy though, and, despite having time off, he shows no interest in going any faster than he has to.

It takes a bit of work to get him trotting at more than a shuffling pace, but pretty soon he is trucking along in a nice rhythm, hindquarters pushing him forward. He stretches his neck down, his back lengthening and his stride opening up.

"Good boy," I tell him. "That looks nice."

I bring him to a walk to give him a break and have him change directions so he gets worked evenly on both sides. Then I do the whole thing over again one more time before finally bring him to a halt.

"Is that enough for him?" I ask, turning to where Lena is leaning on the fence, watching me. I'd nearly forgotten she was there.

She's not alone now, though. Unfortunately, there is a familiar-looking guy on a large bay horse behind her, staring at me with a stony expression. Mia's unsmiling cousin, Josh.

Seriously? Is he planning to spend his life stalking me so he can judge everything I do?

"Perfect," Lena says, coming to open the gate for me and Butterscotch. "You've obviously done this a few times before."

"There were a lot of young horses at my old barn," I say, trying to keep my focus on her and not the scowling guy hovering a few feet away. "I helped with their training quite a bit. Lunging was a big part of that."

"Lucky," she says, taking Butterscotch from me and giving him a pat on the neck. "I love working with youngsters. Josh here is looking for a second horse to bring along. He is thinking of maybe getting a two-year-old."

"Hmmm," I say noncommittally but really, inside, I'm thinking of what a bad idea it is for someone so cold to oversee training a sweet, impressionable baby. "Two is really young to start them. And baby horses need a lot of patience and kindness. Not everyone is cut out to work with them."

Lena blinks at me, her smile slipping a little before she fixes it firmly back in place, and from the corner of my eye I see Josh narrow his gaze at me.

"Are you saying that I'm not capable of being patient and kind?" he asks, raising his eyebrows.

"Pardon?" I turn in surprise, as if noticing him for the first time. "No, sorry, I was just making conversation. I know nothing about you at all." *Except that you are a pretentious ass who told Alice not to hire me because my parents are criminals.*

"Do you two know each other already?" Lena asks in confusion.

"We've met," Josh mutters. "Briefly."

"Josh is very good with the horses," Lena says to me hastily, looking back and forth between the two of us. "Come on, Sidney. We have lots of work to do."

I follow behind her, not giving that jerk the satisfaction of looking back at him a single time, even though I can feel him watching me.

After that I don't have any more time to think about anything except the work in front of me. I'm introduced to the beginner instructor, Samantha, and the herd of adorable little school ponies that are the heart of Barn B.

I am set to work cleaning school tack while Lena and Samantha help a steady stream of children to get their ponies ready.

It's a nice, familiar routine and I feel myself relaxing as I oil the saddles and polish the metal buckles until they shine.

"Wow, everything looks great," Samantha says from the open tack room doorway. "Do you do show prep? Clipping and braiding?"

"Yep, I can do all that."

"Great, I have some hairy fetlocks for you to work on then when you're done cleaning tack."

The morning flies by as I set to work tidying up one of their new school horses, Elmo, who is a handsome, golden Haflinger with a lot of extra hair. And when eleven o'clock rolls around, I realize I don't want to leave at all. I want to stay here all day and bask in this familiar atmosphere.

"It was great meeting you," Lena says when my time is up. "Anna will be home tomorrow and we'll get you into a real routine. I have a feeling that you're going to be a great part of our team, Sidney."

I head reluctantly back to my car, not wanting to break up my lovely morning by going up to the house to spend time with Alice. Which makes me feel a little guilty because she's the only reason I'm here in the first place.

Do it for Oriel, I remind myself firmly. *Think of how happy he will be living in this lovely place.*

To my surprise, Alice is sitting on the front steps when I pull up in front of the house and her face lights up as I let Beans scamper up to her and fling himself into her lap.

She leans down over him, petting his fat body all over and crooning to him under her breath.

"Should we go inside and get started?" I say finally, when she doesn't acknowledge me. "Your dad said…"

"First of, let's agree never to start another sentence with *your dad said.* You have no idea how irritating that is. Secondly, I hate being inside. I'd much rather be out here. Don't you feel that way too?"

"Actually, yes." I sit down beside her and turn to marvel at the view. The massive house sits on a knoll halfway up of the steep hill that Three Sisters is built on. The entire property is a series of wide, flat terraces that rise steadily upward from the lower road beyond Barn B to the upper road that curls about a mile above the house. From my seat on the porch, I can see the entire farm sloping down below us, the pastures full of horses, and beyond to the mountains in the distance. "The view here is amazing."

"Yeah." She sighs and hoists Beans up a little higher. "I really miss that."

"Oh crap. I'm sorry. I shouldn't have said that. I didn't think."

"It's okay. I like it better when people forget. I hate when everyone tiptoes around me like they're afraid of saying the wrong thing."

"What can you see?" I ask curiously, taking the opportunity to ask questions while she's in a good mood.

"Each eye is different," she says after a brief hesitation. "My central vision was ruined in both eyes. So, I can't see things directly in front of me. I see mostly from my side vision, although that's different in each eye too. I can see in the middle-distance best. Things close-up are hard and things far away aren't even on my radar anymore. I remember what those mountains looked like, though. I used to love them."

She gulps and glances down at the dog in her lap.

"What about colour?" I say quickly to keep her talking.

"Yep, I can see colours, but they're not as bright as they used to be, and I miss fine details. Like Beans' eye colour."

"Brown. A nice chocolate brown."

She looks up, flashing a quick, brilliant smile at me that disappears almost instantly.

"Can you read?" I press on.

"No." She shakes her head. "Well, not unless the letters were ginormous or something. And then it's so slow that I don't bother."

"Your dad said...." I break off, remembering how she hates that phrase. "Sorry, I mean, I heard that you have an office set up. Can you use the computer at all?"

She shrugs and shakes her head again. "I think there's some sort of accessibility features built in, but I haven't bothered to look. It's all such a hassle to figure out. Do we really have to talk about all this? It's kind of depressing."

I shake my head, forgetting that she might not see me doing that up close. Alice is right. It *is* depressing. What on earth does she do all day if she can't read or go on the computer or go to the barn to ride? I'd go completely nuts if that was me.

"Sure," I say slowly. "Sorry, I'm trying to figure everything out. Do you listen to audiobooks at least? Or podcasts?"

She frowns. "No. I listen to music, though."

I sit there, kind of stunned, overflowing with pity for this kid. Here she is in a fancy house that belongs in a magazine, with a stable full of horses and all the luxuries that money could buy. And for all that, I think she's probably the loneliest person I've ever met. Lonelier than me, even.

"What are you thinking about?" she asks sharply, as if guessing my thoughts.

"Just thinking about what sort of audiobooks you might like," I say hastily, reaching out to scratch Beans between the ears. "I'm not sure what sort of subjects you are interested in yet."

"None," she says in a hard voice, her body stiffening like I've hit a nerve. "I hate anything to do with school."

"No, but I mean what sort of things did you read for fun?"

"Reading is not *fun*, Sidney. That is for losers who have nothing better to do."

And, abruptly, the old, sneering Alice is back.

"Not even horse books?" I ask calmly, refusing to take the bait. "I'm sure there are training books and podcasts we can find. You must like *something*."

She scowls at me and then lifts Beans abruptly off her lap and sets him firmly on the ground.

"You should go now," she says sharply. "I don't want you here anymore. This visit is over."

"Um, okay. We still have lots of time left, though."

"I'm tired and I'm going to my room. Come back tomorrow."

She spins around and marches into the house, slamming the door behind her with a thud.

I sit there for a second, wondering what on earth I'm

supposed to do now. Is it my job to follow her and coax her out? Are they paying me by the hour here? I have no idea.

Finally, I get up and lead Beans back slowly to my car, wondering what I've gotten myself into. Alice is not a child, so it's not like I can force her to hang out with me. It has to be her decision.

I've just got to get creative. Surely there's something out there that will interest her, eventually. Hopefully.

I am halfway home when my car begins to ring and my sister Eden's number pops up on my display.

I can not hit the answer button fast enough.

"Eden," I practically squeal. "Is everything all right? Are they treating you okay? Have you heard from Leo?"

"Sidney, calm down, everything is fine," she says in her flat, even voice.

"I've been so worried. I haven't heard from either of you."

There is a long silence, and I wonder if we've been disconnected.

"I'm sorry you were worried," she says finally. "Leo sent me a text that he's in Vegas and it's hot, he hates it and he's bored. Oh, and he's mad at you right now."

"Damn. I was afraid of that. And I knew he would hate it there. I wonder if they even remembered to enrol him in school. Or buy him sunscreen. They left all his stuff here, you know. I'm not even sure that he took any books with him. He loves those books."

"Uh-huh," she says. "So, you're still in the house?"

"Only until it sells. You could come stay with me if you like. It's a big house and..."

"No," she says quickly, cutting me off. "But...thanks."

"We should meet for coffee. I have Beans here, we could meet in the park. He'd love to..."

"I'd better go. I have a photo shoot to get to. I just wanted to let you know that I'm doing fine. So, have a nice life. Goodbye, Sidney."

"Eden, wait..."

The line disconnects before I can say anything else, and I find my eyes stinging with tears. Eden and I might not have hung out much in the last few years but she's still my sister and I miss her.

"I can't believe she didn't want to see you, Beans," I say, reaching over to pet his head. "She'll come around eventually though, I'm sure of it. And Leo too."

Beans makes a huffing noise and flops back down on the seat.

I hope that I'm right about my brother and sister. My family seems to be fracturing further apart every day, and it feels like I'm the only one interested in putting it back together.

CHAPTER 17

ALICE

*A*fter Sidney leaves, I stand in our front foyer with my back pressed up against the door, feeling like a complete idiot. I don't move from that position until her car starts and I hear it crunching up the driveway.

The second she's gone, I can breathe freely again. It was dumb of me to panic like that, but her questions had brought up some uncomfortable truths.

I might be intelligent about some things; I like order, logic and I usually know how to get things done, or how to make people do things for me. But I am not smart in the way that impresses teachers. I don't care to analyze boring books and I'm not clever at math. I couldn't care less about science or history or anything like that.

And, while Sidney had been badgering me with questions, I couldn't help but wonder what sort of things I *am* good at now. No teenaged armies to lead, no horse shows to win, no stable to run. Without all those things, what am I? The answer had stood out in front of me as clear as day. *Nothing.* I am a useless lump with zero purpose in life.

The thought had been so terrifying that it had nearly bowled me over. And when I felt that fear, I'd reacted in the only way I knew how, the way my sister Clara had shown me from the time I was a little kid. I'd angrily lashed out at whoever was closest to me.

Fear is for the weak, Clara would say whenever I woke up screaming from nightmares after Mom died or if I came off a pony too hard and didn't want to get back on. *And nobody in this family is weak, understand?*

"Piss off, Clara," I say out loud into the empty hallway. Sometimes, my memories of her are so real that it's like being haunted by a vengeful ghost. I can almost hear her sarcastic voice in my ear, telling me how useless I am.

I take a deep breath and unclench my fists, shaking out my cramping fingers.

Tomorrow, I'll make it right with Sidney. I won't apologize but I'll at least try to act better. I'll show her the stupid school room and see if she can set up the computer properly for me. Especially since I need to her to help me research the Para show jumpers.

Since my dad and Tiffani are still lurking about the house somewhere and I'm not keen to let them know I kicked Sidney out so early, I decide it would be better for me if I disappeared for a few hours.

After stealing a handful of apples and carrots from the kitchen, I throw on my coat and boots and slip quietly outside. I head down the driveway to the barn at a brisk pace, mulling over what I want to do with Jiggs today.

Checkers nickers to me the second I head toward the

paddocks and I stop at his gate first and give him a tiny bit of apple and a scratch behind the ears. Then I turn toward Jiggs.

He's not miraculously at the paddock gate waiting for me or anything. But I can see his blurry shape out behind the shelter. He's watching me with his head flung up.

"That's okay, Jiggs," I tell him. "You don't have to be afraid. We're just going to do the same thing as yesterday."

I have a small plastic tack shed near the paddocks where my brushes and halters are stored. There is room for my saddles too if I ever need them but, since I'm not currently allowed to ride, all my extra things are still stored inside the main tack room. This one doesn't even have a lock on it or anything and my gear is expensive.

Ben has nicely put the lawn chair and the blanket from yesterday in there and I scoop them up and head out to Jiggs' paddock.

Things go much the same as yesterday at first, except that I'm not full of anger and impatience this time. I don't a hundred percent believe in this training process of Ben's, but I'm not totally against it either. It wasn't the fact that Jiggs had come up to get the carrots from me that had half-convinced me. It was that he'd chosen to have a nap beside me afterward. He hadn't walked away after the food was gone, he'd stayed with me and felt safe enough to let his guard down. Jiggs was a notoriously nervous, anxious pony and that moment yesterday had been one of the only times I'd seen him relax at all in all the time I'd owned him.

This time it doesn't take him quite as long to come up and find the carrot I'm holding, and he stands still long enough for me to gently pet his shoulder, although he shivers and moves away a second later.

Then I pick up my chair and move it about ten feet away and pull out another carrot.

At first Jiggs doesn't like the change and he paces a few laps around the paddock before pausing briefly beside me to get a treat and then moving away quickly before I can touch him again.

This time I don't move the chair until he's visited three more times, each time getting a treat. He stays with me longer and longer, occasionally letting me touch his neck or his nose as he eats.

I move the chair again and this time he snorts and scoots backward but then follows me to the place I've chosen near his shelter, waiting patiently next to me while I set the chair up and sit down, draping the blanket across me so I stay warm.

"Hang on," I tell him, laughing as he nudges my leg gently, "I'm getting them. You just wait politely."

Suddenly he throws his head up and skitters backward, retreating toward his shelter in two bounds.

"What's wrong?" I ask. But then I hear Darla's angry voice, followed by Ben's quieter tones. They must be standing outside the barn doorway right around the corner from the paddocks, because I can hear every word.

"That's ridiculous," she snaps. "Why would I even consider something like that?"

"Because it would mean a lot too her," Ben says. "And because you were her coach and that's what you're supposed to do for your students: build them up when they're down."

"No, a good coach concentrates on having a winning team and cuts off the dead weight when needed. She is a liability here and I can't waste my time teaching someone who will never improve. What am I supposed to do? Pull her around a course with a lead-rope like she's five years old? I'm not running the special Olympics here, Ben."

Air whooshes out of my lungs and my whole body goes numb, like someone has dumped a bucket of icy water over me. I don't want to believe it, but Darla is obviously talking about *me*.

"You need to give her a chance," Ben is saying. "You just

dumped her the second she was sidelined. You must see how much that's hurting her."

"Well, the truth hurts, doesn't it? I don't baby my students; I give them hard facts and a dose of reality. Sure, Alice was a talented rider, but she was also a spoiled brat who made me want to slap her at least once a week. The only reason I put up with her was because I knew her mother once. I agree that she worked hard, won ribbons and she could turn tough ponies into gold, but that is not the case anymore. I'm done with her. And good riddance."

"She looks up to you," Ben says, so quietly that I have to strain to hear him.

Darla is silent for a long moment.

"Well, she shouldn't. I am who I am, Ben. I'm here to produce winners and do my job. Anyone who can't be part of that doesn't have a place in this barn."

My heart is thudding so loudly in my chest that I don't hear anything else. Not until a soft muzzle touches my cheek.

I don't jerk backward this time. I freeze so I don't startle him and slowly let out a breath and then inhale again. Tears prick my eyes but I don't bother to wipe them away.

Jiggs huffs his warm breath against my neck then nibbles at my hair, then my coat. He works his way slowly downward until he reaches my hand and gives it a nudge.

Slowly, I lift my hand and rub it against his soft cheek and then scratch under his neatly pulled mane. Instead of pulling away like I'd half expected him to do he leans into the scratch, nearly pushing me off my chair.

"Well, look at him," an amused voice says from the gate. "He seems pretty relaxed."

"Yeah." I wipe my eyes hurriedly with one hand so Josh can't see that I've been crying, but keep the other on Jiggs' neck. "He's getting there."

"Glad to see you're spending time with him. You guys were always such a good team."

"I thought so too. But it turns out that he wouldn't have chosen to work with me at all if he'd had any other options. It's taken me two days to get him to come near me on his own."

"Well, he's been through a lot of changes lately. He always looked like he enjoyed jumping with you. So I don't think he hated everything."

I nod, working my way down Jiggs' neck until I'm scratching his shoulder. He puts his nose near my pocket, snuffling for carrots.

"You did like riding with me, didn't you, buddy? I didn't imagine that."

"So, Alice," Josh says slowly, sounding a little uncomfortable. "I've been meaning to ask you a question but I'm not sure if it's appropriate."

"Um, about what?" For a second I have this wild fantasy that he's going to ask me out or something.

"I'm wondering about your computer setup. I took a semester on adaptive technology last year in my computer science program. I could look at things for you if you like. I know some great apps that can help with low vision."

"Oh." Not asking me on a date then. "You don't have to do that. I was planning to get Sidney to help me with it since we're paying her to hang out with me."

He's quiet for a second before clearing his throat.

"Are you sure you trust her to work here, Alice? Her family is completely crooked. Zara showed me one of the episodes about them on True Dirt. I mean, I know it's a gossip channel but…"

"I really don't care what Zara says," I snap, "she's awful. First of all, I can take care of myself, and secondly, Sidney is way too boring to be a criminal. Besides, she has a great dog."

He chuckles under his breath. "All right, as long as you know what you're doing. I'd still like to help with your computer, though, if that's okay with you. I can at least make sure you have the latest technology."

"Oh, fine," I sigh. This is not exactly how I envisioned spending time with Josh but I suppose I'll take what I can get.

"Tomorrow then?"

"Sure, why not. Thanks."

Gravel crunches under his feet as he turns to leave. "Hey, Alice?"

"Yeah?"

"I bet Anna or Elliot would start giving you lessons when you're ready. They're both talented coaches, you know."

"But they're not..." I break off abruptly. *They're not Darla,* I was about to say. But maybe that's a good thing. Why do I keep waiting around for someone who clearly hates me and who only tolerated me because I was useful to her? And why should I give up doing something I love just because she refuses to teach me anymore?

"I'll think about it," I say finally.

"Good, because you're too talented of a rider to give it up."

He's gone before I can respond to that and I sit there for a long time, quietly petting Jiggs.

CHAPTER 18

SIDNEY

*T*he next morning I get to Three Sisters early, anxious to meet the barn manager Anna for the first time and crossing my fingers that I make a good impression on her.

It turns out that I shouldn't have wasted so much energy worrying because Anna is beyond nice and practically welcomes me with open arms.

"It's so good to meet you," she says breathlessly, running a hand through her short ponytail. "We came in late last night and didn't unload all the gear from the trailer so you're just in time. You can help the girls unpack and then give the trailer a good scrub from top to bottom."

So that's how I spend my morning. By the end, my boots are soaked and my jeans are smeared with mud and hay but I've never been happier. It's almost like being back at Capriole again, being part of a team, everyone working together for the good of the horses.

I am humming under my breath by the time I head up to the house for my session with Alice.

Today it feels like things are finally falling into place for me, despite all the scary changes happening in my life.

See, everything is working out, I tell myself. *Oriel will get to board in this fantastic place and I'm working with a great group of people. I have two jobs that I like and I'm living rent-free for now so I can save up some money. Even Zara and I are on our way to being friends again.*

There is no sign of Alice when I drive to the house, so I leash Beans up and head to the front door.

I had stayed up late last night googling all sorts of different ways to teach someone with low vision, and I'd found lots of adaptive apps and programs that we could use. I'd also dug up a ton of audiobooks and podcasts that I hoped she might like. And I'd saved dozens of YouTube videos of low-sighted people training for Para dressage classes. I knew it wasn't the same as jumping but it would be a start anyway. At least she'd be riding.

A deep chime runs through the house when I press the doorbell and Beans lets out a low woof, scratching his front paw impatiently against the door.

"No, Beans, we have to wait," I tell him, pulling him backward a few steps. The last thing I need is for him to leave claw marks on their expensive door.

Finally, there is a shuffling sound behind the door and it swings open.

"Oh," I say in surprise, stepping backward as an older, grim-looking woman pins me with a sharp, suspicious glare. "Um, I'm here for Alice. I'm Sidney, her...her tutor?"

She narrows her eyes at me and then frowns at Beans who has sat down abruptly to give himself a good scratch behind the ear. "I'm Mrs. Pitts. Leave your boots there on the porch so you don't track mud inside. I hope that dog has been treated for fleas. Alice is upstairs so I expect you know the way."

"Sorry." I kick off my boots and line them up neatly. "Beans has skin allergies so sometimes he's itchy. He's on special food from the vet."

She stares at me blankly.

"Um, I'll go find Alice now." I sidle past her in my socked feet, too intimidated to tell her that I don't really know where I'm going, and head for the stairs as quickly as I can.

Beans seems to think he knows the way, though. He pulls me up the stairs, his nails scuttling on the highly polished wood, and then down the hall, panting and huffing like he's on a mission.

"Good boy, Beans, go find Alice," I say hopefully, although he's not exactly a skilled scent hound.

We hurry down the hall, past rows of closed doors, and finally, at the end, I see an open door and Alice sitting in a chair just inside. She's smiling, for once, and she looks up happily when she sees us. Or at least when she sees Beans.

"There you are," she says, scooping him up into her arms.

"Hey, Alice. I think we're going to have fun today. I stayed up all night researching..."

I break off abruptly when I step fully into the room and realize that we are not alone.

"Oh." I skid to a stop, narrowing my eyes to where Josh is sitting in a plush office chair, staring intently at an oversized computer monitor. "It's you. Hello."

He glances up at me, raises an eyebrow and then turns back to the computer, not saying a word.

Fine then. I perch on the edge of the desk closest to the door and stare at the back of his head, hoping he feels my death-rays boring into his skull.

Alice is still fawning over Beans so I take a second to study the layout of her office.

It's huge, of course, and constructed from the same honey-coloured logs as the rest of the house. Even the furniture is made of wood. There are two heavy tables to act as desks, each big enough for four to six people to sit at, and a wall of couches. A low coffee table, topped with a row of neatly arranged horse and travel magazines, sits in the middle. Over on the far wall, next to the bank of windows with a commanding view over the farm, is a coffee station and a small fridge.

It's more like a fancy corporate conference room than a class-room for a teenager.

"Right, I believe we have you all set up," Josh says finally, ignoring me and turning to Alice. "You think you can remember where everything is and how to use it?"

"Of course." She nods, then hesitates. "But maybe show Sidney too, just in case."

He makes a face and then turns to me reluctantly with a sigh. "All right. I wrote a cheat sheet of all the commands that Alice might need. But I guess you can be backup if she forgets. Which she won't."

"Noted," I say, glaring at him openly.

"Her screen is already magnified but here is the command so she can enlarge documents or photos. Here is the projector func-tion so you can display whatever is on the computer screen right onto the wall. She'll need to get some sort of backdrop to play it on."

"Ooh," I interrupt, "that's handy. Can we play videos too?"

"Like I said, it will play *whatever* is on the desktop." He stares at me like I'm a complete idiot and then goes on. "Everything is also capable of voice assist. All the documents can be read out loud and you can use voice commands instead of the key pad."

"Perfect." I pick up the sheet of commands and then lay it back on the desk. "It's pretty basic, but you saved me setting every-thing up. I googled how to do all this last night."

His jaw tightens and he makes a low, grumbling noise in his throat.

"I really doubt your google-search matches my degree in computer science," he says stiffly.

"Huh, well it looks the same to me. Was it one of those fake degrees they stuff into cereal boxes?"

He huffs out a breath and glowers at me angrily. "I'll have you know that I went to…"

"Save it," I cut him off. "I don't actually care. You can go now. Thanks."

I practically spit out the last word. I know I'm being incredibly rude but I don't know what this jerk's problem is.

"Wow, you two, this is better than reality TV," Alice says, and I turn to see her listening to us with a smirk on her face. "The only thing that would make this better is a bucket of popcorn."

"Sorry, Alice," I say quickly. "I shouldn't be rude to your friends."

Even when they're a stuck-up, judgemental rat, I add in my head.

Josh turns to look at me and for a second, I swear that I see laughter in his eyes. "We're all done here anyway. See you around, Alice."

"Bye," she says, then turns to me with a grin as soon as he's gone. "Wow, he really doesn't like you, does he? What did you do to him?"

I sigh, not really wanting to get into any of this with her. On the other hand, she looks happier than I've seen her so far and it would be nice to keep her in this mood a while longer.

"Nothing that I know of. I guess he hates me because of my parents. Don't worry, I'm used to it; the kids at school were way worse."

"Really? Because of the fraud thing? Why would anyone care?" She shrugs and turns back to her newly-magnified computer screen. "This is kind of amazing. I can actually see the words."

"Well, it's not *just* the fraud, though," I say slowly. "One of the seniors who lost all his money killed himself. It was pretty bad. I'm surprised you didn't hear about it."

She makes a face, still studying the screen.

"Nope. I don't care about the news or anything. And old

people die all the time so I don't see what the big deal is. I wouldn't worry about people not liking me. I'd much rather have them afraid of me. It's so much easier."

"Afraid of you? Why?"

"Because then they do what I say. People are like sheep, if they're afraid then you can control them."

"Alice, that's…"

"Brilliant, I know. My sister Clara taught me that when I was five. You have a lot of catching up to do, Sidney, if you want to crush your enemies like I do."

I stare at her, not sure if the small smile on her face means that she's kidding around or if she's being serious. I have a sinking feeling that I know what the answer is.

"Um, your dad sent me the links to your online classroom this morning," I say finally, deciding that schoolwork is a safer subject, "so maybe we should start with that."

"Oh, I guess so." She leans back in the chair and rubs her eyes as if they're irritating her.

I navigate to the website and log in with the password Mr. Carlisle had sent me, scrolling through the list of subjects. Advanced English, Advanced History, World Economics.

"Alice, these are all advanced classes. I thought you said you hated school."

"Yeah." She looks at me blankly. "I do. I never said I wasn't smart. I'm just not genius smart like my sisters. And I don't care about any of this stuff. Any idiot can memorize things. As far as I'm concerned, it's all a waste of time."

"How did you do so well in school last term when you couldn't see, though?"

"My sight wasn't nearly this bad before the surgery," she says grimly. "I could read enough to get along even though it bothered me. I recorded the teachers' lectures and listened to them later. And then I paid some losers to do my homework. Easy-peasy."

"Wow, that's actually pretty impressive in a twisted way."

"Thank you. I worked hard at it."

"Here's your reading list for English Lit. We can definitely find these on audiobooks."

"Anything interesting?" she asks in a bored voice.

"Um." I scan the list. "That depends. Do you like depressing, thought-provoking books, or more like adventure?"

"I don't like fiction. Why would I want to read about fake people's lives?"

"Fair enough. We have to pick at least one, though. What about *To Kill A Mockingbird*? That's a classic, but it's about a lawyer fighting racism and bigotry in the deep South."

"Hmmm, I do like fighting. Okay, add it to the list, I suppose. What's next?"

It takes us nearly an hour to find her a short list of books that she doesn't completely hate. It's like she has to fuss and argue about every single thing without giving any of the books a chance.

"I'll go grab these on audio for you and then we can pick which one you want to read first," I say, struggling to be patient. I do know how hard this must be for her. Especially if she doesn't even care about school. I wonder what sort of job she'll be able to do once she graduates, even.

"Can't we do it later?" She sighs. "I hate being trapped inside all day like this."

"Well, we could take Beans for a walk. Do you want to come with me and we can listen to one of the books out there?"

"Sure," she says, suddenly looking cheerful again. "Whatever it takes so we don't have to be cooped up in this stupid house all day. I feel like I'm in a cage all the time."

"It's a pretty fancy cage." I smile at her.

"Whatever. It's still a cage. Come on. I don't care about which book. Just pick one."

I start to scroll down the list but Alice is already out the door with Beans' leash in hand, so I hurriedly stuff my phone in my pocket and follow her. For someone with low vision she's a quick mover, but I don't trust Beans not to pull her right down the stairs.

"Wait, Alice."

But she's there at the end of the hall right near the first step, her back stiff and head tilted to one side as if she's trying to figure something out. She holds the leash tight in both hands. Beans is scrabbling on the wooden floor, straining toward the stairs.

"Beans," I say sharply. "Stop that. Sit."

Remarkably, he does sit, staring at us both in confusion.

"Are you all right, Alice?" I ask her carefully.

"Does this spot on the floor seem extra slippery to you?" she asks tightly.

"The floor?" I look down at the shiny boards and shrug. "I mean, it all looks polished if that's what you're wondering. The whole house does."

"No, I mean is this exact spot more slippery than the rest of the hall?"

I look at her pale tense face, not quite sure what's going on. Not sure what's upset her so much.

"Um, hold on." I slide my socked feet beside her and then shuffle down the hall in the direction we'd come before heading back to where she and Beans are waiting. I pay special attention when I get close to her, then shake my head.

"Nope, it all feels the same to me. The whole hall is slippery, though. You should wear shoes inside if you're worried. These stairs are scary."

"No," she huffs out a relieved breath, "that's all right. I just wasn't sure..." She breaks off for a second. "Sometimes I wonder if Mrs. Pitts is trying to get even with me with all the stuff I put her through growing up. Sometimes when I slip or bump into things that shouldn't be there, I wonder."

"Oh, Alice, the housekeeper? Do you really think she'd do that?"

She looks down at the floor and lets out a deep breath. "No, she probably isn't the type. It's only…do you believe in karma?"

"Like the universe punishing you when you do bad things? No, I don't. I've seen too many rich people lie and steal money from clients with zero accountability for me to believe in karma. And Barb, the owner of the barn where Oriel lives, is horrible to everyone and she hasn't been hit by lightning yet or anything."

"Yeah, that's what I thought. I guess it's silly but sometimes I wonder if that's why I went blind so suddenly; payback for all the bad things I've done."

I study her face, which is full of fear and defiance. How must it feel for such an independent and strong-willed person to be suddenly so vulnerable? Especially since she apparently has a history of treating people badly.

"Alice, you're fourteen, how bad can your list of crimes be?" I say finally, trying to make her laugh.

She flashes a grim smile. "You'd be surprised, Sidney. Well, let's go walk this dog then."

I stay right beside her as we go down the stairs one step at a time. She doesn't complain but it's obvious how uncomfortable this is making her. The slippery steps and the fact that walls, ceiling and stairs all blend together in a sea of brown wood must be a nightmare for her.

For the first time I feel a surge of protectiveness toward Alice and I wonder why her family doesn't seem to notice that she's struggling. How hard would it be to put a carpet down in the hall or fix the lighting so it's not glaring off every surface? Or get her an online library filled with audiobooks?

Would it be weird to bring it up with her parents, though? I've barely worked here a day and I don't even know these people.

I'll just wait and see, I decide finally. *Maybe Alice doesn't even want my help.*

CHAPTER 19

SIDNEY

I feel strange walking into the barn at Happy Acres, knowing that this will most likely be my last month here. My first week at Three Sisters has flown by, but I already know that I love it and that I want to stay.

Surprisingly enough, there are parts of Happy Acres that I'm going to miss. And some people too.

"Are these really for me?" Val asks, staring down at the bag of books with wide eyes and an incredulous smile.

"Of course they are," I say, gulping. I haven't told her yet that the books are kind of a going-away present, that I will probably be leaving and taking Oriel with me. Now that school is about to start, Val will only be here on the weekends so I might not have too many more chances to say goodbye.

I have the feeling she's not going to take it well.

"*Dressage, Centered Riding.* Oooh, *Massage for the Performance Horse.*" She lets out a little squeal and jumps up and down with excitement. "Can we try this one right now? Can we try on Diva? She's a performance horse."

Well, she was once, I think, *before Barb wrecked her.*

"Yes, of course. You brush her and get her into cross-ties first and then we'll practice some things."

It's my first day off from Three Sisters. I've already ridden Oriel and cleaned his stall, and now I'm waiting around hoping to talk to Barb. So far, she hasn't set foot in the barn today, which worries me because school starts in a few days and she's about to lose all her free child labour. Who will be doing morning feeds and turning out the horses then?

I'm also not looking forward to telling Barb that Oriel might be leaving. I'd decided to tell a bit of a lie and say that he's going for training, just in case things don't work out at Three Sisters and I need to bring him back here suddenly.

It feels too scary to put all my eggs in one basket and trust that this new job will work out. Even though I'm starting to like Alice, she is still far too unpredictable for me to depend on her.

"Okay, she's all clean," Val calls, and I look over to see poor Diva standing sourly in the cross-ties, a wary expression on her face.

"Hey, pretty girl," I croon, even though right now she looks far from pretty. Her head is up and her nostrils pinched as if she expects nothing but trouble from us. She's actually a well put-together horse, but a year of being treated like a machine and not a living creature has taken its toll on her. She's only ten years old but she already looks like she's in her late teens. If I had all the money in the world, I'd buy her just to get her out of this place. She'd be an amazing kid's horse once she wasn't in pain anymore.

Val hops around excitedly at her shoulder, oblivious to the mare flinching away from her with every leap.

"Softly, Val," I say, "let's think relaxing thoughts so she can enjoy her massage."

"Like my mom at the spa," Val says, laughing loudly. "We need some lavender oil and mood music."

"Maybe next time." I smile and hold my hand out so Diva can see the carrot I have for her. "At least we have snacks. She probably likes those better than lavender oil."

Diva gives the carrot a suspicious look before snatching it from my palm and crunching it angrily. Which is kind of typical for her.

"Now, let's see where we should start."

Val and I look down at the book together, staring at the figure outlining the different muscle groups of the horse. I used to massage Oriel all the time, but I must admit that it's been a while and I've forgotten almost everything.

"I think her neck bothers her," Val says thoughtfully. "She doesn't arch her neck like Oriel does. Hers is stiff, like a board."

"Good observation. And that can be from both pain and from the wrong muscles being developed. Do you think we should start there?"

"Yep." Val grins at me.

"Okay, you do the lower part here and I'll work on the section up top near her poll. Let's see if we can get her feeling more comfortable."

Diva looks furious when I gently touch the area next to her ears, but after I make a few light circles across her coat, her ears slowly unpin and she lets out the smallest of sighs.

"There you go, girl," I say softly, "nothing to be suspicious of. We're going to make you feel better."

After a minute of glaring, Diva finally snorts out a loud breath and drops her head.

"She likes it," Val whispers excitedly.

From behind us, a door slams, making all three of us jump.

"What's going on here?" Barb bellows.

Diva's hooves scrabble on the concrete aisle as she pulls briefly at her cross-ties.

"Whoa, Diva, it's okay." I lay a hand on the mare's shoulder and then turn to glare at Barb. Who shouts like that around horses for no reason?

"We're just giving Diva a massage," Val says in a tiny voice from where she's tucked herself behind the mare. "Sidney gave me a book about it."

"What have I told you about teaching *lessons?*" Barb narrows her eyes at me nastily.

She looks awful. Worse than usual, if that's possible. Her face is puffy and blotched pink and white with a faint sheen of sweat glistening on her nose and cheeks. Her eyes are bloodshot and she seems to be having trouble focusing on us.

"I wasn't teaching. We were looking at the book and trying some things out," I say soothingly, hoping that I can keep her from blowing up. "You can't be mad over that."

"Don't you tell me what I can or can't be mad about," Barb barks. She sways slightly and for the first time I notice the bottle clutched in her hand. "You think I don't see the way you walk around here like you're better than everyone else. Judging me and my students."

"No, I never judge your students," I say quietly, glancing back at Val. "They do the best they can with the few skills you give them."

"Oh, so you're judging *me* then, Miss High and Mighty?" Barb snarls. "You come out here with your rich clothes and fancy horse and think that you're better than me. But you're not. Don't think I don't know all about the trash family you come from. You act like you're queen of the dressage girls but really you're just garbage."

I suck in a breath, not shocked by the words so much as the venom behind them.

"No she's not," Val says furiously. "You can't talk about my friend like that."

"Val, it's okay," I say quietly, "maybe you should put Diva away now."

"Yes," Barb hisses, "put her away because that's the last time you'll be seeing her. Both of you need to get off my property right now."

"What are you talking about?" I ask incredulously. "You can't kick us out. I pay board here. And Val's parents pay for her lease. We haven't done anything wrong."

"I'll be the judge of that," Barb says coldly. "Don't think I didn't see all the times you've given this brat lessons when I specifically told you not to. I won't have devious rule-breakers around here. I won't tolerate it."

"Barb," I say, trying to sound reasonable. She is obviously drunk and maybe she won't even remember any of this when she sobers up. "We apologize if we broke any of your rules. And I can move Oriel if that's really what you want. But Val didn't do anything…"

"No more chances!" Barb screeches, her cheeks flaming beet red. She clenches the bottle in both hands like she's itching to hit something with it. "After all I do for you people and this is how you repay me."

Suddenly, she bursts into angry tears, which is almost scarier than her yelling.

"I give everything to you kids and all you do is go behind my back and take advantage of my kindness. Exactly like my witch of a sister. I work my fingers to the bone and she wants to take everything away from me when it's *mine.* It's not fair!" She breaks off into a wail and stumbles sideways until she's leaning heavily against the wall, sobbing loudly.

I stare at her in horror, wondering what on earth to do. Should I call the police or the ambulance or just get out of there as fast as possible?

"Val, put Diva away now," I say firmly. "And then call your mom and see if she can pick you up. Tell her it's an emergency."

Val nods wordlessly and unclips Diva, leading the mare hurriedly back to her stall.

"Barb?" I say cautiously, taking a step toward where she's slumped against the wall. "Um, are you okay?"

"Get out," she slurs. "I won't have people judging me in my own home."

"I'm not judging you, Barb. I just want my horse to be in a safe place and to be taken care of properly. It's not a lot to ask."

"It's too much," Barb says heavily. "Everyone asks too much of me. I'm a giver and everyone else only takes from me. But you," she looks up suddenly and the animosity glimmering in her eyes is enough for me to back up a few steps in alarm. "*You* won't take anything from me anymore. You need to get your overpriced horse out of here today. I don't care where he goes or what you do with him. Just get out or I'll call the cops and make you get out. You're lucky I'm too nice to put a bullet in him."

"Okay, okay." I hold up my shaking hands placatingly and take another step backward. "I'll find someone to pick him up. Give me a few minutes."

"Do it outside then," she mumbles, sliding another few inches down the wall like she's about to pass out. "You're not to step foot inside this barn again. And that goes for that brat too. You both have one hour to get out and then I'm calling the cops."

She sends a final glare at me and then lurches clumsily into her office.

I heave out a shuddering breath when the door slams shut behind her, my entire body shaking with adrenaline.

Barb has always been an awful person but I'd never seen her act so crazy before.

I have to get Oriel out of this place. Nobody should be leaving their horses or their children with this woman. She is completely unstable.

Val. I quickly head toward Diva's stall, thinking of how terrified the kid must be.

"Hey, Val? Are you in there?" I keep my voice light as I peer into Diva's stall. The mare isn't at her hay pile. Instead, she is standing in the far corner with her head hanging low, inches above where Val is sitting cross-legged in the shavings. She pins her ears at me when I hover in the doorway.

"Are you protecting her, Diva?" I ask softly. "What a good girl. Everything is okay."

"Is it?" Val looks up at me with a pale, tear-stained face.

"It will be," I say as firmly as I can, hoping I've hidden the tremor in my voice. "Did you call your mom?"

"Yeah, she's coming to pick me up. I told her what happened and I don't think she's going to let me ride here anymore, even if Barb does change her mind. Sidney, what's going to happen to Diva?"

I look at the tired, cranky mare, and shake my head.

"I'm so sorry, I don't know," I say honestly. "With any luck maybe Barb will sell her to a better home someday. In the meantime, you could start riding somewhere better. Would your mom let you take lessons at Three Sisters?"

Val shrugs and looks down at the book in her lap.

"Maybe, if it's not too expensive. But it won't be with Diva. I don't want to leave her behind."

Tears pool in her eyes and she sniffles loudly. "This is all my fault, isn't it? It's because I got you to teach me stuff, that's what made Barb mad."

"No way," I say quickly. "Something like this would have happened anyway. Barb has been getting more and more unpredictable lately. Will you be okay here for a few minutes while I make some phone calls?"

She nods again, reaching up to gently pet Diva's cheek.

I'm surprised that Diva hasn't moved back to her hay. The mare has never acted overly fond of Val, or of anyone for that matter. But she seems to sense that something bad is happening here.

"I'll be right outside. You call me if you need anything." I head down the aisle to a spot just outside the barn, where I can keep an eye on Barb's office door. I don't want her drunken self going anywhere near Val right now.

"Come on, pick up, pick up," I whisper as Elliot's phone rings and rings before going to voicemail.

"Um, hey," I say, trying to keep my voice steady. "It's Sidney. Can you call me back? Something happened at Oriel's barn and I need your help. It's kind of an emergency. Thanks."

I hang up and stare at my phone. Fifteen minutes have passed since Barb first told me to get out or she'd call the police. For all I know she's passed out in her office right now, completely oblivious, but on the other hand she could be just waiting to make that call and have the police haul me away.

I know that I probably have some rights because I've paid board for the month already, but there is no way I'm keeping Oriel here a second longer. But what if I can't get hold of Elliot? Where are we going to go?

Breathe, I remind myself, *just breathe. You can handle this. Who else do you know who can help?*

Ben. I don't have his phone number but Alice probably does. I hate to call her for help with anything but I can't see any other options right now.

She answers almost before it's had a chance to ring.

"Sidney," she says sharply. "You'd better not be calling to quit already."

"Um, hi Alice. No, I kind of have an emergency here. Do you have Ben's number?"

She's silent for a moment. "Maybe. Why?"

I bite the inside of my cheek in frustration. "Because it's an emergency, Alice. I need his help. My horse has to leave his barn and…"

"Bring him here," she cuts in excitedly. "He can come here today."

A tiny shiver skates up my back at the eager, almost predatory, note in her voice. Taking him to Three Sisters is the obvious choice, but my instincts are kicking into overdrive, like a warning light flashing on my car's dashboard.

"That's nice of you to offer," I say slowly, "but we're not done with our trial and..."

"Why are you arguing? Look, Ben and Elliot are at some clinic, but I know somebody who can help with the trailer. Tell me where you are and I'll figure it out."

"Alice, I..."

"Tick-tock, Sidney. Is it an emergency or not?"

"Yes, but..."

"Then give me the address."

I give in, finally. But I don't feel great about it.

There is something about Alice that I still don't trust, and I can't help but feel that Oriel and I are jumping out of one bad situation into another.

I check in on Val again before I clean out my locker. Diva has returned to her hay and Val is quietly reading the horse massage book. Her tears have dried up but she looks pale and sad.

Barb is still shut up in her office, and there isn't a sound coming out of it, not even the music she usually blares.

There isn't much to take out of my locker. I keep most of my stuff at home anyway since things have a habit of going missing here. But I take my grooming kit and small stack of saddle pads, Oriel's padded bridle, and my tub full of neatly wrapped polos and boots.

I put everything in my car, and then sit myself down on one of the big, decorative rocks that line the driveway so I have both a good view of the road and of the barn aisle.

I think of Oriel out in the pasture with his friends, not even guessing that his life is about to dramatically change. Again. Will he even like Three Sisters? Will he make new friends? Am I no better than my parents dragging us along in their roller-coaster lives, not even noticing how their decisions affect us?

No, I decide, *it's not the same at all.* Because I'm always thinking about Oriel and trying to do better by him. I would never abandon him.

From down the road, I hear the heavy sound of a truck and trailer approaching.

Well, this is it, I think as I pull myself slowly to my feet, *there's no going back now.*

But when I see who is driving the fancy black truck towing the three-horse trailer with the Three Sisters logo emblazoned on the sides, I nearly bail on the entire plan.

There, in the driver's seat, is annoying Josh. And Alice is perched beside him with a small, triumphant smile on her face.

My heart sinks.

To be fair, Josh doesn't seem any more pleased about this than I am.

"Hello," he says stiffly, rolling down the window and looking at the crumbling barn with his lip curled in distaste.

Despite the fact that I myself have put down Happy Acres many times, I still want to slap that condescending look right off his face.

Alice opens her door and slides down carefully, her expression bright with interest. I have no idea how much she can see of the shabby property but she turns in a slow circle, tilting her head as if to get a proper look.

"Thanks for coming," I say through gritted teeth. "Alice, you didn't tell me you were roping Josh into this, I thought one of the grooms maybe…"

"Beggars can't be choosers, Sidney." She laughs in a not very nice way and shakes her head. "Now where is this horse?"

In the end, I don't really have much of a choice but to go get Oriel and load him in the trailer. There is a part of me that almost wishes that he would balk and refuse to get in, but of course he just steps in obligingly, trusting that I know what's best for both of us.

Alice stands well back during the loading but her face still has that avid look on it, as if she's gotten something she wanted very badly. It makes me more uneasy than ever.

"He's well put together," Josh says grudgingly as he shuts the rear trailer door. But I don't bother to answer because my attention is now fixed on the small figure standing forlornly in the barn doorway.

"Oh Val," I say as she stumbles toward me, hiccupping with tears, "I'm so sorry."

"You're leaving," she sobs, "and I'll never get to see you or Oriel again."

"Don't say that," I say as soothingly as I can. "We don't know what the future will bring. We'll meet up again."

She shakes her head and then pulls away, wiping furiously at her eyes and cheeks.

"My mom's here," she says as a dark SUV rolls up next to us. "I have to go. Can you at least let me know that Oriel is okay in his new home? Can you send me a picture?"

"Yeah, of course, I can do that. See if your mom will let you start riding at Three Sisters."

"It won't be the same without Diva," she says glumly. "Thanks for everything, Sidney. For the books, and the lessons. And, well, for being nice to me."

"Bye," I whisper, feeling a little teary-eyed myself. This whole week has been so full of goodbyes.

Val's mom gives me a tired half-smile as her daughter climbs onto the back seat, and then revs the car out of the parking lot.

Poor kid, I think, *I hope she doesn't have to give up riding completely.*

"Can we speed this up?" Alice calls impatiently out of the truck window. "We're wasting time here. I want to get this horse home."

I look over to see Josh watching me with a strange expression on his face.

"Anna has spots for scholarship students in her camps," he says quietly. "There will be one over winter break. You should ask her if there's still room."

Before I can get over my astonishment that he's said something civil to me, he's back in the truck and starting the engine. I scramble over to my own car so I can follow them back to Three Sisters.

I drive right behind them, not taking my eyes off the trailer carrying my precious cargo. I can't help the churning feeling in my gut telling me that if I let that truck out of my sight for an instant that Oriel is going to be driven out of my life forever.

CHAPTER 20

ALICE

*W*ell, today has been one of the most interesting days I've had in a while. I would almost say that it was *great.*

I'd gotten up early to say goodbye to Trin before she headed off to boarding school, which is something that I'm not even close to ready for. I know she'll get to come home on weekends sometimes but I'm still going to miss her like crazy.

Pearl had already been trailered out yesterday to get set up in her fancy new stall at the school and Trin has been wild with excitement ever since.

"I'm going to miss you so much," I say, crushing her into a tight hug.

"Me too." She presses her face against my shoulder. "Are you sure you're going to be okay without me?"

"Of course," I lie. "Totally fine. You're going to have the best time at school. Pearl will be the fanciest pony there."

She laughs and then nods, pulling away from me. "See you soon?"

"Absolutely."

"Alice, Mrs. Pitts is around if you need anything," my dad says. "We'll be back late this afternoon just in time to take you to your counselling session with Donna. Make sure you let somebody know if you go down to the barn. And no riding. I'm letting you be around the horses again, but it's a privilege, not a right, and I want you to make good choices."

"Right, yeah, yeah," I say, barely restraining myself from rolling my eyes. He hasn't even noticed that I'd been going down to the barn on my own for days. "See you this afternoon."

I turn away before either he or Tiffani can heap any more unwanted advice on me and head into the kitchen to load my pockets with apples and carrots and grab a few granola bars for myself.

I spend the rest of the morning hanging out with Jiggs. I have never spent so much time doing absolutely nothing with a horse in my life but it's become one of my favourite things to do now. It's kind of peaceful.

Jiggs isn't bothered by me being in his paddock now that he knows I'm not going to ask him to do anything. In fact, he's become a bit playful and funny. He lips at my hair and tugs on my sleeves, something I would have never let him do in the past. Somewhere along the line I'd been taught that letting a horse into your space was bad and that you always had to stay on top of them or they'd walk all over you. But maybe I'd been missing out on something too by keeping my ponies at such a distance.

After a few minutes of hanging out with me, Jiggs wanders back to his hay pile. He is so much more relaxed now that it's like he's a different pony. He doesn't even anxiously trot around his paddock when I show up anymore.

"What should we listen to today, Jiggs?" I ask, pulling out my gigantic phone. Sidney had set my phone up with both audio-book and podcast apps and she'd picked out a few things already for me to try.

Last night I'd spent hours in bed listening to some trainer who'd ridden across Mongolia on horseback. It had been fascinating and afterward I'd had the first peaceful, uninterrupted sleep I'd had in ages.

I settle in to listen to the rest of the story and I'm so caught up in it that the sudden ringing of my phone makes me jump nearly out of my seat.

A giant S appears on the display and I hit the button in irritation.

"What?" I snap. "You'd better not be calling to quit already."

But my irritation quickly turns into disbelief, and then triumph, as she starts talking. It's like all my plans are falling into place at once.

After I hang up on her, it doesn't take me long to track down Josh. Any of the grooms would probably want to check with my dad or Darla before helping me, but not Josh. He just nods and quietly goes to hook up the trailer.

The entire time we're driving to the crappy barn where Sidney has been boarding her horse, it's like there is a happy orchestra playing in my head. I'm humming the whole time.

"It's nice of you to help Sidney," Josh says, peering down at the GPS before making a left-hand turn.

I glance over at him, startled. All I'd been thinking about was getting my new horse home.

"Right, well, she sounded desperate. It's the least I can do."

"I just hope she's not taking advantage of the situation. She's only worked at Three Sisters for a few days. Truthfully, she's not as bad as I expected, and Anna and Lena like her, but you never know."

"Well, if it doesn't work out then I can always fire her and keep the horse. I've always wanted a Friesian."

I start laughing and it's a few seconds before I realize that Josh is not laughing with me.

"I'm kidding," I add quickly, but he doesn't say anything else.

I can't see much of Happy Acres when we get there but I can sense that it's a dump. It smells like rotting manure and the barn is like this dark, depressing blob.

Sidney takes so long getting her horse from the pasture that I start to nervously wonder if she's going to change her mind and not bring him to Three Sisters at all.

But finally, he's standing there in front of me with his big hooves planted at the bottom of the ramp.

I stand back at the perfect spot so I can take in as much of him as possible with my peripheral vision, and he is drop dead gorgeous. All rippling muscle and elegant lines, just like I remembered from when I'd seen him online. I can't wait to see him without his blanket on. I can't wait to ride him.

I heave a sigh of relief when the trailer doors shut behind him and he's locked safely inside.

There is yet another delay while Sidney talks to a random sobbing little girl who appears out of nowhere, and then we are finally off.

The whole drive back I'm overflowing with excitement, it feels like Christmas morning.

Josh has fallen into one of his moody silences so I turn up the radio and hum along to it.

I make myself scarce when we arrive because suddenly there are grooms everywhere and Sidney is sniffling with tears while she's unloading, which is ridiculous when you consider how lucky she is right now.

I don't need to be around when all that chaos is going on. It will take a while for Oriel to settle in and I want to meet him properly on my own, once he's quiet and more relaxed and there are not so many people around.

I head toward the house for a well-deserved lunch, cutting through the parking lot in front of the barn.

"What do you mean you're leaving?" a familiar voice demands loudly. "My lesson was supposed to start ten minutes ago."

I jolt and hurriedly duck behind one of the oversized pickup trucks parked near the barn, hoping that Marsha hasn't seen me.

Marsha is my least-favourite boarder and I try to avoid her at all costs. She is unbearably loud and she picks the worst horses to buy. Not that the horses themselves are bad, they're just awful matches for her terrible riding. She's completely ruined two horses in the time I've known her and she's currently working on a third.

"I'm sorry, Marsha," Darla says in her no-nonsense voice, not sounding sorry at all. "I have a family emergency. Your lesson will be rescheduled."

"My lesson *is* an emergency," Marsha bellows. "This horse is out of control and I have a show coming up. What can be more important than that?"

"I received a phone call telling me that my sister has been rushed to the hospital. Not that that's any of your business. Now get out of my way."

Marsha makes an outraged huffing sound and I hear Darla's boots crunching on the gravel. A few seconds later, her little Porsche revs up and peels out of the parking lot.

I wait until I'm sure Marsha has gone back inside the barn and then make a break for the house. I hadn't even known that Darla had a sister; she'd never mentioned her in all the time I'd known her.

She didn't bother to visit me in the hospital. Not after that one time she was forced to. But she'll rush off to the bedside of a sister she never even talks about.

I squash down the hurt before it can take up residence in my chest. I have a new horse to think about now. I don't want to dwell on Darla.

Mrs. Pitts pounces on me the second I walk in the front door.

"Lunch is ready," she says, looming up in front of me in the hallway before my eyes have a chance to adjust to the dimmer lighting.

I have a brief thought that maybe *now* is her perfect opportunity to get her revenge on me. My family is gone for the day, we are all alone together and nobody is around to hear my screams.

But the smell of her famous chilli simmering on the stove is enough to make my stomach growl so I follow her to the kitchen. At least I'll die full and happy if she has poisoned my lunch.

"This is so good, you could open a restaurant," I say, piling chilli onto one of the cheese buns Mrs. Pitts has toasted for me.

"Thank you, it's a family recipe. My great-great-great grandmother from Mexico passed it down."

"Your family is from Mexico?" Pitty has always been as pale as a ghost and she doesn't have an accent.

"My ancestors on one side, yes, but that was a long time ago. I suppose I'm from a bit of everywhere now."

"Huh." I think of our Scottish family crest hanging in the hallway and the genealogy charts framed on the wall in my dad's office. Long lines of ancestors who'd come together to form *me*. I've never really thought of anyone else's history but my own.

It's weird to think of someone as uninspiring as Mrs. Pitts as having her own past and her own stories. I guess she was young once too. Did she ever dream of a different future than the life she has now?

It's such a startling thought that I don't say another word until I've polished off two bowls.

I'd made Josh promise to text me when Sidney finally left, and the second my phone chimes, I stack my dishes in the sink and head back down to the barn as quickly as I can.

Up ahead I hear a high-pitched, greedy nicker.

"Hey, Checkers," I call softly. "Yes, I'm coming."

Jiggs doesn't make a sound but I can hear his compact hooves thudding on the ground as he paces in circles. Having a new arrival has set his anxiety off again.

Another nicker, deeper and louder, joins the chorus and I feel my heart skip a beat.

"Hi friend, don't worry, I brought you a treat too."

I head to Checkers first, letting him greedily grab the small apple slice from my palm, crunching it up before nudging me rudely for more.

"No, that's enough for you. You're on rations, remember? Here, Jiggs, do you want your treat?"

His pacing doesn't stop but he does head my way, delicately taking his apple slice from me before moving on, slipping away from my outstretched hand before I can pet him. It's a little thing but it's still progress.

I turn to the large horse in the paddock next to him. The real reason that I'm here.

"Wow, I didn't realize how big you'd be up close," I say softly. I offer him a piece of apple, wondering belatedly if he's a biter or has any nasty habits I don't know about. It's weird because I can't see his expression. I just have to trust that he'll behave.

He reaches for his apple gently, lipping at my hand and then quietly crunching his treat. His warm breath puffs on my cheek, sweet and sugary from the apple, and his untrimmed whiskers tickle against my skin making me laugh a little.

I inhale slowly, breathing in the scent of him, and then carefully I reach out and touch his silky neck, running my hand down to his shoulder, which is as far as I can reach from this side of the fence. He does not feel like a flabby retired old horse. This guy is fit, all muscle, and I can feel the proud arch in his neck. His mane is thick and wavy, like it had recently been braided and falls well past his shoulder. I run my fingers through the silky strands.

All the horses here have neatly pulled manes about two inches long that always sit perfectly flat against their necks with rarely a hair out of place.

This guy has a feeling of wildness to him. I can imagine him galloping down a long beach next to the ocean, his hooves crashing in the surf and his mane blowing in the wind.

He snorts abruptly, like he can picture it too, and I smile.

"You and I are going to be friends, aren't we, big guy? Sidney doesn't know it yet but I'll be riding you in no time."

I get my chair and blanket from the storage shed and sit down outside his paddock, right near the fence separating him and Jiggs, and pull out my phone.

I don't open the audiobook about Mongolia this time. Instead I pull up the podcast app and find the one that Sidney had saved for me. The one I'd avoided listening to so far.

Sidney had been so excited when she'd told me about it. The No Limits podcast was run by two girls, one who was blind and one in a wheelchair, who were both riders and Paralympians. Their content was basically interviews with other athletes who had to overcome physical challenges. One of the girls was even heading up a movement to include show jumping at the Paralympic games.

But the whole idea of their show had made me feel sick and angry at first. Because, I don't want to fit in with those type of girls. I don't want to be defined by my vision loss or the fact that I'm no longer normal. I want to be a regular rider, not a disabled rider. I don't want people feeling sorry for me, or thinking I'm all noble for carrying on in the face of adversity.

I'd been sort of rude to Sidney when she'd first mentioned it; I'd yelled at her, in fact, but I hadn't deleted the podcast from my list.

And now, there is something about Oriel being here that makes me want to listen to it. Nothing is going to change the fact that I'm partially blind. That is not miraculously going to go away. But maybe I can find a different way to move forward.

"We'll give it a try, Oriel. If we hate it, then we'll delete the whole thing."

He stomps a heavy hoof and I take that as agreement.

Time slips away as I listen and I pull the blanket tighter around me as the temperature drops another notch. Both Oriel and Jiggs drift toward my corner of the fence and it feels good just hanging out with them. Like they're quietly supporting me on either side.

I owe Sidney an apology, I think, *this podcast is amazing.*

"Alice?"

I jerk sideways, caught off guard, which alarms Jiggs and sends him trotting away.

"Dad," I snap. "What are you doing here?"

"That's a nice greeting for your father. We just arrived home and you have your appointment with Donna this afternoon, remember? She was nice enough to see you on a weekend so we can't be late."

"Oh, right. I forgot. Sorry."

"So, this is the new guy, hey? He looks fancy."

I smile despite myself. "Yes, I think so too. I can't wait to start lessons with him."

"Did Sidney agree to that?" I hear the frown in my dad's voice. "Is this horse even safe?"

"He's twenty years old, Dad, of course he's safe," I say, because my dad doesn't need to know that an older horse can be as lethal as a young one in the wrong circumstances. "He's like a big puppy dog."

"Well, if Elliot and Sidney agree that he's safe and appropriate, then I don't see the harm. I'd love to see you back riding again, even if you can't jump."

I suck in a sharp breath, all ready to fight with him and then slowly, painfully, I squash my anger down.

He's said I'm allowed to ride again, so what's the point in arguing with him now, when he can revoke his decision at any second? He's basically my prison guard.

The girls on the No Limits podcast found a way to jump so I will too, even if I have to wait until I'm old enough to move out on my own. In the meantime, I guess I'll just have to play the game.

"Right," I say, gritting my teeth. "Let's get this counselling session over then."

∾

The ride to Donna's is mostly silent, at least for me. My dad ends up having to take a bunch of work calls on his phone, even though it's the weekend, as there is some sort of crucial emergency at his office.

It isn't even interesting listening in on his conversations because they are dead boring even in a so-called crisis. Lots of middle-aged men pretending that price fluctuations on some foreign stock is earth-shattering.

I put in my headphones and open my podcast again. It's much more pleasant to spend time with inspiring riders than with my stressed-out dad.

"Do you want me to go up with you?" he asks, hanging up on his last call when we reach the parking garage. He turns toward me but there's a distracted note in his voice and I can tell he's just dying to make his next call.

"No, don't worry about it. I know the way."

For a second, I hesitate, wondering if I should tell him about the little café downstairs that makes the lemon loaf. Maybe we could go there after my session and I could tell him about the podcast. Maybe...

But, before I can say anything, he already has his phone up to his ear and I am forgotten.

I stare at him for a moment and then climb out of the car, shaking my head at how ridiculous this whole situation is. Yes, I can navigate the parking lot and the elevator myself, but I'm still legally blind. What if I got lost or hit by a car or something? How is it okay to leave your nearly-blind daughter to navigate a large building full of strangers on her own but not to ride a pony around a small course? It doesn't make any sense.

Pondering the absurdity of it all, I make it to Donna's office right on time.

"Alice," she says warmly, meeting me in the otherwise empty waiting room, "it's good to see you. How is your week progressing? How are things with your pony?"

"Great. Jiggs is good. I've been hanging out with him and gaining his trust again. He's coming around. But, more importantly, we had a new horse arrive today. He's technically my tutor's horse, but I'm going to be riding him eventually. His name is Oriel."

"Alice, that's fantastic. That's nice of her to let you ride him. So will you be starting with dressage then?"

"Yes." I shrug. "At least until I figure out a way to start jumping. You were right about that, by the way. There are blind riders who jump and I'm following these girls who have their own podcast now. They're trying to make show jumping part of the Paralympics. But, until then Oriel will make it a bit easier to suffer through dressage."

Donna laughs softly. "Well, Kira says that she loves dressage almost as much as jumping so it can't be too bad."

"Like watching paint dry. And I'll have to ride with annoying Elliot for my coach."

"You don't like her?" Donna sounds amused.

"She's fine, I guess. My sister Isabelle raved about her. But I don't get what all the fuss is about. She's so slow and methodical and wants everything to be done correctly. It's boring. Riding with Darla was always fast and exciting. I loved it."

"She won't teach you now?"

I tap my foot up and down, one of my rare anxious habits, and accidentally kick the edge of her desk with a thud.

"Sorry. That was an accident. No, Darla won't teach me anymore. She doesn't care about dressage. And she's busy coaching other riders. And, I heard her sister is sick so...." I break off, biting the inside of my cheek.

"I'm sorry to hear that. You must miss riding with her."

I nod, feeling a hard lump forming in my throat.

"I do. I miss a lot of things."

"I'm glad you have your first lesson with Elliot and Oriel to look forward to then. Did you talk to your dad about keeping Jiggs around longer?"

"Jiggs? Oh, no, I kind of forgot. Nobody is going to buy him anyway. We're coming into winter and he's still hot and spooky. Besides, my dad is too busy to have a conversation with me. I'd have to make an appointment or something to spend more than five minutes with him."

"Oh, that sounds frustrating. So did you make one?"

"One what?"

"An appointment to speak with your dad. I thought that talking to him about keeping Jiggs was on the list of things you wanted to work on. At our last session you said that was important to you."

"Right, I meant to talk to Dad but there's been so much going on. And Oriel's here now so...."

There is a long silence and I feel my cheeks flush. I wonder if it sounds like I'm just dumping Jiggs now that he's not useful to me. Now that I have Oriel. I'm not doing that, am I?

"It's not like my dad would let me jump him anyway," I say defensively, "and Jiggs would hate dressage."

"I'm not here to judge you, Alice. We are working on your goals, not mine. But last week you said that you were enjoying spending time with Jiggs, that you were learning a few different horse-handling techniques. Has that changed?"

"No," I say sullenly, "it hasn't. I like working with him. It's like having a project horse again, in a different way."

My chair feels uncomfortable suddenly; too hard with seams in all the wrong places. I get up and walk to the window, staring out at the hazy blue. Somewhere down there is the harbour and I think I can almost make out the contrast between the shore and water.

"Are there boats down there right now?"

She pushes back her chair and moves to stand beside me. "A few. There are some rowers practicing and way down to the left there is a float plane about to take off."

"What colour?"

"Orange with a blue stripe."

I nod and heave a small sigh. "I wish I'd come here more often before I lost my vision. I love the water. When I was small, Mom used to bring my sisters and me down here for ice cream sometimes. We'd sit down by the inner harbour and watch the boats and the people. Do they still have those musicians and street shows down there?"

"They do," Donna says, and I can hear the smile in her voice. "Artists, comedians, and all sorts of strange acts. There was a mime when I was there last time. Not my favourite, honestly."

"Same," I say. "Mimes and clowns are creepy."

"Some people love them but I can't help but agree with you. Did your stepsister leave for school yet?"

I move back to my chair, glad that we're on to easier topics. And for the rest of the hour I talk about Trin, Beans, and the No Limits podcast, and about how I'm not finding Sidney completely awful as a tutor.

"Well, Alice. Our session is up," she says when I finally pause for breath. "It's always a pleasure to talk to you. I look forward to hearing about your adventures at our next session."

The transition is so abrupt that I want to protest, to *make* her let me stay. Like last time, I do not want to leave.

"Okay, goodbye I guess." I get up reluctantly and head toward the door, feeling like I still have so much left to talk about.

Maybe Donna plans it that way, like a television show ending on a cliff-hanger so that viewers will come back for more. Well, if that's her plan then it's working. I'm already counting down the days until I can come back.

CHAPTER 21

SIDNEY

*T*oday has been one of the worst days of my life and I am exhausted. I'd hardly been able to force myself to leave Oriel behind at Three Sisters, even though he looked completely content in his paddock in front of a pile of leafy, green hay.

Worst of all was when I'd sent a text to Val to let her know Oriel had made it safely, she'd told me that some of the girls at Happy Acres had seen Barb being taken away by ambulance. And nobody knew if she was going to be okay.

I'd cried all the way home, not because I was particularly attached to Barb but from the stress of it all. She had looked, and acted, so awful when she'd confronted us. Maybe I should have realized that she wasn't well and at least checked on her.

When I finally stumble into the house, all I want is to have a long, hot shower, to crawl into bed and forget that this day ever happened.

And that's right about when I get Zara's text.

Hope you're ready for tonight. I'll be at your place in an hour.

I stare at the phone in disbelief, my heart sinking. Damn. I am in no way prepared to have people over tonight. I can't deal with any more drama.

But when I call Zara to cancel, she overrules me right away.

"No way," she says when I try to explain about everything that had happened, "you aren't going to wallow all alone in your misery. You need friends around to take your mind off things."

"You're sure it would be only a few people?" I ask, too fragile after my day of chaos to even put up much of a fight.

"Oh yes, absolutely, just a small group. I'll come early and we can hang out and get ready together."

"I'm not sure what we'll eat." I think of the dwindling food supply in my fridge and freezer.

"Don't even think about that. I have it all handled."

Even though the way she says that last word is a little ominous, I finally give in.

Zara arrives at four o'clock on the dot and, to my complete disappointment, her friends Brittani and Mia are standing on the doorstep behind her.

"Girl, you look rough," Zara says as soon as I open the door. "But, don't worry, we'll fix that right up. Luckily, I brought reinforcements."

"Oh, great." I try to force my face into some sort of welcoming smile.

"It will be fantastic. You'll see." She reaches out suddenly and pulls me into a hug. "It's good to see you. Come on, girls, let's get this party started."

Mia gives me a sympathetic look as she steps into the hall and I wonder if Josh has already told her about me having to move Oriel. What am I thinking? Of course he has. He's probably told everyone at the barn about how pathetic I am. Maybe he already posted it to True Dirt too, give them a little more ammunition to fire at our family.

"Thanks for letting us have the party here, Sidney." Brittani's smile is about as insincere as you can get, all teeth and glittering eyes, and I wish I could push her right back out the front door. "This will be epic."

"Nice to see you too, Britt," I say with as much enthusiasm as I can muster. I've known her since middle school and she's always seemed like a complete fake to me. I'd never understood why Zara had gone over to the dark side and started hanging out with her last year. Or why Britt is standing in my foyer now.

"Your house is gorgeous," she says, looking around with envious eyes. "I bet you'll get a fortune for it if it ever sells in this market. I can't believe you get to live here all by yourself. You're so lucky that your parents don't care what you do. Mine are so protective that they barely let me out of their sight. I'd be having parties every night if I were in your shoes."

Before I can respond to any of that, there is a scuffling sound in the hall and then Mia lets out an excited squeal and leans down to scoop up Beans who has woken up from his nap and come to join us.

"He is so adorable," Mia says, squishing him against her chest. She doesn't seem to care when he licks her chin. "I miss having a dog."

"Oh, you girls and your animals." Zara rolls her eyes and Brittani gives a little smirk. "They are so gross."

"What? How can you not love this guy?" Mia sets Beans down with a final kiss on his forehead and beams at us all.

I smile back at her tentatively. She doesn't seem so bad, really. Better than her sulky cousin Josh, anyway. Maybe not all Zara's new friends are awful.

"We should go sit by the pool," I say, remembering my manners. "I have crackers and cheese set out and..."

"Never mind the carbs, Sid. Nobody needs those. We have wine." Zara pulls a bottle out of the large duffel bag she's carried in and dumped in the middle of the hall. "Now, this is your night so you don't have to worry about a thing. We have it all organized. I know I missed your birthday and Christmas, so this is my way of making up for it."

"Oh, you don't have to do that," I say quickly. "And it's only going to be a few people, right? I'm not really up for a…"

"Ladies, pour this girl a glass of wine," Zara commands and then leads the way toward the pool while the rest of us trail in her wake.

There was a time when Zara practically lived here in the summers. Her own family is big and noisy, including four brothers heavily into hockey, so their place was always chaos. I'd loved it but Zara used to take every chance she could to get away from them. Apparently she still remembers her way around.

"So, tell us all about your horse," Mia says as soon as we're seated at one of the small tables near the pool and Zara has pushed an overflowing glass of wine into my hand. "Josh said he arrived today. Wow, this cheese is good. I love the nippy stuff."

Although Britt and Zara avoid everything but the wine, Mia doesn't seem to have any problem with carbs, and she's been picking away steadily at the snack platter I'd set out earlier.

"He seems to be settling in well," I say cautiously. "His name is Oriel. He's a Friesian and we do dressage." I take a sip of the wine, hoping that it eases some of my anxiety. I'm out of practice being social. Having any sort of conversation feels weird and stilted.

"Oh, yeah, dressage. I tried that once and it's so not for me. There are only so many circles around the ring you can do. I was bored out of my mind."

"Well, that was the wrong type of dressage then," I say, laughing. "I can't get enough of it. It's like sculpting, dancing and martial arts all in one. It's addicting."

She wrinkles her forehead and studies me thoughtfully. "I've never heard it described like that before."

"No? Well, my old coach, Pablo, was really into classical dressage. He wanted to elevate everything into an art form. Even at the walk. We rode to music almost every day to stay inspired. He was intense, but amazing too."

"He was a certified weirdo," Zara calls from where she and Brit are now fiddling with the epic sound system my dad had installed around the pool. "I'm so glad I stopped riding there."

I take another sip of wine so I don't have to respond to that. Zara had never been a dedicated rider and she hated doing any sort of chore outside of the riding itself. She didn't even want to groom her horse because she thought they were too dirty. She hadn't lasted long at Pablo's and had quit riding altogether shortly after that.

"Maybe we could go on a trail ride one day," Mia says eagerly. "My girl, Nim, loves the trails way better than riding in the ring."

"You take lessons with Darla, right?" I ask, surprised that I'm finding myself liking Mia. I'd always resented her, blamed her even, for taking Zara away from me last year, but she seems nice so far.

"Kind of." She frowns and snags another piece of cheese. "We have to take lessons with her if we want to board there, that's part of the rules, but I'd rather ride for fun. Josh is the serious equestrian in the family."

"Okay, you two can't talk about *horses* all night," Zara says loudly, sashaying up to the table. "We have a party to get ready for. Where are we setting up the food, Sidney?"

"Um, the kitchen counter?"

"Ugh, no way." Zara rolls her eyes like I've suggested something offensive. "We're not barbarians. We'll have proper tables delivered; I just need to know where to put them. Brittani's mom runs a catering company so she's bringing all the stuff. By the pool, maybe?"

"Catering company? How many people are we feeding?"

They've already turned away, not listening to me at all, and

Mia shrugs.

"Sorry," she whispers, "I'm as clueless as you. Zara invited me last minute. I hope you don't mind."

"No," I say, realizing that it's true. She seems quite nice, and having another friendly face at the barn, maybe even someone to ride with, can't hurt either. "So, you live at Josh's house?"

"Yes, with Josh and Oliver's family. My Uncle Silas is Josh's dad and he's married to Oliver's mom, who is great. I'm just staying with them for a few years while my parents are doing some field-work trips. They're archeologists so they're in the middle of a big research project."

"Oh, wow. You didn't want to go with them?"

I watch her expression closely, wondering if she feels abandoned.

"No," she says slowly, "I've travelled with them a lot already. I wanted to finish high school in one place and enjoy riding my horse. I'll catch up with them again in a few years. Plus, living at Uncle Silas's house is great. I always wanted a brother growing up and now I have two. Do you have any siblings?"

"Yes, a little brother, Leo, who is with my parents in Vegas right now, and my sister, Eden, who is an actress."

"You're lucky. Being an only child kind of sucks sometimes."

I nod, but honestly I've spent so little time with my own brother and sister lately that it sometimes feels like I'm an only child too.

"All right, girls, we're running out of time here. We only have a few hours to get ready. So we need to get Sidney fixed up so that Zack can't take his eyes off her."

"Yes." Brit leans forward with a gleam in her eyes. "Let's talk makeover."

"Wait, what?" My face floods with heat. "I didn't think Zack was really coming. I don't need to wear anything special. I thought we were all just hanging out. I…"

"Sidney, stop panicking," Zara orders. "We do not panic when a hot guy likes us."

"You mean Zack is coming tonight?" Mia asks slowly, and I turn to see her staring at Zara with a strange expression on her face.

Zara looks alarmed for a second and then she laughs, shaking her head. "Of course he is. He and Sidney really hit it off this summer."

"Did they now?" Mia turns to look at me, frowning.

"Yes, they have," Brit says quickly, defensively. "What, you don't think Sidney is good enough for him or something? Way to be judgemental, Mia."

"No, that's not it, I just thought..." She turns to me with a concerned expression on her face.

"This night is not for *thinking*, Mia," Zara snaps. "We're here for Sidney, right? And if you can't be supportive of her then you need to leave, *now*."

Mia's eyes widen in surprise and then she shrugs and takes another cracker off the platter. "I'm never one to miss out on a good party. I'll stay."

I look from one face to another, trying to figure out what they're talking about. Why would Mia care if Zack and I liked each other? Did she have a thing for him or something?

"Good, that's settled." Zara grins at all of us and holds the bottle of wine in the air. "Now, let's get started."

***It turns out that the oversized duffel bag that Zara had left in my front hallway is packed full of skimpy dresses, makeup, hair products and two more bottles of wine. I don't even know how one person can own so many clothes and beauty supplies. I could practically fit my whole closet in there.

"No, not that one," Zara calls over the music blaring in my room as I squeeze myself into yet another clingy dress.

"No?" I look into the mirror, smiling at the way the silky, gold material glitters under the lights. It covers way more skin than any of the others have, which is more my style. "I like it though."

"I agree," Mia says from her spot on the end of my bed where she is leafing through a pile of my old horse magazines, "it suits you."

"Too boring." Brit turns around from where she's applying another coat of blood-red lipstick in front of my bathroom mirror. "You look like a nun."

"Um, I'm pretty sure nuns don't dress like that," Mia says, laughing.

"Well, a librarian then," Brit snaps, sending Mia a pointed look. Ever since that weird conversation earlier, there has been a bit of tension between the three of them. "Sidney, keep looking."

"There's not much left," I say, fishing around in the bottom of the bag. "Only these, but they're…"

"The green one," Zara squeals as I hold up a tiny scrap of fabric. "That will look perfect on you."

"Um, is it in two pieces?" I ask doubtfully.

"Don't be silly, the material is stretchy. Just put it on."

I'm already feeling tipsy from the wine and at the stage where everything seems funny. So, instead of arguing, I shimmy into the thing and then look at myself in the mirror.

"Wow," I say, blinking at my reflection. It's short, tight and shows way too much skin, but the effect is also beautiful. The colour is perfect against my skin and it looks like it was painted on, like it was made for me.

"Yeah, wow," Zara echoes, "that's the one."

"Oh, no, I couldn't wear this in front of other people," I say quickly. It's worse that the skimpy bikini she's already picked out for me.

"Sure you can. You're hot, Sidney; it's time for you to own that and stop being a pathetic, mousy little horse girl who would rather read moldy old books than talk to a real guy."

There's a sharp bite in her voice but when I spin to look at her, she's smiling.

"Sorry, too harsh, I'm a bit drunk already. Don't mind me. My point is that you look like a million bucks and you should flaunt that. Right, girls?"

"Definitely," Brittani says; "once we do your makeup and hair, Zack will be throwing himself all over you."

Her phone beeps and she glances down at it. "Sweet, the food is here. I'll be right back."

"I'm coming too," Zara says. "You're on babysitting duty, Mia, don't let her get changed."

It's a bit of relief when the two of them and their nonstop chatter are gone. I had forgotten how much Zara likes to talk and gossip, as if she has to fill in every second of silence with noise. I walk over and turn down the music and then study my reflection again.

"Is it awful, Mia?"

"No, of course not. It's beautiful. As long as you're comfortable in it, that's all that matters. It's just a dress."

"Yeah." I smile in the mirror, studying the girl who is me and yet also a stranger. "It's like becoming a character in a play, isn't it?"

Mia laughs and nods. "Exactly, that's why dressing up is fun. You get to be another person for a night. This room is great, by the way. It suits you."

She looks around at the bookshelves appreciatively.

"Thanks, I love it."

"Can you actually read in all these different languages?" She leans forward to study the shelf closest to her.

"Sure. Some of the older books I'm interested in were never translated into English so I do a lot of translating. I have older horse training books in French, Spanish and German."

"And are these all your ribbons from horse shows?" She stands up and goes over to the wall by the door where my wooden display case of ribbons and trophies stands.

"Yep, Oriel and I showed a lot over the years. He's amazing."

"So, if you're like this talented rider who speaks multiple languages and is obviously crazy-smart, then how on earth can you be interested in someone like Zack?"

"What?" My stomach does a funny little flip-flop and I put a hand over it, suddenly feeling a bit ill.

"No offense," she says quickly, "heaven knows that I'm the last person who should be giving relationship advice and I know that he's Zara's friend and all, but you seem, uh…better than him?"

"Oh, no," I say quickly, "Zack is way out of my league. He's popular and has all those followers. And he can be really sweet and sensitive sometimes. He writes songs and poetry and…" I break off, embarrassed. It's not like he needs me to defend him or anything, so I'm not sure why I'm trying so hard to convince her. Or myself.

"Okay, okay. If you say so. I was just checking. I don't know him that well, but if you say he's a good guy then I'll take your word on it. Come on, I can help you with your hair if you like. That's one thing I do know something about."

By the time Mia and I leave my room I'm feeling confident again. With my hair piled on top of my head in soft waves, and some waterproof makeup in place, I'm looking like a million bucks.

And it turns out that in the short time Zara and Britt have been away, that my entire house has been transformed.

First, there is a catering truck parked outside and no less than six employees bustled around getting things ready.

My front foyer has been filled with golden helium balloons that bump gently against the ceiling. And the pool area has been transformed with fairy lights, lanterns and five tables loaded with all sorts of food. There is a whole table just for wine and a separate table with a keg and about a million gold plastic cups.

"Sidney!" Zara squeals, coming up behind us. "Isn't this amazing? Don't you love it?"

"It's, uh, beautiful," I say, still in a bit of shock, "but, there are so many tables and so much food. How many people are we…"

"Don't start with that again," Zara says sharply. "Britt worked hard to make this happen so don't sound unappreciative. They're leftover things from this wedding her mom did so it's no big deal, we're trying to set the right mood here."

"No, it's really nice. But…"

"Sidney." Zara links her arm with mine and gives me a little shake. "Relax. Stop worrying. You're supposed to be having fun, letting loose, and not being such an uptight nerd. Got it? You're going to have fun tonight whether you like it or not."

"Right." I take in a deep breath and let it slowly out. *I can do this, I can let go and have a good time for once in my life.*

"That's right, just relax and enjoy yourself. Everything is going to be fine."

And at first it *is* fine. People start showing up around seven o'clock and they're mostly people I knew from high school. Old friends and people I've lost touch with. Gone is their icy indifference from last year. All the guests seem happy to see me and everyone is excited about free food and alcohol. It's like the whole scandal had never happened and this painful last year has been erased.

It doesn't take more than a half an hour before people are stripping down to their bathing suits and hopping into the steaming pool.

The wine is flowing and everyone is laughing and joking around.

More people pour in, and sure, half of them might be strangers but that doesn't seem like a bad thing anymore. The night is warm and everyone is happy and having a good time. Maybe my parents were right about something after all. Maybe I should spend more time being young and enjoying life, and less time worrying.

"Sidney!" Mia bounces over to me and to my disappointment,

she is dragging her reluctant cousin, Josh, by one hand. "Look who showed up. I nearly had to twist his arm to get him to leave the house but here he is."

My heart sinks when I see his sullen face. Why on earth would he show up here since he hates me so much? Is he here to check out the house of the infamous criminals he despises so much? Or to heap on a little more judgement?

To be fair, he looks extremely uncomfortable, like he'd rather be anywhere but here, and I almost feel a pang of sympathy for him. I'm the same way at most parties. It's where I'm at my most awkward.

"Ah, our future Olympian," I say, raising my eyebrows at him and giving him what I hope is a scathing look. But it's ruined a bit when I wobble on my too-high heels and barely keep myself from falling.

His mouth turns up in the smallest of smiles and for a second his gaze flicks over my barely-there dress before he locks it firmly onto my face again.

"It's good to see you, Sidney. You look…great," he says, a faint tinge of pink crawling up his neck to his jawline.

"Oooh, those are some big words coming from this guy," Mia squeals. Her face is flushed and her eyes are glittering. "Ah, the dressage rider and the jumper. It's like a smutty romance novel unfolding in front of my eyes."

"You're drunk, Mia," he says disapprovingly, but she just laughs and disappears into the crowd.

He looks around a bit desperately before finally turning back to me with a sigh.

"Sorry to crash your party." He sounds stiff and uncomfortable. "Mia has been on a mission to get me to go out and have fun ever since she moved in. She says that I'm too boring, so she's taken me on as her project."

I snort back a laugh and am surprised when his lips curve up in a real smile. It lights up his whole face and makes him look almost tolerable.

"And how is the experiment going so far? Are you having fun?"

He shrugs his shoulders. "Sometimes. Has your horse settled in all right?"

"Yes, and thank you for trailering him. That was very nice of you." I have to force the words out. Because as nice and polite as he's being now, I'm not about to forget how cold, and downright hostile, he's been for the last week.

"No trouble. Alice was very persuasive."

"Yeah, she does know how to get her way." I sigh.

There's another long awkward pause where we stare anywhere but at each other.

"Are you enjoying working at Three Sisters so far?" he asks finally.

"Yes, you must be disappointed that they haven't fired me yet." I mean it as a joke, but the words come out sharper than I'd intended. It's what I've been thinking ever since he showed up with that trailer to collect Oriel.

"What?" He blinks at me in surprise.

"Um." I take a gulp of wine, desperately trying to think of a smooth exit out of this conversation. "Well, Alice told me the first time I met her that you think my parents are criminals and that I probably am one too and that she shouldn't hire me."

"Oh, god, seriously?" He groans and rubs his face. "That kid."

"Yep." I cross my arms over my chest and look away, feeling silly and childish all of a sudden. It should feel good to finally confront him but it doesn't. It's just embarrassing.

"Sorry about that," he says, his worried gaze fixed on my face. "I shouldn't have jumped to conclusions. I was looking out for Alice. She is a menace but I still don't want her to get hurt, especially not now."

"And I'm clearly the type who hurts children. Well, enjoy the party. The appetizer tables are over there if you get bored."

I wave toward the overflowing tables and then turn to walk away. Time to get myself as far away from him as possible. He's definitely ruining my buzz.

"Sidney, wait." He reaches out and catches my hand in his and for a second I'm caught off guard. His grip is firm but gentle too and I can feel the work-calluses on his palm rubbing against my wrist. Which surprises me. I mean, I know he rides a lot but he doesn't strike me as an outdoorsy type of guy who likes manual labour.

I look down at our joined hands, feeling the steady warmth of his skin against mine, and then back up to meet his gaze. I'd never really studied him closely before, but he's not the worst looking guy in the world. In fact, his brown eyes are sort of lovely. And, when he's not scowling at me like he usually is, he almost looks...nice.

"Sorry, what?" I say, clearing my throat a couple of times to get the words out.

"I truly apologize. I was wrong. I was an ass. Alice is like a little sister to me and I wanted to protect her. But that's no excuse for making judgements before I even knew you. Let me make it up to you?"

For a second I'm tempted, but then I shake my head. "Don't worry about it. It's forgotten. Besides, I'm used to way worse treatment than that. Last year at school makes anything you can throw at me a piece of cake in comparison."

His expression clouds over and his soft grip on my hand tightens.

"That's terrible. I'd like to..."

"Sidney," Zara cries out, swooping up between us like a drunken bird of prey and breaking our linked hands roughly apart, "you can't have *all* the boys to yourself. Josh is mine tonight."

Josh's eyes widen like a deer facing oncoming headlights. I almost feel sorry for him.

"Besides, Zack is here."

"He is?" My heart jolts hard in my chest as I turn to see him striding across the lawn toward us like a young Greek god, an entourage of beautiful people flowing in his wake.

Suddenly, Josh is forgotten and all the doubts I'd been having about me and Zack dissolve instantly when I catch sight of him. He's exactly like I remember. Same brooding eyes, chiselled jaw and perfect hair.

When he walks in, dozens of heads turn like he's a magnet and the whole party shifts toward him, as if he has his own gravitational force that pulls everything in.

Zara floats away from me, laughing and throwing her head back as she greets him. She leans in close, running her fingers down his arm like they're old friends, and whispers something in his ear that makes him laugh.

My stomach dips for a moment but then she's grabbing his hand and tugging him in our direction.

"Do you know that guy?" Josh says in a disapproving voice.

I glance at him, surprised at the dark note in his voice, but before I can answer Zack is there beside me and the second I look in his sea-green eyes everything else melts away.

"Hey, gorgeous," he says in that husky voice that's nearly a growl. "You look amazing."

"So do you," I say lamely, my voice coming out a squeak.

Suddenly noticing Josh, his eyes narrow and he drops an arm possessively around my shoulders, pulling me tight against his side.

I freeze, my breath catching in my throat. Zack, after all these months of calls, texts and messages, is actually here. And he's touching me. This is the most perfect moment ever.

"Prescott," he says, staring at Josh. "Nice of you to show up to my girl Sidney's party."

"Zack," Josh says, tightening his jaw and shooting a quick glance at me before looking away again.

I can almost see the tension crackling in the air between them.

Zack's arm tightens possessively around me until it's almost uncomfortably tight.

"Hot tub's on, babe," he says, leaning in so his breath tickles my ear. "I want to see you in that smoking hot bikini I've heard so much about."

Josh blinks, his gaze suddenly fixed on mine as my cheeks begin to burn.

"Come on, cousin," Mia says, appearing beside us and tugging on Josh's hand. "This is a party. Let's mingle."

"Right." Josh nods stiffly at Zack, his eyes lingering on me for a second before he turns and disappears into the crowd.

"Arrogant prick," Zack mutters, dropping his arm off my shoulder abruptly.

"Do you know Josh?" I ask in confusion.

"I've seen him at some music gigs with Zara. He's always been weird. Come on, forget about him. Let's get naked."

My cheeks flush again which makes him laugh and grab my hand, tugging me toward the hot tub. Of course, there will be no real nakedness. That was just a figure of speech, right?

"You need more wine, girl," Zara says, appearing beside me and topping my still-half-full glass up with the bottle in her hand. It's so full that the golden liquid sloshes over the top.

I take a grateful sip, feeling the liquid burn all the way down. Here I am, living by myself in a huge house, hosting my first party. And the best guy here has his gaze riveted on me like I'm the only person who exists for him right now.

If I don't think about debt, or my flaky parents, or the fact that I'm about to be homeless, then I would say I'm quite possibly the luckiest girl in the world.

CHAPTER 22

SIDNEY

I am not lucky.

I am very, very unlucky. And stupid. And so, so gross.

I stare into the empty toilet bowl, waiting for the next wave of nausea to sweep over me and wish that I was anywhere else but here.

Somewhere outside the bathroom the party is still raging. The music is so loud that it shakes the whole house. I can feel it vibrating through the floor into my knees.

I groan and clutch my head, wishing it would all just stop. I only want to crawl into my bed and sleep. But I can't. Because there are a bunch of strangers in my room doing *things* that I don't even want to know about.

They'd laughed at me when I'd begged them to get out and then slammed the door in my face. I hadn't even been able to grab a change of clothes, so here I am shivering on the cold bathroom tiles wrapped only in a towel and my own shame.

I don't know where Zack went. He isn't here holding my hair back while I puke and telling me everything is going to be okay, that's for sure. Not after what I'd done.

How was I supposed to know that you're not supposed to spend a lot of time in a hot tub if you'd been drinking? That it can make you suddenly, violently, sick?

Everything had gone so well until that moment, too.

Our hot tub is huge, big enough for ten people, but it was crowded with probably double that amount of scantily clad people at the time of the incident.

Everyone was laughing and drinking and telling ridiculous stories about things that had happened at other parties in the past. I was tucked up against Zack's warm, chiselled side while he absently ran one hand up and down my arm in a way that sent shivers through me from head to toe.

I'm doing this, I thought in delight. *I'm in the middle of this party, fitting in with Zack and all these beautiful people like I belong.*

I wasn't even regretting the tiny bikini Zara had made me stuff myself into anymore. I looked just like everyone else, after all.

A warm glow of happiness bubbled up inside of me and for a second everything was completely perfect in the world. Then my stomach gave an abrupt lurch.

Oh. I put a hand over my mouth.

"Um, I'll be right back," I said, starting to push myself out of the water, wondering how long I had to make it to the bathroom.

"No way, you're not going anywhere, sexy." Zack wrapped his arm tightly around me, squeezing hard as I squirmed to get away. "You're staying right here with me."

"I really need to…" But it was too late. The nausea came on so fast that I didn't even have time to turn my head before I was spewing the entire contents of my stomach into the hot tub.

There was an instant of horrified silence right before the screaming began. Like a scene in a horror movie, everyone was lunging out of the tub, pushing and clambering over the fallen bodies of their friends, like they were being attacked by sharks.

Zack pushed me away from him so hard that I fell out of the hot tub, my elbows smacking against the smooth tiles that lined the grotto.

"I'm so sorry," I cried desperately. "It was an accident. I didn't mean..."

But he'd already hoisted himself out of the hot tub and was standing as far away from me as possible, staring at me like I was some sort of revolting insect.

I pushed myself upright, legs shaking and my whole body trembling. I was pretty sure I was going to be sick again. I needed to get out of here. I needed Zack to say something comforting, to stop looking at me like I was dirt.

"Oh, babe. Are you all right?"

I felt overwhelming relief when I heard Zara's voice. But she was not speaking to me; she wasn't even looking at me. She had her hand wrapped around Zack's perfect bicep and she was looking up at him like he had narrowly escaped mortal danger or something.

The screams had died down and now everyone was laughing hysterically, half of them holding up their phones.

"That's it, Zara," Zack said coldly, yanking his arm out of her grasp. "I'm done with this crap. She's disgusting and I have better things to do. This is not worth the money."

"It's okay," she said soothingly, still not looking at me. "We have enough. I got the whole thing on video."

A flash went off right by my face, blinding me, and I took it as my cue to get out of there. I bolted through the crowd toward the house.

"Sidney, what's going on?" Josh stepped out in front of me, his expression unreadable, but I couldn't deal with him right then. I was dying inside.

So here I am, hours later, locked in the big guest bathroom, naked except for a towel because there is no way I'm putting that bathing suit on ever again, still vomiting all those delicious appetizers away.

I'd left my phone somewhere by the grotto so I can't even text anyone for help. Not that anyone would help me anyway.

I don't dare open the bathroom door and flag someone down because there is some sort of keg-chugging game going on right in the hall outside the door, and I'm afraid that if I open it then some gross drunk guy is going to think my naked self is an invitation or something.

I rest my head against the toilet and heave for the millionth time.

How much longer can this endless party go on? Surely people will start going home any minute. Right?

Nope. It turns out that parties can go for an eternity. Or at least that's what it feels like to me.

When I am reasonably sure that I'm not going to throw up anymore, I stumble to the bathtub and fill it with the hottest water that I can stand. Then I slip inside to stop the shivers wracking my body.

My eyes close in relief as the hot water wraps around me like an insulating blanket. My elbows sting from where I'd hit the deck and I feel weak and hollow inside. I can still see the way Zack looked at me; like I was leftover garbage, and I feel my earlier shame wash over me again.

You're so stupid. Tears sting my eyes. *You should have never trusted him. You knew that him liking you was too good to be true and you went along with it anyway. It's your own fault. It serves you right for being so dumb.*

I don't know exactly what Zack and Zara have been up to but it's obviously bad. They had both been playing me all this time and I'd been too dumb to put the pieces together. Had Zack even written those poems and lyrics for me or had that been Zara all this time? Had any of it been real?

I lie in the tub, waiting for the music to die down and for people to leave, but if anything, the party gets louder and more out of control. I can hear things crashing and bottles breaking. The music shakes the walls and people keep laughing and shouting at the top of their lungs. I wonder what the neighbours are thinking.

I have my answer to that soon enough because suddenly sirens are blaring through the music. There is the sound of thudding feet, slamming doors and some yelling. Then the music stops abruptly. There is no other sound but the faucet dripping into my cooling tub of water.

I wait another few minutes to make sure they're really gone and then I climb shakily out onto the sodden bath mat and wrap myself in two towels.

Taking a deep breath, I open the door.

The hallway is a disaster. Cans and empty bottles lie scattered everywhere and there is a fine spray of broken glass right outside the door. Something red, I'm guessing a bottle of wine, has been smashed against the wall, leaving a bloody stain dripping down the light grey paint.

I make a wide berth around the glass, tip-toeing in my bare feet to my bedroom.

The door is hanging open and when I flick on the light, I nearly get sick again. Everything has been trashed. All my books have been pulled off my shelves and lie heaped in a pile on the floor. My wooden case with all my ribbons, trophies, and photos in it has been toppled over and there are big cracks in the glass doors. My dresser drawers have been wrenched out and heaped on the floor; clothes are strewn everywhere. A bunch of my bras have been strung up from the overhead ceiling fan, rotating slowly around like the world's most embarrassing mobile.

The bed has clearly been used and the rumpled sheets have been piled in an ominous lump in the middle.

I push my way to the fallen drawers, managing to grab warm

socks and a shirt and yoga pants. I can't deal with all this right now. The second I'm dressed, I back out and shut the door tightly behind me, feeling sick and violated. I don't want to ever step foot in there again.

A low whine sounds from somewhere down the hall.

Oh my gosh. How could I have forgotten about him?

"Beans?" My voice catches in my throat. "Where are you, buddy?"

The whine comes again, followed by the frantic sound of scratching.

"Hang on, I'm coming."

The living room actually looks better than the hallway does. A large vase is lying on its side and there is a blank spot on the wall where our television once hung.

My parents are going to kill me. I can't believe someone literally took our television off the wall. What kind of animal would do something like that?

The distressed whine comes again and I spin around, trying to figure out where he is.

"Come on, Beans. Where are you?"

He begins to bark frantically. Something he never does unless he's really upset.

I hurry into the kitchen, looking around in confusion in the semi-darkness. Where on earth could he be?

An upper cupboard rattles and I rush over and throw it open.

"Oh, buddy. I'm so sorry." I pull his wriggling body out and clutch him to my chest, nearly sobbing with relief.

He scrambles to get down, running to the back door because he clearly has to go to the bathroom and probably has for hours. I can't believe somebody had stuck him up there. I'm lucky that's all that happened. If something awful had been done to him it would have been all my fault.

Guilt churns through me as I let him out and I sag against the back door, staring out at the garbage-strewn back lawn. I am a terrible pet owner. I'm desperately trying to afford Oriel. I can't protect my dog properly. I am officially an awful person.

Somewhere in the darkness I can hear him snuffling and snorting.

"Come on, Beans," I call, stepping out onto the stone patio, suddenly worried that I shouldn't have let him out here at all. There is probably food spilled everywhere and his digestion is never the best, even when he's eating his special vet kibble. "Buddy?"

Claws clack toward me and suddenly he's there, wriggling and snuffling excitedly, already forgiving me for letting him down so badly.

But when he dances into the kitchen, my heart shudders to a stop in my chest. For a second, I'm living my worst nightmare because it looks like he is covered in blood. Large slashes crisscross his body and there is a circle of red around his eye. But in the next instant I realize that it's lipstick that's been smeared on him. Somebody *drew* on my sweet, trusting, senior dog in lipstick and shoved him in a cupboard.

An image of Brittani standing in front of the mirror covering her mouth in this very shade swims to life in front of me. A wave of rage washes over me, so strong that I have to reach out and grip the counter with both hands to keep from falling down. Bile rises in my throat and I wonder if I'm going to be sick again.

Beans stops and looks up at me, wagging his stump of a tail and clearly wondering why we're up in the middle of the night when we should be in bed sleeping.

"I'm so sorry," I say softly, hoisting him into my arms as I lock the door to the patio and then go and do the same thing to the front door, which has been apparently hanging open all this time.

I carry him down the hall to the bathroom, too numb and worn out to cry, even though I want to. I put him in the bathtub where I'd spent half the night and carefully wash the offensive red streaks off his coat. Only once he's clean can I breathe freely again.

Wrapping him up in an oversized bath towel I step out into the ravaged hallway, strewn with glass, bottles and deflating balloons.

I will deal with this mess in the morning, but right now I need to find a safe place for us both to sleep. I really hope it's not the bathroom again.

My room is out of the question, as is my parents' old room which has been trashed too. But for some reason, Leo's bedroom door is still closed and his room is completely untouched. His planet models still hang undisturbed from the ceiling. His books are still arranged carefully on the bookshelf in alphabetical order, unlike mine which are probably ruined.

I crawl into his narrow bed with an audible sigh of relief and let Beans burrow under the covers next to me. He circles a few times and then plants his body against my side, feeling warm and solid against me.

I am asleep before my head even hits the pillow.

CHAPTER 23

SIDNEY

*B*eep, beep, beep.

I wake up and groan painfully, shutting my eyes tight, and burying my head under my pillow to make the noise stop. My head feels like it has a jackhammer pounding away behind my eyes.

Beep. Then a sort of metallic clunking sound and men's voices talking right outside my bedroom window.

Not my window, Leo's window, and his room faces directly onto the road in front of our house.

Wincing and squinting against the sunlight, I twitch the curtains sideways and peer out onto the street.

"No." I scramble to my feet, ignoring the throbbing pain in my skull. I'd been so distracted yesterday afternoon that I'd parked my car right in front of the house instead of a few blocks away. And now it is being loaded onto the bed of a tow truck.

"No, no, no." I sprint down the hall in my bare feet, leaping over broken glass, cans and deflated balloons.

"Hey!" I yell, throwing open the front door and running across the frost-covered lawn toward my car. "You can't take that. It's mine."

Both men swivel toward me with identical looks of astonishment. I don't even want to know what I look like after my hellish night, but by the expressions on their faces, it's not great.

"Nora Jones?" the man closest to me says, pulling out a clipboard and studying the page in front of him.

"No, that's my mom. But this is my car."

"Sorry, that's not what the paperwork says. It's being repossessed for non-payment of the lease. You might be able to call the dealer and work something out but you'll have to do it in the next five minutes or we're taking it away."

"Okay, please don't take it away. I need to find my phone. I'll call my mom right now."

I sprint back into the house, my heart thudding wildly. They can't take my car. I need it for work. Where was the last place I saw my phone?

It's impossible to find anything in this mess. I scour the house and then finally remember that I might have left it at the pool. I run outside and stare at the bottom of the hot tub where a familiar black rectangle is resting peacefully. The water is thankfully clear now but I still cringe as I step in and fish it out.

I wipe the water off on my shirt and push the power button desperately, but of course, it's dead after spending a night in the hot tub.

"This can't be happening," I say out loud. My heart is pounding in my chest and I have no idea what to do. I need my car. I have two jobs to get to.

I can figure this out. Surely, if I explain my situation I can reason with them.

From out front I hear the tow truck rumble to life and I dart back through the house. But, by the time I reach the front door, I'm just in time to see my car being ferried down the street.

I lean heavily against the porch railing. Everything around me blurs and my lungs don't seem to be working properly. With a low groan I sink down to the steps, tears rolling down my face. I can't handle all this. It's too much. I want to go back two years ago when I was still a kid who got to ride her horse and read books all day. I hate this life.

A door slams across the street and I look up to see one of our neighbours standing on his own front step with a cup of coffee in his hand just watching my life collapse like I'm a Netflix documentary. He's wearing a bathrobe that barely covers his hairy knees and a pair of fluffy blue slippers. He doesn't bother to look away when he sees that I'm watching him.

"Glad I can entertain you," I mutter, struggling to my feet and stumbling back into the house. I slam the door behind me extra hard to make a point.

To be fair, the party had probably kept the whole street up all night. And it's not like the neighbours loved us anyway, not since the news vans had first showed up on our quiet street and had camped on our lawn for months. Thank goodness there were none around to see me now. We were old news as far as the media was concerned.

Don't panic, think. I lean against the wall and stare dully at the dozens of half-deflated balloons floating around the foyer. First, I need to call my parents and to do that, I need a working phone.

I hurry to the kitchen and rummage through the cupboards until I find a bag of rice. That's what you're supposed to do when your phone gets wet, right? Cover it in rice? I drop the phone in the bag, seal it back up and give the thing a good shake, hoping it works best if you coat it. Like Shake n' Bake chicken.

"Okay, Beans," I say, looking down at where he's licking cider from a tipped-over bottle. "We need to clean this place up."

I put on shoes first, so I can navigate the garbage-strewn floors without cutting my feet, then scoop Beans up and take him back to Leo's room where I've set up a temporary base. It feels like the only safe place in the house right now.

Leaving him there, I step out into the hall, looking around with a sinking feeling in the pit of my stomach. How am I ever going to clean all this up? Where do I start?

I head to the kitchen and rummage around until I find a jumbo box of garbage bags. I guess I'll worry about making the floor safe for Beans first. The last thing I need is to rush him to the vet because he ate something bad or stepped on something sharp.

As gross as this is, cleaning helps clear my head so I can think.

How am I going to get to work? Today is my day off from both Three Sisters and the Shrimp Shack but I still need to go and see Oriel. I can't just dump him in a new place and then not show up to make sure he's okay.

The city bus. It must go out to the farm. And there's probably a way to look up the routes online and how much to pay for them. I've never ridden the bus in my life, but there's a first time for everything.

An hour later, the main hallway is at least safe and clear of debris, although the rest of the house is still a disaster. I don't even want to think about what the back yard and the pool must look like.

I check my phone to see if it's working yet but the screen stays stubbornly black. So I stuff it back in its rice bath and cross my fingers that hopefully it just needs more time.

When I check on Beans, he's already dry. He prances toward me, huffing and wagging his stumpy tail.

"Do you need to go out, friend? Okay, I could use a break too."

There are a million things I need to do to get my life in order right now and I don't even know where to start, but walking the dog is something I can handle and I owe it to him after the horrible night he'd had.

Even though I still feel sick and hung over, the fresh air and the gentle sunshine outside makes me feel a bit better. And instead of just circling the block once, I let Beans drag me toward the dog park, which is his favourite place to go.

I sit on a bench in the sunshine and let him play with the other dogs, putting off going home as long as I possibly can.

Over an hour passes before he's tired himself out and I clip him back on his lead and head toward the disaster waiting for me at home.

It turns out that a lot can happen when you're away from home for an hour.

When I finally make it back to the house, the first thing I see is a pale, lavender business card stuck in the front door.

I pull it out slowly, raising my sunglasses to squint at the writing.

Oh, crap. Lisette. My parents' real estate agent friend.

There's nothing on the card, just her name, phone number and logo. Weird.

I push open the front door and notice right away that the air smells different. Less like stale alcohol and pot smoke and more like the cinnamon and lavender room spray that my parents use before they show a house to potential clients.

"Hello?" I call cautiously, closing the front door behind me and taking a few steps inside.

There is no answer. But when I get to the kitchen, I see a large piece of stationery with Lisette's flowery letterhead on the top.

Unacceptable, is scrawled in slashing capital letters at the top.

Sidney, I have left you and your parents multiple messages. My clients expect better than this. We will be discussing this further.

So disappointing,

Lisette

.   .   .

I stare down at the message, gulping. Lisette is another agent in the firm my parents worked for and she is not a nice person. I've met her at a few events and have always avoided her sour face and sharp tongue. She becomes a completely different person when her clients are around. But for the rest of us she's like a grumpy, rabid, raccoon.

And, if she brought clients here *today* of all days, she's going to be livid.

I hurry over to the bag of rice that I left on the counter and cross my fingers and toes as I fish my phone out. I brush off the stray grains of basmati that cling to it and hold my breath as I push the power button.

It wakes up slowly, which is natural after a near-death experience, I suppose, and then runs some update that takes a few more minutes before I'm finally taken to my familiar home screen.

My heart sinks.

Voicemail. Thirty text message notifications. Fifteen missed calls from my parents. I am in so much trouble.

I listen to the voicemail first. Most of them are from my parents demanding that I call them. I listen to them one by one with a sinking heart and delete them as I go. Three are from Mia, though, which is surprising because I didn't even know she had my number.

Hey, it's Mia, just making sure you're okay. I heard you got sick but we can't find you at the party anywhere. Answer your phone. Hope everything is all right.

The last one was from later this morning, somewhere around the time my car was getting repossessed.

.   .   .

Hey, we haven't heard from you. Just call to let us know you're alive. I heard about the police and everything. Hope you're not in too much trouble. Bye.

After a moment's hesitation I delete her messages too. She'd seemed nice enough yesterday. But who knew how much of that was an act. I'd thought Zara was my friend and look where that had landed me. It was best to move on and get them all out of my life for good.

The messages from my parents range from disappointed to downright angry.

I don't work up the courage to call them for another hour.

"Darling," my mother's voice trills through the phone, not sounding angry at all, which is surprising. "I know your father and I left you some stern messages, but it's all been sorted now so I don't want you to worry about it."

"You're not mad? Mom, I'm so sorry, I…"

"Hey, slugger," my dad comes on the line with her. "We know we asked you to spread your wings, loosen up and act like a normal teenager, so part of this is on us. But, that being said, selling the house is pretty important right now. We can't have potential clients walking out on a sale."

"I know. I feel so bad about all the mess. The party got out of control and I was so sick and scared. I had to spend the night…"

"It's all arranged!" my mom says brightly, cutting me off before I can tell her about my awful night. "Lisette has organized a cleaning crew to come in and get everything back in shape. Our own furnishings were a little dated anyway so she'll get rid of the old things and have a staging company come in. That way everything will look ready to sell."

"Er, all right?"

"So, kiddo." My dad heaves an audible sigh. "Once it's staged, I'm afraid we can't have you living there anymore. You understand, I'm sure. It's just business. We can't move forward in the direction we'd like until the house sells and frees up some capital. It's a bit of a time-crunch actually."

"So, what should I do?" I say, feeling small and afraid.

"We can't decide your path for you, darling," Mom says. "You're on your own journey. But, we think you should really take Nanna up on her offer of staying at her place until you get on your feet. Even if it's just for a few months. Your father and I are willing to send you a plane ticket to Alberta. And, with your amount of hustle, it won't be long until you find a job and are able to make your own way in the world."

"That's what I did," my dad pipes up, "I was only a bit older than you when I went to intern at the real estate company. I started from nothing and built an empire. Anyone with a little motivation can..."

"I'm not going to live with Nanna," I interrupt angrily, rubbing my face in frustration. "Right now, I have a more urgent problem. My car just got taken away. I need to get to the barn. And to work."

"Oh dear," my mother says in a breathy voice. "I completely forgot about the car. You didn't park it in front of the house, did you? We told you..."

"Yeah, well, it's gone. Look..." I gulp hard, hating what I'm about to say. "I'll put off going to school for another year. Can you dissolve my education fund and give me that money now so I can find another place to live? It's kind of an emergency."

There is a very long silence on the other end. I look at my phone, wondering if we've been disconnected.

"Well, you *see*, Sidney." My dad clears his throat a few times. "We thought it best if we reinvested your education fund for you until you really need it."

"What?" Everything inside of me goes very still and I hear a sharp buzzing sound in my ears.

"It was for your own benefit," my mother says, not sounding

quite so breezy. "When Manifest Now takes off, I think you will be thanking us. We've just hit a few short-term roadblocks."

"You used my education fund to invest in your stupid company?"

"Hey now," my dad breaks in, "no need for that negative talk. I hear your frustration and uncertainty about the future, Sidney. Change is hard. But sometimes we need to make sacrifices in order to…"

"Dad, you need to stop. Are you saying that there is absolutely no money left in the education fund that Nanna set up for me?"

Another long silence and I can hear muffled whispering in the background.

"Sidney," my mother says. "I'm putting money in your bank account right now. It's not much, but it's what we can spare for the next few months. And of course you'll get your royalties when Manifest Now takes off. I'm afraid it's the best we can do for you now."

"And Sidney," my dad cuts in, "don't forget that struggles are our opportunity to grow and let go."

"Yep, thanks," I say flatly, "thanks for the money, Mom. Keep in touch."

I disconnect the call before they can say anything else and then sit there, staring down at the phone in my hands. I'd forgotten to ask about how poor Leo was doing. Or what was going to happen to our stuff. Nobody had mentioned anything about it going into storage. All Leo's things were still here. And mine too.

Beans nudges my arm with his wet nose and I reach out and pull him into my lap, holding him tightly against my chest.

"We're going to figure this out, Beans," I whisper to him. "No matter what, I'm not giving up on you and Oriel."

CHAPTER 24

SIDNEY

"Five thousand dollars," I say out loud, staring numbly at the screen showing my bank account.

Nanna had started an education fund for me years ago and had been paying into it all this time. Which is amazing when you considered that she didn't even really like me.

"This way at least one of my grandchildren will make something of themselves," she'd told me when I was small. "Lord knows your parents won't see to it."

There had been at least twenty thousand dollars in there, maybe more, and now it's all gone. Even if I manage to somehow scrape up enough to survive this next year, that's still the end of my dreams of going to university overseas.

There is a tiny possibility that Manifest Now will take off and my parents will pay the money back. But I doubt it.

Another wave of nausea sweeps over me. Five thousand dollars sounds like a lot of money on paper but I know for a fact that it is not. Not when I have to somehow buy a vehicle and pay for an apartment by the end of the week. Rents here are crazy; I could easily spend two thousand a month just to have a roof over my head, and that wouldn't include food and the electric bill. And most landlords expect you to pay an extra month in advance plus a damage deposit. Plus extra for having a pet.

I suck in a ragged breath, feeling the walls closing in on me, and put my hands over my eyes to block everything out.

It will all be okay, it will all be okay, I say over and over, desperately trying to believe that.

Beans snuffles at my feet, dancing up and down so his little claws click against the floor. And then he gives an excited woof and prances toward the front door. A second later the bell rings.

Oh no, what now?

I tread cautiously to the door. With my luck it's some gangster coming to collect more money. But when I peek through the spy hole in the door I blink in surprise. Not a bill collector; it's Mia, and behind her is Josh.

I close my eyes briefly, swearing under my breath. How could this weekend possibly get any more mortifying?

I briefly wonder if I can pretend not to be home but Beans is already scratching excitedly on the inside of the door, ready to welcome any guests who will pet him.

"Hello," I say, cracking the door open a hair so they can't see the disaster inside.

"Oh, Sidney, you're alive," Mia says, looking relieved. "We left you a ton of messages but we weren't sure if you were okay. You just disappeared last night after…"

"I'm fine. Thanks for checking." I start to shut the door but Josh puts a hand out to stop me.

"Can we come in and make sure?" he asks, his expression serious as he studies my face through the small crack in the door.

"It's not a great time, actually. I'm kind of busy."

"Sidney, we had nothing to do with what happened last night,"

Mia says, pressing her hands against her chest. "I didn't know about it until afterward. Honestly, I only started hanging out with Zara again last month. She swore that she'd changed and that she'd forgiven you. I thought you were friends again. I didn't know…"

"Wait, stop. What do you mean?" I let the door swing open and Beans scampers out to greet them, huffing and wiggling.

"Zara was selling stories about you to True Dirt. I want you to know that I would never be part of something like that. I didn't know she'd planned to trash your house. Or sell all those pictures and videos."

Mia's voice is thick with tears and Josh lays a hand on her shoulder.

"Ah, so that explains it," I say woodenly, turning toward the living room. I feel the overwhelming need to sit down.

"I'm so sorry. I was sure that she'd stopped. I haven't hung out with her in months and she swore that you two were friends again and that she'd told you everything. It wasn't until last night when she said Zack was coming over that I started to get suspicious."

"Do you know why Zara did all this?" My voice sounds odd, flat and faraway as if I'm speaking through a tunnel.

"Her grandmother had to go into a nursing home after she lost all that money in the condo scandal. It costs the family thousands of dollars a month to keep her there and they're struggling to afford other things. Zara's always been bitter about that. And True Dirt was paying her a lot."

I nod, feeling a bit of relief mixed in with the hurt and sadness. At least I know the whole truth now. I don't have to mourn my friendship with Zara anymore. Or with Zack.

"Wow, this place is a disaster." Mia looks around with wide eyes. "It didn't look this bad when we left."

"We should have stayed longer last night," Josh says grimly. "You look awful, Sidney. Zara said she'd taken care of you or we would have stayed to make sure you were all right. We didn't know what had really happened until hours later."

"It's fine." I pull myself together with supreme effort. I can't afford to melt down in front of these two. I need that job at Three Sisters more than ever now.

"I should have known something bad was going to happen when I saw you in that dress," Josh mutters. "The way that jerk Zack was looking at you, and you were obviously drunk. I should have guessed..."

He breaks off as both Mia and I swivel to stare at him.

"Sorry, what?" I narrow my eyes. "I really hope you're not saying that all this happened because I was wearing a stupid dress."

"No?" He gulps, looking desperately at Mia for backup. "Well, it was kind of short and didn't look like something you'd normally..."

"Josh, sweetie, you're not helping," Mia says, giving him a little push toward the door. "How about you go outside and get some fresh air so I can have a chat with my girl, Sidney."

"But—"

"Bye." She shoves him out the door, ignoring his protests. "Sorry about that. I love my cousin dearly but sometimes I swear he should have been born in the 1700s. Just ignore him."

"He's so...."

"Judgy? Old-fashioned? Opinionated? Believe me, I know. He's a work in progress but he does have a lot of potential. He's actually a good guy." She smiles at me reassuringly.

"You sure about that?" There is no hiding the skepticism in my voice.

"Yep. Positive. He just operates by this unnaturally high moral code that nobody could ever live up to. Including himself. Both his parents were in the military and I guess they were pretty strict. His dad, my Uncle Silas, is nice now, but I don't think it was always that way."

She hesitates and then shrugs.

"Josh gets protective about the people he cares about. But he goes about it in all the wrong ways sometimes. Like what he said about your dress. You can bet he's going to be kicking himself about that for weeks."

"Well, I guess he wasn't totally wrong. It *was* too short and I..."

"Nope, no way. You're allowed to look hot in a perfectly normal dress without people taking advantage of you. Look, Sidney, I need to ask you if anything else happened last night. Like anything bad. We can go to the police right now if..."

"No." I shake my head. "I locked myself in the bathroom all night. It was awful but I didn't get hurt. Poor Beans, though..." I break off abruptly, studying her warily. If Zara and Zack had been playing with me all this time, then what reason do I have to believe that Mia is on my side now? It could easily be another trick that stupid me was falling for yet again.

"What?" Mia looks at me in confusion.

"Why are you being so nice to me all of a sudden? I thought you and Zara were friends."

"We were. But I don't stay friends with people who do stuff like that. Life is hard enough without us turning on each other, we girls have to stick together. Right?"

"Right. I guess."

"I swear I'm on your side. And I feel awful about last night. Please tell me how I can help."

"I don't think there's anything you can do to help me." I sigh heavily. "Unless you can find me a new car and a place to live."

"Don't you have a car and a place to live?"

"No." I look into her kind, calm face and decide to take a risk. "This morning the dealership towed my car away because my parents defaulted on their lease payments."

"Oh," she says in a surprised voice.

"And then the real estate agent who is trying to sell the house popped by with some clients."

"Oh."

"Exactly. So now I have to be out of here by the end of the week. And I don't have any money to live on because it turns out that my parents invested my entire education fund into their stupid company so there's hardly anything left. So now I have to figure out how to find a car and a place to live. And my parents are just getting rid of all the stuff in the house, including all the things my little brother left behind. And I know it's stupid to be attached to things, but he saved up all his money for that telescope and for those stupid planets that hang from the ceiling and..."

I break off, realizing that I'm crying and that Mia is patting my hand sympathetically.

I pull away from her and wipe my eyes furiously, a wave of shame sweeping over me.

"I'm so sorry," she says quietly, "that is a lot to happen all at once."

I nod, gulping back tears, and pull in a shuddering breath. And that's when I look up and see Josh staring at me from the doorway.

His expression is unreadable but all I can think of is how pathetic and weak I must look right now. And how maybe he was right not to trust me to be at the farm and tutor Alice. My life is a disaster. He's probably going to run to the Carlisles and tell them to fire me right now.

"Sorry," I say dully. "Thanks for checking on me. You guys should go now."

There is a long silence and then Mia lays her hand on my wrist.

"As if we'd leave you with all this, Sidney. We're here to help. Now, the first thing you need is a place to live."

"I'll figure something out." I sniff, keeping my eyes glued to the floor to avoid Mia's sympathy and Josh's look of disgust. "I'm sure you have better places to be."

Josh makes a grumbling noise under his breath but when I look up, he's texting furiously away on his phone, ignoring both of us.

"Of course we don't. So, you need a place to live and a car to drive; that's only two problems to solve. Do you have any money saved at all?"

There is no judgement in the way she asks. It's just a question and I barely hesitate before answering.

"My parents sent me a bit of money so I have around six thousand in the bank. But I'll have to pay a damage deposit wherever I rent and probably a pet deposit too. So that will take up half of it. And I need to pay Oriel's board. I don't even know how much they're charging me to keep him at Three Sisters."

"Right," she says slowly, her mouth pulling down into a frown.

"And I have a week to find a place. I need to be out by next weekend."

"It's all settled," Josh says abruptly from his place in the doorway. "Not the car, but a place to live anyway."

We both look up at him blankly.

"Three Sisters," he says to us as if it's obvious. "There are the dorms for working students upstairs in the big barn. They didn't get lived in last year because Darla put a stop to the program. They'd work in an emergency, though, right?"

"There are apartments upstairs?" I hadn't even taken a proper tour of the big barn yet; I'd been too busy working for Anna down the hill and Alice up at the house. Even Oriel's things had been put in the storage shed by his paddock, not in the tack room in the barn.

"That's what I said."

"It's brilliant," Mia cuts in quickly. "Who do we have to ask if Sidney can live there?"

"It's already done. I sent Alice a message and she's arranging it."

"She is?" My heart sinks and a shiver rolls down my spine. Alice doesn't seem like the type to help someone without wanting something big in return.

"Yeah, she said she owes you for letting her do a part-lease on Oriel."

For a second there is a roaring sound in my ears and I have trouble getting air into my lungs. My throat is tight and it's like I'm choking. I want to get out of here, drive to Three Sisters, stuff Oriel in a trailer and get him as far away from there as possible.

But I can't. Because I'm poor and stuck.

"Sidney, are you okay?" Mia asks.

"Yeah," I say finally, forcing myself to inhale. "All good. Um, tell Alice thanks."

I don't look at Josh. I'm afraid that if I look up that he'll see the complete panic in my eyes. But the truth is that, even though I hate the thought of giving in and letting Alice ride Oriel, this might be my only chance at surviving right now.

I have a home for Beans, Oriel and myself. We're safe and I probably won't have to pay very much rent. This might be a good thing.

At least that's what I'll tell myself to keep from falling apart.

CHAPTER 25

ALICE

*T*he early morning sun streams through my window as I blink myself awake.

What time is it? I roll over and hit the top of my alarm.

It is eight, thirty, a.m., the robotic voice says.

I don't think I've been up this early since the surgery. For a moment I sit there, wondering why I feel so different, like something is missing.

I'm not angry, I realize suddenly. The familiar rage that usually accompanies my every waking moment is gone. I feel lighter and, well, *happy*.

Oriel is out in his paddock waiting for me. I have Jiggs too. I can spend all morning hanging out with them.

I doubt Sidney will let me ride Oriel any time soon, but I can at least get to know him, and make friends with him. When she sees how much he likes me she'll have to see what a good idea it is to let me lease him.

Humming under my breath, I get dressed and head downstairs, following the delicious smell of bacon and fresh coffee to the kitchen.

"Good morning, Pitty. What's for breakfast?" I call out happily. "It smells amazing."

"Hello, Alice." The quiet voice does not belong to Mrs. Pitts; it's annoying Tiffani instead.

"Oh, hi. I thought you and Dad were leaving for work early today." I try to sound polite but it's probably hard to miss the irritation in my voice.

"I'm working from home today. Mrs. Pitts made pancakes with a side order of bacon if you'd like some."

"Uh, that would be great." I slide slowly, reluctantly into my chair. I don't want to eat with Tiffani but it would be beyond rude to walk away now. Plus, I don't want to miss out on the bacon.

"Oh, you're here early, Alice. I'll put your toast on." Mrs. Pitts appears beside me. "Here's your coffee."

"Thank you."

She hesitates for a second, most likely stunned that I'm thanking her. "You're welcome."

"Did you hear from Trin yet?" I ask Tiffani, trying to fill in the silence.

"Yes, she called last night. She's having a great time so far. And Pearl is settling in well. She likes her lessons and they've already been on some trail rides with the other girls too."

"Lucky," I say before I can stop myself.

She takes a sip of her coffee and then clears her throat.

"You know, if you ever wanted to go on a trail ride, Alice, then I would go with you. You could even ride Paddington if you like and I could take out a school horse. I know you used to ride him for Clara sometimes."

I open my mouth to say no and then stop myself. Tiffani had inherited Paddington when my sister Clara was banished overseas. He is older now but he'd been Clara's main hunter back in the day and I always had really liked him.

"I'd like that," I say finally. "Thanks."

Before she can start a full-blown conversation with me, I set my phone on the table and flick on a podcast. I'm not trying to be rude but this is the most polite conversation I've had with Tiffani in forever and I don't want to jinx it by us continuing it any longer.

I happily tuck into the food that Pitty sets in front of me, not even glancing up when Tiffani leaves to go to her office.

When I'm finished, I pocket my phone and take my dishes to the sink and then head to the barn.

The air smells delicious outside. It still feels like fall but there are warm currents wafting around me, bringing the scents of horses, hay and earth; all the things I like best.

I hum under my breath as I walk down the hill toward the paddocks. And to my delight, all three horses nicker when they see me coming.

"Hi guys," I call out. "I brought you snacks."

I move from gate to gate, giving them each a small piece of carrot, lingering the longest in front of Oriel.

"You and I are going to be good friends, aren't we?"

He whuffles my hair softly and I rest my hand on the wide spot between his eyes and then trace my fingers down to his nose. His head is double the size of Jiggs' head. And he has a thick forelock that runs nearly all the way down to his nostrils.

I move away from him reluctantly, wishing for a second that *he* was my project horse to work with instead of Jiggs. But I push the thought away and go to the little storage shed to get my folding chair. This time I grab my grooming tote as well. I'm not sure if Jiggs will let me groom him while he's loose, but I'm going to see what happens.

He doesn't take off trotting when I come into his paddock. Instead, he marches over, and I actually have to back him out of my space this time. Which is an improvement considering that even a few days ago he didn't want to come anywhere near me.

"Are you getting pushy, Jiggs?" I scratch under his mane as he nuzzles my pockets. Besides listening to the blog run by the Para equestrian riders, I'd also been listening to some of trainer podcasts Sidney had suggested. And one of them did an episode on helping horses who had lost their confidence. One of the things he'd talked about was getting horses interested in exploring their world. He suggested getting them to be curious about things rather than them automatically fearing anything new.

I hadn't realized how much of my old relationship with Jiggs involved me saying "no" all the time. I was always telling him not to move around, or not to spook, or not to push into my space or look for treats. I hadn't really been giving him any positive cues or encouraging him to do anything outside of riding. I hated to admit it, but he'd actually been scared of me even though I'd never been intentionally mean. Yes, I'd managed his nervous nature well, but I hadn't done much to help him become a brave or confident pony. To tell the truth, maybe I'd *liked* having him be spicy and nearly unmanageable because that made him more fun to ride.

Jiggs reaches out tentatively toward my grooming tote, so I set it on the ground in front of me and unfold my chair, letting him nudge the brushes around to his heart's content.

"Is that fun, Jiggs?" I pull a small curry comb out of the tote and run a few circles down his neck. He doesn't pull away like I half-expected him to, and I feel a strange sense of happiness blossom in my chest. It's such a little thing, but having him stand here loose while I brush him feels incredible right now. He knows he could leave any time but he's choosing not to.

"I'm going to take off your blanket, okay? Will you stand still for that?"

He doesn't even look up from the brushes he's playing with

while I feel my way around his coat, unclipping his leg straps and then the clasps under his blanket. I undo the front buckles last and the slowly pull it off him. He gives a little shiver as it slides free but doesn't leave, and I set to work giving him a good grooming from ears to tail.

He stands still for the most part. A couple of times he wanders away to go get a drink or grab a mouthful of hay, but he always returns.

"There you go, that's enough for today," I tell him finally when he's been groomed within an inch of his life and his blanket is back on. "Tomorrow we'll see if we can get you interested in putting your halter on."

I actually don't really care about working him in a halter, but it would be nicer for him if other people could catch him without having to have a dramatic chase.

And he might still sell this year. His new owners will probably be kinder to him if he's easy to handle.

I put my stuff away and then wander over to lean on Oriel's gate.

He rumbles low in his throat, striding over to me without hesitation. He's so tall that he blocks out the sun and is a dark shadow in front of me. But I'm not scared. He radiates a sort of regal kindness that makes my heart stutter in my chest. I don't think I've ever been in love with a horse at first sight, or first meeting I should say, but I now am overwhelmed with the feeling that I need to own this horse. Or at least ride him. He belongs with me.

And that's when I get the first text from Josh. It takes me a while to read the whole thing letter by letter but when I'm finished, I do an excited whoop of disbelief that has all three horses throwing their heads up.

Sidney is being kicked out of her place and needs a place to live.

"No way," I say out loud, grinning and doing a happy little

dance that makes Oriel snort in surprise. "This day can't get any better."

All my plans are falling into place one by one like clockwork. Like the universe is trying to apologize for taking my sight.

"Looks like you and I are going to be spending a lot of time together, Oriel," I tell him, reaching out impulsively to hug him around the neck.

He stands still for a second and then sidles away from me, but I don't care. I text Josh back as fast as I can manage and then I send a message to Elliot.

We need to organize some lessons ASAP, I write. *I have a horse to ride.*

CHAPTER 26

SIDNEY

I make it through the next few hours by staying completely numb.

I shower and get dressed and then somehow I am being into bundled into the back seat of Josh's low-slung sports car and shuttled to Three Sisters.

I nearly lose it when I see Oriel. All I want to do is wrap my arms around him and sob. This whole weekend has been almost too much for me to handle.

But Mia and Josh are right there, so I just feed him a carrot and pat him woodenly on the neck, afraid that if I let any of my emotions slip it will be like a raging river crashing through a dam. If I start crying again now then I will never stop.

Ben meets us in the barn aisle, smiling at us in his usual kind way. I don't know how much Alice has told him or, for that matter, how much Josh has told Alice, but he seems to understand the situation.

"The dorms haven't been used in a while," Ben warns.

"They're meant for working students since all our full-time employees live off-site. We used to have quite a few foreign workers from Europe and all over the world, but Darla put a stop to that last year."

"Why?" I ask, curiosity piercing my fog for a moment.

"She doesn't like foreign accents," he says with a shrug. "She says they irritate her. So we put a hold on the program for now. We do like to have someone here to do a late night check, though, and sort of be night security if anything happens. You could commit to that?"

"Yes, of course," I say, although I'm not sure how any of this is going to work yet. My shift at the Shrimp Shack usually ends at eleven, but without a car I'm going to have to bus here somehow. Do the buses even run that late?

He ushers us up the stairs and into a huge living room area with dark leather furniture and paintings of horses on the wall. There is a massive picture window that has a view right down into the indoor arena. A spotless kitchen area sits off to one side with a big fridge and an expensive looking coffee machine.

"Wow, this is amazing," I say. It looks like it belongs in a magazine.

"Well, this is the boarders' lounge too, so you have to share it with them during barn hours. You'd have to keep everything neat and tidy too and clean up after yourself."

"No problem," I say quickly, looking around at the impeccable kitchen and thinking of our messy counters and unwashed dishes that usually fill the sink at home.

"The bathroom is here. It's shared too so you'll need to be mindful of that and keep it clean. The dorm rooms are meant to sleep four, but of course you'll have a room all to yourself for now. Here's a key so you can lock your door. There are mini fridges in each room but you'll have to cook in the main area."

He pushes a key into my trembling fingers and then leads me down a short hallway and opens a door on the left.

I peer inside, noting the two sets of bunk beds and a couple of small dressers. It's very basic, like being back at summer camp.

"Closets are there," he says, pointing off to the left where there are two small closets with mirrored, sliding doors. "And that's it. What do you think?"

"It's great," I say, trying to sound enthusiastic. Everyone is going out of their way to help me here so the least I can do is appear grateful even though the room is a little depressing. "And they're okay if Beans is here with me?"

"Alice said she talked to her dad and he okayed it," Ben says, frowning a little. "She has sure taken a shine to you, Sidney. It's not like her to go out of her way to help anyone. It's nice to see that side of her."

"Yeah." I nearly choke on the word. "Nice."

Ben studies me for a second. "Are you doing okay, kid? You look a little rough."

"Er, yes. It was a long night. One I'd rather forget."

"Well, I know it's your day off, but we're a little short-staffed today. Do you think you could do those back paddocks where Oriel is?"

"Of course, no problem."

"Great, and maybe you can help us with lunch feed when you're done."

Mia and Josh head out for their trail ride and then I follow Ben out behind the barn to where the wheelbarrows, forks and shovels are kept tucked neatly out of sight. This is where the manure bins are kept as well as the bags of bedding. No gigantic pile of half-rotted bedding here, like at Happy Acres. These portions are individually wrapped so you can just open them in each stall.

The sight cheers me up somehow. Because even though my own life is chaos, there is still order like this in the world. Everything neatly stacked in its place.

As crazy as it sounds, there is nothing I'd rather be doing right now. My ordinary routine, taking care of Oriel and cleaning paddocks, is exactly what I need to clear my head and feel grounded again.

"All right, big guy, let's get your home cleaned up," I say, dropping my wheelbarrow for a second so I can scratch his neck.

He leans into me, closing his eyes while I scrub my nails back and forth through his coat in the way he likes. Finally he sighs and ambles away to finish his hay.

His paddock here isn't overly large but the footing is nice, soft sand and I can already see body prints in it from where he's rolled and napped. The wooden shelter at the back is lined with rubber mats and the shavings are nice and deep. It's luxurious, but I know he's going to miss his big, wild herd of horses. I'll have to see if I can get him some pasture time, once I'm sure that we're both staying here long-term.

It doesn't take me long to get him all tidied away before I move on to the ponies. I hadn't had much time to meet them yesterday when Oriel had arrived; I'd been too overwhelmed by everything to pay attention to them.

Checkers, the tiny pinto pony, marches right up to me and sticks his nose directly in my face and then begins searching my pockets for cookies.

"Sorry, kid, I don't have anything for you," I tell him, laughing at the disappointed look on his face. "You look like you need to stick to your diet anyway."

Ears drooping, he moves back to his hay net, not interested in me at all anymore.

My thoughts drift as I clean and I wonder how I'm going to get home this afternoon and back to work tomorrow. I'm supposed to work both jobs on Monday and I have no idea how I'll manage it and where I'll find time to buy a vehicle.

I need a dependable car that is big enough to put feed and tack into. But what can I afford? Would any dealership even give me a loan?

The final paddock has Alice's pony, Jiggs, in it and I see what they mean about him being hot and unpredictable.

The second I get into the paddock, he is on high alert, head held high and snorting like I'm a wild cougar about to kill him and not some barn help trying to clean up his manure.

"Come on, pony," I tell him. "You must have seen a wheelbarrow every day of your life. This is no big deal."

But Jiggs doesn't believe me. He takes off in a brisk trot, circling his paddock in an anxious circle the whole time I'm cleaning. And nothing I can say or do will make him relax.

"All right, fine, just don't run me over and I'll get out of here as soon as possible."

It's a little disconcerting to clean with him prancing around like that nonstop but I get the job done as fast as I can, breathing a sigh of relief when I can shut the paddock gate behind me.

I dump my wheelbarrow into one of the large manure bins out behind the barn, which are a sharp contrast to the towering manure-mountain back at Happy Acres, and put my things away.

Then, I get to work helping Ben feed the horses their lunch.

"So Ben, where is the bus stop around here anyway?" I ask casually as I load an overflowing net into the hay-cart.

"Oh, there's one down the road from Barn B, I think, but it's about a twenty-minute walk. Why? Is something wrong with your car?"

"Um, it went back to the dealership but I'm getting a new one," I say quickly, before he can pry any further. "I need a few days to sort it out."

"I see. Well, it's a long walk on foot. I know that Lena used to catch the bus, but she had her bike so it wasn't so bad."

"Okay, thanks," I say as brightly as possible, inwardly cringing. I'm not exactly a hiker and a walk like that is going to make this endless day even longer. "You don't know how to pay for the bus, do you? Do they take credit cards?"

Ben coughs back a laugh and shakes his head.

"I don't think so, Sidney. You need coins, or a bus pass. How about I drive you home today? I have to go into town anyway."

"Really? I don't want you to go out of your way. I can totally figure out the bus on my own."

"Not a problem," he says. "Now, help me hang up the rest of these nets."

~

I help Ben all afternoon. I'm just so grateful that he and the entire Three Sisters family has gone out on a limb for me like this. I mean, they barely even know me. But I also have one eye on the clock, thinking about the hours ticking by. The car dealerships will probably close early on a Sunday, and I have to work both jobs all week long. So my window of opportunity to search for a new vehicle is dwindling by the minute.

And next weekend I'll have to move out of my house and into the Three Sisters dorm. I'll need a vehicle for that since the thought of asking anyone here to help move my things is beyond mortifying.

"Are you ready to go, Sidney?" Mia pops up beside me out of nowhere, grinning just as I'm bringing my second horse in from the pasture. She has a smudge of dirt across one cheek and a tangle of leaves in her hair so I'm guessing that she had a good trail ride.

"Are we going somewhere?"

"Car shopping." She tilts her head at me like I'm a bit slow. "Josh and I made a list of all the dealerships that are open on Sundays. But we need to leave now before they close."

"Um." I look questioningly at Ben but he waves me away.

"Go on. I'll see you tomorrow. Thanks for your help."

Josh doesn't say a word while he drives, and I am kind of sorry that I've ruined his day. I mean, he can barely stand to be in the same room with me normally, and here he's been forced to spend hours in my company, helping me clean up my dumpster-fire life.

Which makes the ride to the first dealership beyond awkward, even though Mia keeps up a constant stream of chatter to fill in the silence.

I mostly block her out while I study the spec sheets on my phone. I can't afford anything fancy like my old car now. No, what I'm looking for is something used but dependable. A fuel-efficient car that is only a few years old and maybe still under warranty. There is a small SUV on the dealership website that I have a good feeling about.

I am not my parents' daughter for nothing. Despite their sketchy history with fraud, they are actually very clever with money most of the time. I know how to balance a budget and how interest rates and financing works.

My dad had had quite the collection of exotic cars for a while there too, so I'm not a complete beginner when it comes to buying vehicles.

I wish we could have stopped off first at my house to get changed since I'm still in my dirty barn clothes, but, as Alice says, beggars can't be choosers and I'm a little desperate here.

"I'll come with you," Josh says, when we pull into the parking lot. "These salesmen can be..."

But I'm out of the car before he can unbuckle his seat belt.

"No need," I say hastily as his window rolls down and he gives me a dark look, "I've got this. Thanks."

The last thing I want is judgemental Josh hovering behind me and second-guessing my decisions. I cross through the back parking lot of the dealership and head straight to the SUV that caught my eye online. It's only a few years old and has sleek lines and a leather interior and the kilometers on it aren't so bad. It's not as nice as my old car, of course, but it will do the job.

"Hi!"

I jump as a salesman materializes from nowhere behind me,

his megawatt grin reminding me suspiciously of my dad's when he's about to make a sales pitch.

"Hello," I say, giving him the barest of smiles. "I'm looking for a quality used vehicle. And I think this one might work for me."

"Good choice," he says, whipping out a clipboard and a pen from somewhere. "Why don't you sit inside and I'll tell you all about it."

I don't want to seem too interested, but I know as soon as I slide onto the leather seats that I already love it. I keep my voice neutral, bored even, while the salesman gives his spiel and then we take it for a quick test drive.

"It's not bad," I say casually when we get back. "I guess it will do."

"Great, I'll grab your financial information and then let's go in and make a deal," he says, grinning.

As he fills out the paperwork, I am silently congratulating myself on being an adult and making my first huge life purchase.

"So, we have a bit of an issue with your credit score," he says, looking up from his computer. He's not smiling anymore.

"Why? I don't owe anyone any money." I have a brief flash of terror wondering if my parents used my name to take out more credit cards or something.

"No, that's not it." He shuffles some papers back and forth on his desk. "It's that your credit is nonexistent. You haven't developed a rating yet. Do you have someone who can co-sign for you?"

I shake my head. "I brought a substantial deposit. I want to put three thousand down and finance the rest. Your advertisement said three percent interest, I believe."

"Um, yes." He clears his throat. "The three percent interest is for those with a top credit score, though. You must understand that, in terms of loans, you're a bit high-risk. For you we could only offer thirteen percent."

"*Thirteen?*" The word comes out a high-pitched squeak as I do some quick calculations in my head. "That's crazy. My payments would be nearly a thousand dollars a month."

"Sorry," he winces. "That's just the way it is. We're taking the risk, you see."

All the happy confidence I'd been feeling drains out of me, leaving me feeling incredibly tired and sad. I'd thought I had this made. My parents had financed things to the hilt and nobody had ever given them a hassle. How is it that people who are already rich get the good deals and poor people who are barely keeping afloat and might need a car desperately, have to pay even more money? It doesn't seem fair at all.

"Well, thank you for your time," I say glumly, shuffling to my feet. "I guess I won't be buying it after all."

"Did you know we have a clearance lot?" he asks quickly, following me to the door. "If you have three thousand for a deposit, then we might be able to find you something you could drive away today."

"Clearance lot?" I feel a spark of interest again. "Tell me more."

And that's how I find myself, an hour later, driving away from the dealership in my new truck. Well, new to me anyway. It has rock chips in the paint, it rattles and wheezes and it doesn't have anything fancy like a backup camera or navigation like my old car did. But it runs and has enough space in the back for a whole stack of hay.

Mia squeals with excitement when she sees it and Josh raises his eyebrows into his hairline but somehow manages to choke back his opinion.

I thank them a million times for driving me and then head toward home.

It's not what I'd come there for but I'm feeling strangely proud as I drive it off the lot. It might not be perfect but I bought it myself, and somehow, it feels like a good start to my new life.

CHAPTER 27

ALICE

I must admit that I'm a little nervous as I head down to the barn after breakfast. It will be my first time facing Sidney since I arranged for her and Beans to move in here and I'm honestly not sure how she's going to react.

I kind of hope that she'll be filled with love and undying gratitude toward me, but I somehow doubt that. I'm forcing her into leasing Oriel to me, after all, and that's not something I'm going to take back. Either I ride that horse or she finds a new place to live.

The three geldings are eating their hay when I reach the paddocks but they all nicker eagerly when they see me. It's the carrots in my pocket, I know that, but it still feels nice to have somebody glad to see me.

I visit with each of them and then I grab my grooming tote and head in to see Jiggs. He's right at the gate, waiting, and I have to shoo him back a few steps so I can get inside. Then he follows me, his nose right at my elbow.

"Let's get your blanket off, kid," I tell him softly, feeling around for the familiar buckles so I can unclip them. I've just undone the last snap when he suddenly throws up his head and takes a few hesitant steps backward.

"Hello, Alice." Sidney's voice is quiet and I can't tell from her tone if she's angry with me.

"Um, hey," I say, swallowing hard. "What are you doing here so early?"

"Anna doesn't need me right now so I came to clean the paddocks."

I nod, reaching out to lay a reassuring hand on Jiggs' neck. "It's okay, boy, Sidney won't hurt you."

He snorts hard and then nudges me with his nose, taking a step closer to me as if I'm going to protect him.

"He's kind of jumpy, isn't he?" Sidney asks. The paddock gate makes a creaking sound and I know she's leaning on it, watching us.

"Yes, but he's getting better."

"He seems to trust you, anyway." She's silent for a moment and she heaves a deep sigh. "I'm not happy that you forced me into letting you ride Oriel."

I hold my breath, waiting her out.

"But I appreciate having a place to stay. And I have you to thank for that, I suppose. You can ride Oriel after the paddocks are done. Just a trial, mind you. If it goes well then you can lease him a few days per week."

She sounds sad and resigned. I should probably feel guilty about that but I don't. Riding Oriel is the only thing that matters.

"Great," say, relieved. "I'd love that. I'll help you clean paddocks."

I say those last words before I have a chance to think them through. Even though we have staff, I'd cleaned lots of stalls and paddocks in the past. No matter how spoiled people think I am, I'm not afraid to take care of my own horses. But that had been back before the surgery. How is blind-me supposed to help with paddocks now?

But Sidney is already wordlessly trudging away to get the wheelbarrow and the manure forks so I turn my attention back to brushing my pony.

Jiggs snorts when he hears the wheelbarrow bumping across the grass toward us but he doesn't move, even when Sidney bangs the gate open.

"He's much more relaxed when you're around," she says. "Here's your manure fork if you really want to help."

"All right." I give Jiggs a final pat. "I'm not sure how much help I'll be, though."

"Well, do your best." She sounds distracted, like she doesn't really care what I do.

I grab the remaining fork and turn to survey the paddock. I can see the piles from further away but they disappear when I get up close. Still, it's not impossible. No worse than navigating a flight of heavily-polished stairs, so I get to work, carefully scooping the piles into the wheelbarrow. It's not perfect, or accurate, and Sidney ends up tidying up the bits that I drop but it still feels good, like part of my normal routine is back.

Jiggs trails along after me, lipping at the fork, nudging the wheelbarrow, and generally getting in the way.

"He's like a completely different pony from when I saw Kira riding him," Sidney says, dropping her fork into the wheelbarrow and steering it toward the gate. "I don't know why you just don't ride him. He seems fine."

"He *is* fine." I gave Jiggs a final pat before I follow Sidney. "He's hot and forward, but he's fun to ride and he doesn't do anything dirty."

"So, what's the problem then? Why are you so set on riding *my* horse?"

Heat creeps up my neck. I guess she's not as okay with me riding Oriel as I'd hoped. "I made a mistake when I got out of the hospital and I jumped him when I shouldn't have and we crashed. My dad and Tiffani saw the whole thing and sort of freaked out. That's why Dad put the ponies up for sale and grounded me from riding. He's never going to be okay with me riding Jiggs after that; he knows I'm going to try and jump again. It's what Jiggs is bred for."

She doesn't say anything while she steers us into Checkers' paddock and shuts the gate behind me.

"Would you try and jump again, even though it's dangerous?"

"Yes," I say without hesitating. "That's all I want to do."

"Well, Oriel is not a jumper, so you're out of luck there."

"I know," I say quickly, "I didn't mean I'd try and jump *him*. I need to do the dressage thing for a while and win some competitions, maybe get on a team. Then Dad will relax, stop fussing over me and go back to forgetting I exist like usual."

She drags her fork tines across the ground with a sharp rasping sound, sifting bits of manure out of the sand. "I still don't understand why you want Oriel. You are surrounded by fancy horses that you can ride."

I shake my head. "Not experienced dressage horses. I need to improve fast if I'm going to start winning things. Oriel knows what he's doing already, and the horses here don't. I hope you're not backing out on our deal, Sidney. I found you a place to live and a great farm to board your horse at. I'm not asking much."

"No," she says quietly, after a long silence. "I'm not backing out of our deal. I'll let you ride Oriel, for now, but if there is ever a second that you don't treat him right then our deal is off."

"Of course," I say quickly. "I won't do anything to hurt him."

"Fine. Let's get these paddocks cleaned then and then we'll tack him up."

Sidney doesn't say anything else the whole time we're cleaning paddocks. She works away steadily, ignoring me while I do my best to keep up.

I know she's still mad at me, and I'm even a little sorry for that, but mostly all I feel is excitement.

"So this is how it's going to happen," Sidney says firmly after she comes back from putting the wheelbarrow away. "We will groom and tack him up here. Then I will ride him in the ring. It will be his first time riding here and he can get overexcited in new environments. Afterwards, you will cool him down *at a walk only* and I will go over the basics with you. If you do one thing to hurt this horse or put him or yourself at risk then I will tell you to get off him. Do you understand me?"

"Yes," I say, nodding. Normally I wouldn't let anyone talk to me like that but I know that Sidney is just being overprotective. I'm the same way with my ponies so I get it. "Don't worry. You won't regret this."

She laughs sharply, but there is no humour in it. "Let's get this over with."

I can hardly contain myself as I brush Oriel's silky coat. He's so tall that I couldn't even get near his head if he didn't want me to. Luckily, he lowers it gently, letting me run a soft brush over his ears and down his neck.

I'm practically dancing with impatience as Sidney tacks him up. She is incredibly slow about the whole thing, fussing over his saddle pad and polos and making sure his girth is lying smooth against his skin. And yes, I understand the importance of making sure your horse is comfortable, but I have the feeling that she's stalling for time.

Finally, she can't put it off any longer and she leads Oriel to the mounting block that is just outside the doorway of Barn A.

I trail after her, wishing it was me up there riding him down to the ring.

His big hooves make a satisfying clop, clop, clop on the gravel, much different then the sound my ponies' hooves make.

There isn't anyone using the dressage ring, which is not surprising because Three Sisters is officially a hunter/jumper barn and it was only through the efforts of my sister Isabelle that there is a speck of dressage here at all.

Sidney doesn't say anything as she rides Oriel into the ring and it isn't until she's completed three laps at a walk that she pauses down at my end.

"He's twenty years old," she says in a tight voice, "so you can't rush his warmup. Ten to fifteen minutes of walk, then the same amount of trot work on a loose rein. Understand?"

"Yes, okay," I say quickly, even though I'd just been wondering why she was spending so much time letting him drag around rather than putting him to work.

"What sort of lateral work are you used to doing?"

"Um, leg yields? Oh, and shoulder-in," I fumble with my words, caught off guard. I'd been to some clinics that focused on lateral work, but it wasn't something I did all the time or anything. Of course, I knew that top riders did tons of schooling on the flat but it wasn't really my cup of tea.

She's silent again and I hear Oriel's footfalls break into a trot. I can only see him when he's down at my end of the ring but I like the rhythmic sound he makes, like he's completely in balance and flowing.

I study them as well as I can in the low, overcast light, impatiently waiting for my turn.

Sidney takes her time, though, although she does move to my end of the ring more and more often.

"Can you see what we're doing?" she asks, trotting him in a circle in front of me.

I frown in concentration. I can't see her aids at all but I can see the way Oriel is moving, the smooth, inward curve of his body and neck. His circle gets smaller, then widens.

"Spirals?" I guess.

"Right. This is a good exercise for him since he tends to get stiff and a good one for you to make sure your outside aids are solid. I make sure to do this at least twice per session and in both directions."

She moves him up into a canter and then they're off again, moving down to the far end of the ring in a series of huge bounds.

His stride is huge, which is a surprise, and for the first time I wonder uneasily what it feels like to sit on that much power.

Finally, Sidney trots him back toward me and then halts near the gate.

"All right, I guess it's your turn," she says, dully. "You can cool him out. You're just going to walk and get a feel of him."

"Yep," I say, bouncing up and down impatiently. "I'm ready."

I slip through the gate and move toward the mounting block where Sidney has already positioned Oriel.

"Climb up and I'll fix your stirrups. Don't touch the reins yet."

Ignoring her tone, I pause to scratch Oriel's neck before I step lightly into the saddle.

"Oh, it's so weird," I say, because this is my first time sitting in a dressage saddle and the feel of it is completely different to my usual close contact saddles. The cantle rises up behind me and there are slabs of leather angled above my knees, along my upper thighs.

"When I first started riding him it took a while to get used to his stride," she says shortly. "So Pablo found me a saddle with thigh blocks to keep my seat more secure. I don't need them anymore but I love my saddle and didn't want to alter it."

She shortens my stirrups but they still feel strangely long.

"It will take a while for your legs to adapt to this position. Let them stretch down and relax. Today is about getting a feel for him."

I nod, nudging the irons with my toes and letting my legs drape around Oriel's sides. My center of gravity feels a bit wonky and I lean forward a little, trying to fit into this odd saddle.

"Sit back, use your core to support yourself instead of leaning forward," Sidney says, sighing heavily like this whole thing is exhausting her. "You can pick up the reins if you like; just make sure it's a soft feel."

I nod and gently pick up the reins, trying not to feel too offended that she's obviously hating every second of this.

Oriel mouths the bit softly as I pick up the lightest contact possible. I barely have to think about moving forward and he's already striding out, his powerful hind end propelling him forward in the biggest walk I've ever sat.

I've ridden my sisters' horses in the past, it's not like I've only ever sat on ponies, but this...this is something else. Each step shifts my hips from side to side like I'm swaying on top of an elephant. He's not even that tall of a horse but his stride is massive.

"That's right," Sidney says from beside his left shoulder. "Can you see that you're approaching the corner at M?"

"Um." I sweep my head sideways, looking for the letters that I know must be there. I can see a few feet out and the faint outline of the fence but not the letters."

"Okay, turn left here, outside aids please. Do you feel how he drifted?"

"Yes, I'm..."

"H is coming up so you'll need to anticipate the turn. Having low vision means that you're going to have to stay on focus all the time if you don't want to get hurt. Oriel doesn't know that you can't see very well so he'll try and do what you're asking of him. I don't want him run into a fence."

"Obviously," I say, starting to feel irritated. "I'm not being blind on purpose, you know."

"No, but I'm not sure if you take your responsibility to these horses seriously either. You're just focused on your own goals."

I open my mouth to argue and then shut it again. "Okay. Fine, I won't run anyone into a fence. I'll take everything you say seriously. I promise."

She sighs, probably knowing that this is the nearest to an apology that she's going to get from me.

"All right, well, you're doing fine. You have light hands and he seems to like you."

"Does he?" A little jolt of excitement shivers through me. "How can you tell?"

"His ears are pricked, he's listening to you and he hasn't bucked you off yet. So those are good signs."

I laugh and feel myself truly relaxing for the first time since I climbed on board and, after a second, Sidney laughs too.

This is all going to work out, I think happily, *exactly like I planned.*

CHAPTER 28

ALICE

I'd expected Sidney to put off my lessons with Elliot indefinitely but instead she sets one up for the very next day.

"Thank you so much for this," I tell her as we walk down toward the ring. She's riding Oriel again and I'm at his shoulder, trying to keep up with his giant walk.

She's still mad at me. Even though I've done my best to stay polite in the face of her frosty attitude, she's barely said three words to me all morning.

"It's more for Oriel than for you," she says grudgingly. "I want him to have a good ride. He hasn't been ridden by anyone else but me in a long time. He's not as easy as he looks."

"I believe you. But I've been riding difficult ponies my whole life. I am a good rider."

A part of me wants her to trust me and be her friendly self again but another part of me is really irritated by her attitude. I know I forced her into this but she should be grateful that she has a place to live and a great place to board her horse. And, also that *I'm* the one riding her horse and not some amateur.

"So everyone keeps telling me."

When we get to the ring I go and lean against the fence while Sidney takes Oriel inside. She's going to warm him up for me so he's not so fresh and then I'll have my lesson.

"Today's the big day, is it?" Josh says, strolling up beside me and leaning his elbows on the upper rail next to me.

"Yes, how does he look?"

"Really nice. He's an impressive horse. Sidney rides him well."

"Does she?" I wish I could see them. I'd never paid attention to dressage back when I had my sight; maybe I caught a few minutes during the Olympics or something, but that was it. So, I didn't have a clue what it was supposed to look like.

"Surprisingly well. She's not what I expected."

I turn to him, trying to understand the strange note in his voice. "Are you still thinking about her parents? The criminal thing? I think you need to let that go."

He laughs and nudges me with his elbow. "I have. I was an idiot. I shouldn't have told you not to hire her."

"Is she pretty? Is that why you're having regrets now?" I am genuinely curious. I only have a vague idea of what Sidney looks like, and I'm also not sure why Josh is so bothered about being mean. I'm mean to people all the time and it certainly doesn't keep me up at night.

"She's beautiful," he says. "Not in a flashy way but in a real, genuine way that creeps up on you. And she's a good person too. She cares deeply about things and she's smart and…"

I tune him out, already regretting that I'd asked the question. But, as irritating as it is that Josh obviously likes someone who isn't me, I suddenly see a way to stop Sidney from being so mad at me about Oriel.

"You should ask her out." I say the words quickly, before I can change my mind. "She could use some fun in her life."

It's an astonishingly generous move on my part, since my ridiculous feelings for Josh are still alive and kicking, but it's the least I can do after forcing Sidney to let me ride Oriel. Maybe she'll be less cranky if she's dating someone.

"What?" He turns to me in astonishment.

"You know, like take her to dinner or a movie or something." I am beginning to see why my sister Clara had a hard time with this guy. He might be great with horses but he's a bit dense socially.

"Oh, I don't... I mean, she wouldn't. Why would you even..."

"Just think about it," I say quickly. "Oh, look, here's Elliot. I'd better go. Time to ride."

Thankful to escape any more of that awkward conversation, I head to the gate, reaching it at the same time Elliot does.

"Hey, Alice, this is exciting," she says, opening the gate for me. "I'm so glad you get to ride him. I think you'll be a good match."

Clearly Sidney hasn't told her anything about why I am riding Oriel, which is a relief. At least I won't have both of them mad at me.

I follow Elliot to the mounting block, my stomach fluttering with unfamiliar butterflies. I don't usually get nervous riding, but today feels momentous somehow. As if a new chapter of my life is beginning.

"We're going to start on the lunge line so you can get a feel of him. Then we'll work on a plan to help you navigate the ring safely on your own."

"The lunge line?" Irritation bubbles up inside of me. "I'm not a baby, Elliot. I can ride."

"Nobody knows that more than me, Alice. I've seen you ride. I think you're brilliant or I wouldn't have suggested Oriel as a horse for you."

I blink at her, caught off guard. I'd always assumed that Elliot hated me for some reason. That she lumped me in with Clara because I'd been my sister's sidekick for a while. I never expected her to say I was brilliant.

"Um, okay. Thanks. So why the lunge line then?"

"To develop both your seat and your confidence. Oriel's expressive gaits are going to catch you off guard at first and there's no way around that. We want to make sure you're comfortable with him before you have to deal with figuring out how to navigate the ring safely."

"All right, fine. Although, I think you're fussing way too much."

"Well, prove me wrong then. Let's get to work."

So, that's what we do. And, even though I feel like a ridiculous beginner at first, Elliot was right about me needing to get a feel for Oriel.

That first trot stride rocks me back in the saddle and there are a few dicey seconds where I struggle to figure out my posting diagonals, especially in this strange saddle with my legs dangling inches below where they usually are.

But, after a few minutes, with Elliot coaching relentlessly from the end of the lunge line, I am able to relax into him and begin to enjoy the ride.

"Wait until you get to feel him open up and extend down the long side," Sidney says, forgetting she's angry with me for a second. "It's like flying."

The canter is surprisingly easier than his trot, even though it's big too. After that first leap forward, he's like sitting on a gigantic rocking horse and I can't help but laugh out loud with the sheer joy of it. I've missed this so much.

"All right, that was great. That's enough for him today," Elliot says, bringing us down to a walk.

"That was amazing." I lean forward and impulsively wrap my arms around Oriel's neck, giving him an appreciative hug. "Unclip him and I'll cool him out."

"Oh, I'm not sure that's a good idea," Elliot says.

"It's fine." Sidney appears at our side before I can argue and then unclips the line, stepping back. "Just walk. Nothing else."

"I know. I will." I hear Elliot muttering something but I ignore it. I'm not planning to do anything stupid to mess this up, even though that's apparently what everyone expects.

It's a bit like riding into a void with Oriel. If I turn my head slowly, I can map our surroundings within about ten feet. And I can see the outline of the rail but not the letters until I get right up to them. And in the upper half of the ring, where it's shadowed by nearby trees, it's even worse.

"You're about fifteen feet from the rail at A," Sidney says quietly, appearing beside me.

"What letter comes next again?"

"All King Edward's Horses Can Manage Big Fences," Sidney says, reminding me of that old rhyme we'd used to memorize our letters back in Pony Club, before Clara had gotten us all kicked out.

"Right, A-K-E-H-C-M-B-F. Where am I now?"

"H, coming up on C."

Now we're out of the shadows and I can see the rail again, but not the letters. From the jumper ring next door, a horse breaks into a thudding canter and Oriel lifts his head and makes a questioning sound that rumbles through his body.

"Never you mind about those horses," Sidney tells him affectionately, "you just pay attention to Alice."

A warm feeling steals over me. For a second I feel this sort of connection to the two of them, like I'm part of a team.

"Can I ride him up to the barn?" I ask.

"Sure," Sidney's voice is flat and distant again, "whatever you want."

CHAPTER 29

SIDNEY

*T*he entire week is beyond exhausting. But on the plus side, it means that I'm too tired to worry about all the crappy things that have happened to my life.

I work at Three Sisters and at the Shrimp Shack every day, and at night Beans and I fall into my narrow dorm bed above the barn and instantly fall asleep.

I could have slept in my own bed at home, of course, I still have time before moving day, but I can't bring myself to do that. The night of the party had changed things for me and I don't feel like my old house is home anymore. I drop in every day to pick up a few things and then get out as fast as I can.

It isn't until Saturday that I finally have time to pack all my stuff up into the dozens of cardboard boxes that I'd brought home from the Shrimp Shack.

Most of my books had survived the night of the party, although there were some cracked spines and torn pages that were beyond repair. My beautiful wooden display case was still on its side, too heavy for me to lift back into place. I'd just swept up the broken glass and carefully fished out all the pictures, ribbons and trophies that I'd won over the years.

After my room is empty, I walk through the house, looking for anything else I'd like to keep, but there isn't much. A decorator had picked out all our artwork and furniture and, although it is all nice to look at, I'm not attached to anything.

But my brother's things are another story. I know that it might be a long time before I saw him again, but I can't bring myself to abandon his stuff. His models, his telescope, and his weird action-figure collection. These things were all important to him. And I knew that he'd have never left them behind if my mom hadn't promised to ship them to Vegas. Which had basically been a lie.

Even though I really don't have room for much at Three Sisters, I pack everything of Leo's up and ferry the boxes out to the truck.

By the time I'm done, the entire truck bed is full of boxes and so is the back seat.

"Goodbye, house," I say, shutting the door behind me a final time. I'd loved this house and my pool and my spacious room. I doubt that I'll ever be able to afford to live somewhere so nice again. But it's time to move on.

It's nearly dusk by the time I'm done ferrying all my stuff up the narrow hallway to the dorm at Three Sisters. Darla had apparently cancelled her lessons so there were only a handful of riders around and they mostly ignore me.

By the time I'm done, I'm limp with exhaustion and just want to flop onto my child-sized bunk bed and never get up, but Beans starts squeaking and prancing almost immediately in the way he does when he needs to go out.

"All right, all right," I say wearily, heaving myself to my feet. "Fine. Where's your leash?"

He huffs at me and barks, spinning in a happy circle as I head toward the door. I snap his leash to his collar and let him tow me down the stairs.

The dusky sky is even darker now. Clouds have closed in overhead and it feels like the temperature is steadily dropping.

"Not too far, Beans," I say, drawing him toward the back of the barn where Oriel's paddock is. "It looks like a storm is coming."

But Beans wants a proper walk after being cooped up all day. Huffing and lunging, he tugs on his collar, bouncing ahead in the direction of the upper grass jumping field that is lined with trees.

"Okay, fine." Despite how tired I am after a half-day of moving, it's nice to see him looking so happy with our new home. "Let's go explore a bit then."

I pick up the pace, letting him drag me up the hill and off toward the huge grassy field. Most of the jumps have already been packed away for winter but there are a handful left. Solid timber logs that look like they belong on a cross country course.

"I wonder what it's like," I say out loud, looking at the heavy obstacles. I have only jumped a few times in my life and never over anything impressive like this.

Beans sniffs at the base of the jump, lifts his leg for a second, and then tugs me toward the nearby forest.

"Okay, not so fast, buddy. It's getting dark so we can't go too far."

Up ahead, I can see that there is a clearing in the trees where a wide, straight trail has been cut. Even in the dim light I can see the imprints of dozens of hooves in the soft ground, so this is obviously part of the bridle paths that wind around Three Sisters.

Wow, this is beautiful. I suddenly can't wait until my next day off when I can ride Oriel here. He loves trail riding.

Beans gives a sudden yank on the leash, jarring my fingers painfully and jerking the leather clasp right out of my hand.

"Wait, Beans." I leap forward to catch the trailing lead but he chooses that moment to shoot off up the path, completely ignoring me.

Damn it. I break into a run because as cute as Beans is, he is not that smart. And I doubt he'd be able to find his way home if he got lost in the woods. He'd probably get his leash wrapped around a tree and end up stuck.

"Beans!"

My voice is drowned out by a deep, hollow thudding sound and I realize, too late, that a horse and rider are flying down the trail toward us.

Beans is oblivious, sniffing in the very middle of the trail as the dark horse powers toward him.

They can't see him, they'll run him over. Waving my arms, I run toward them, my heart thudding a million miles a minute as I see the whole thing unfolding in front of me.

Beans looks up at the last second and lets out a bloodcurdling shriek that sounds like he's been murdered and, instead of running, he rolls over on his back with his paws in the air.

The horse does his best to stop. He sits on his hindquarters, front feet paddling the air as he tries to slow his forward momentum. At the last second, he powers upward in a leap that takes him right over Beans' astonished head and lands directly into my path before bowling me over and knocking me head over heels into the woods.

The breath whooshes out of me and I lie there in a clump of ferns, wheezing and gasping for air.

"Sidney? Sidney?" A face looms over me and I groan and shut my eyes. Why couldn't it be any other person at all? Why did it have to be Josh? "Are you okay?"

"I think so." I blink a few times to clear my vision. "Where's Beans?"

"He's fine. He took off into the woods but we didn't hit him."

"Your horse..."

"Is also fine. Why are you asking about everyone but yourself? You're the one who got sent flying."

I laugh at his outraged expression, then groan as my ribs spasm.

"Don't move. That was a hard fall. You might have broken something."

I lie still for another second, doing a mental inventory of my body. Nothing broken, but I'm going to be sore tomorrow.

"I'm all right. I have to find my dog, though."

He reaches down and holds me by both elbows before I can push myself to my feet.

"Take it slowly," he says, pulling me upright. "You might have a concussion."

"I must have one. Because you're being way too nice to me."

His solemn face breaks into the smallest of smiles.

"I've been an ass, haven't I?"

"Don't worry about it." I try and shake him off but when I go to take a step forward, my ankle buckles underneath me and I yelp, sucking in my breath.

"You *are* hurt," he says, wrapping his arm around my shoulder. "Here, lean on me and we'll take a look at that foot when we get to the path."

I'm in too much pain to argue as he helps me hobble out of the undergrowth. The impact had thrown me about six feet off the trail into some dense brush. I was lucky that nothing more than my ankle was hurt.

Josh's horse Heck is grazing peacefully at the edge of the trail, rooting through the half-dead grass for tasty things.

"If I give you a leg up could you ride him back?" Josh asks. "It's a long way back to hobble."

"Oh no, don't worry. I'm okay. I'll just rest here for a second and then I'll be fine. I've got this."

He raises his eyebrows at me and shakes his head. "Sidney, I'm not leaving you here in the dark to find your way back. What kind of monster do you think I am?"

The kind of monster who tried to keep me from getting hired, I think but don't say out loud. He's been uncharacteristically nice to me over the last few days anyway, so I don't even think I'm angry at him anymore. It's probably time to let that go.

"Sidney?" I look back to find him watching me, all traces of his earlier smile gone. "Please let me help."

I let my breath out through my teeth and then nod. "I can't leave until I find Beans. He's too old to be out here on his own."

"Right. You stay with Heck and I'll be right back."

I don't love the idea of being left in the dark woods on my own, but I can't see a better plan and Josh is already gone anyway,

The second I'm alone, all my aches and pains come flaring to life. I'm going to have bruises everywhere and my ankle is throbbing.

Please don't be broken, I think, suddenly realizing what being hurt means right now. If I can't walk then I can't work. And if I can't work then I can't take care of Beans and Oriel.

Determinedly, I wiggle my toes one by one and then gently move my ankle. It hurts. A lot. But it's functional. If I wrap it and take some pain control, then I should be able to manage.

Beside me the horse snorts and grazes a little closer to where I'm sitting.

"Hey, horse," I say to him softly. "I'm sorry we ran into you. I hope you're not hurt too."

He doesn't look injured at all, but horses are surprisingly delicate for such big animals. A slide on slippery ground like that can pull a suspensory ligament in a heartbeat. And I didn't want to be responsible for ruining an expensive animal. Especially one belonging to Josh.

It feels like forever before I hear footsteps crunching up the trail and the sound of snorting and huffing.

"You found him," I call excitedly. "Thank you so much."

"He was stuck," Josh says grimly and even in the semi-darkness I can see the scratch on his face. He deposits a wriggling and totally unrepentant Beans on my lap. "I had to unwind him from a prickle bush."

"Oh, Beans." I squish his little body against me and breathe out a sigh of relief.

"Come on, let's get you back. How's your ankle?"

"Not broken," I say quickly, just in case he's wondering about my ability to work. "I'm sure if I rest and ice it tonight it will be fine."

I pull myself to my feet before he can help me but the first step is like fire shooting up my leg.

"Come on, I'll give you a leg up."

Every part of me wants to argue. But the thought of walking, or hobbling, all the way down the hill sounds like a nightmare right now.

"All right, thanks."

"Wow, that was easier than I'd expected. I thought I'd have to spend at least fifteen minutes arguing with you."

"It's been a long day," I say tiredly. "I don't have anything left in me."

He stares at me for a second, frowning, and then goes over to retrieve Heck from his patch of grass.

"On three," he says, as I place my hands on the saddle. He cups my knee and boosts me up.

I hiss sharply as the stirrup iron bangs against my foot.

"You okay?"

"Yep." I nod, letting my breath out slowly. Okay is not exactly the word I'd use to describe what I'm feeling, but there isn't any point being a baby about it.

We walk along in silence for a moment, only the sound of Beans' heavy breathing breaking up the quiet.

"You surprise me every time I meet you, Sidney," Josh says finally. "You're never what I expect."

"Oh, did you expect something from me?"

"Well, yes, I..." He breaks off suddenly, reaching down to untangle Beans from a tuft of tall grass that has snagged the leash.

"You mean because of who my parents are?" I say, feeling a wash of disappointment. I wonder how many years it's going to take before I can escape their messed-up legacy. The lawsuits are going to drag on for years. Maybe I can change my name, move to a place where nobody knows me and start over.

"No, I mean, yes. I just..."

"Don't worry about it," I say heavily. "I get it."

There is a long silence before Josh clears his throat.

"So, I have this habit of judging people."

"You don't say."

"Yes, I know, shocking. Did Mia tell you that both my parents were in the military?"

"Yes." I nod.

"Yeah, that's where they met. I was raised on bases all over the world when I was a kid. At least until my mom was killed serving in Iraq."

"Oh, Josh, I'm sorry. I didn't know."

"My dad was pretty messed up when she died. He'd always been strict, but afterwards he sort of got crazy about it. He had this unbreakable moral code that you couldn't deviate from one inch. It was all about truth and honor for him. It was impossible to live up to his standards when I was a kid."

"He probably would not have liked my criminal parents very much then."

"Probably not. But, I can tell you it's not much fun being raised by someone like that either. Over the years he's mellowed out. Marrying Oliver's mom has helped a lot and he's not like he used to be. But still, those sort of things rub off on you even when you don't want them to. Mia calls me Mr. Uptight, which is why she's constantly dragging me to all these stupid parties and events to try and loosen me up."

I can't help but burst out laughing.

"Oh, so that's why you showed up at my disastrous party. I wondered why you'd come."

He's silent for a minute. "Actually, no. Mia called me and said she was worried about you. She had a feeling that Zara was up to something."

I can't see his expression in the dark but heat creeps up my neck as I remember that night.

"Let's get back to the barn. I need to ice this before it swells any more." That's the truth. I'm a little worried about how I'll get my boot back on once I take it off.

A few minutes later and we're finally riding up to the open barn doorway.

"Hey, Josh, you're back," Ben says, "we were beginning to wonder." Then he catches sight of me and his eyes widen.

"We had a bit of an accident on the trail," Josh says. "Can we use the first aid kit?"

Ben nods wordlessly and disappears toward the tack room.

"Come on, swing down, I'll catch you." Josh is standing right below me, his hand on Heck's shoulder, the light washing over his too-serious face, and for a second he looks like a different person. Like a knight out of a storybook or something.

For some reason I find myself blushing. I swing my leg over the saddle but my movements are off, and I knock my ankle clumsily against Heck's rump on my way down.

Pain sears through me and I shut my eyes tightly, biting my cheek again hard in an effort not to cry out.

"You're okay, I've got you. Just lean on me."

Strong arms wrap around me and for a second I let myself rest against the solid, comforting weight of him before pulling away.

"Thanks. Sorry."

"Here, I can take her," Ben says, appearing beside us.

Josh tightens his arm around my shoulder slightly, as if he's reluctant to let go and then releases me.

I limp silently beside Ben to the tack room, worrying the whole time that I'm going to be fired for getting hurt.

"I'm sorry," I say the second I sit down. "It was a stupid accident and it was all my fault. Heck could have been hurt. I can still work, though. If we wrap it up tight then…"

"Sidney…"

"Please don't fire me."

Ben looks at me in surprise and then laughs. "Calm down. Nobody is firing you."

"You're not?"

"No, the barn work is only part of your job, right? You're here for Alice."

"Yeah, but…" I hiss out a breath as my boot comes off, but a second later the pain eases even though the swelling looks awful.

Ben pokes and prods at it, frowning. "I don't think it's broken but if there's no improvement in a few days then we should take you in for x-rays. For now we'll wrap it and ice it. You need to take it easy for a few days, okay?"

"All right."

"So, you and Josh are friendly, are you?" He doesn't look at me, just busies himself wrapping my ankle in a layer of bandage.

"No, I barely know him. He's sort of, um, rescued me a few times lately. It's a bit embarrassing, honestly."

"Well, I should probably tell you now that there is a rule at the barn against staff dating the boarders or riders."

"Of course. I mean, that's fine. I would never…we are just friends. Not even friends. Acquaintances."

"Huh. Well, I'm only making sure you know the rules. No dating clients and no bringing any guests to the dorms. Of course, if you weren't working here, I'd say that the two of you would make a nice…"

"I am," I say quickly. "Working here, I mean. You have no idea how badly I need this job, Ben. I won't do anything to mess it up."

"No, I know you won't. All right, all wrapped up. There are ice packs in the freezer upstairs. Do you need a hand getting up there?"

I stand up and tentatively put weight on my wrapped foot. It still hurts, but it's bearable.

"Nope, I've got this. Thanks so much, Ben."

When I get back to the aisle there is no sign of Josh so I limp my way to the stairs and slowly make the upward climb, wincing and inwardly cursing at every step.

But when I make it to the viewing room, I have to laugh at the scene in front of me. There on the couch is Josh and Beans is flopped down beside him with his fat belly exposed, his tongue lolling out, and all four paws waving in the air.

"Your dog is ridiculous, you know," Josh says, raising an eyebrow at me. His lip twitches slightly and that's the only thing that gives away that he's laughing.

"Oh, I know." I hobble the last few steps to the couch and then sink into it gratefully, closing my eyes in relief.

"Did you take anything for the pain?"

I shake my head, eyes still closed. "Not yet. I will in a bit, though. I want to just sit here and do nothing for a second."

He gets up and I can hear him bustling around the kitchen but I don't bother to open my eyes.

"Here, tea, aspirin and an icepack."

I crack my eyes open and peer up at him. "Tea?"

"Come on, don't tell me you're not a tea drinker. My mom used to say that tea was the cure for anything."

"Huh, my mom would probably say that about wine." I ease myself upright and carefully take the mug he's holding out. The liquid is a milky golden brown and I take a cautious sip. It's sweet and has a hint of cinnamon.

"It's good, right? Spiced chai with milk."

I nod and take another sip, then reach for the aspirin he's holding out to me.

"Thanks. You don't have to take care of me, but I appreciate it."

"Well, I did sort of run you over." He sits down beside me and carefully lays the icepack on my wrapped ankle. "It's the least I can do."

I hiss involuntarily as the cold hits my throbbing foot. "No, my dog nearly took out your expensive horse. That was totally our fault."

"Does that feel okay?"

"Uh-huh." Which is a lie but I don't think there's anything but time that's going to make me feel better.

"Well, I'd better go. Mia has some concert she wants to drag me to."

"Right. Thanks again."

He takes a deep breath like he's going to say something else and then he's gone, shutting the door quietly behind him.

Beans looks up when the door clicks shut and lets out a little whine.

"Yeah, I agree, he's nicer than I thought. But don't get too attached," I tell him. "Plus, you nearly killed him when you ran under his horse. I hope you're ashamed of yourself."

Beans looks over at me, eyes rolling, and then flops back down on the couch with a grunt. Completely shameless.

CHAPTER 30

SIDNEY

*S*unday morning is the first day in a week where I don't have to instantly leap out of bed to rush off to do something. I lie there for a few minutes, blinking at the sunlight streaming into the room and the piles of boxes that I still need to deal with.

The dorm already looks a little less strange, and more like a home, with all my stuff heaped around me. This the first time I haven't felt like an intruder, like my existing in this space at all is somehow shameful.

Beans stretches out beside me with a sleepy groan and then roots back under the covers, looking for the warmest spot.

I stretch too, pleased that the pain in my ankle is less agonizing than it had been the night before, and let out a contented sigh. There is nothing at all on my to-do list today except to organize my living space and take care of Oriel. Not a thing. I frown, wondering why I feel like I'm forgetting something important.

The thought nags at me until I finally reach over and grab my phone, pulling up my reminders.

Eden's Birthday. I rub my eyes to wake myself up and scootch up into a sitting position. It's probably too early to call her but I do it anyway. Back when she was small, I'd always woken my sister up on her birthday and given her whatever present I'd picked out. Our parents weren't big on remembering special occasions, although they always gave generous gifts of cash once we reminded them.

But small gifts that meant something, that showed that you actually knew the person and cared about what they liked, were a tradition that Eden, Leo and I had always done quietly between us.

Luckily, I'd already organized her present weeks ago, before our family had fallen apart completely.

I expect to get her voicemail but by some miracle she answers.

"Hello?" she mumbles into the phone, sounding both sleepy and annoyed.

"Hey, Eden, it's me. I wanted to wish you a happy birthday."

"Oh." There's a long silence. "You remembered."

"Of course I did. You're my sister. Sorry I didn't have a lot of extra cash this year for a present, but I bought you a gift certificate to that costume store you like downtown. They should be emailing it to you today. I know it's not much but hopefully you can use it."

"Oh, thanks, Sidney. I really like that shop." For a second, she sounds ten years old again and I wish like anything that she was here with me.

"Are you doing okay?" I ask. "Are they treating you right there?"

"Yeah, it's fine. Just a little crowded, I guess. They had a cake for me last night though, at a restaurant. They made the waiters sing and everything."

"That sounds like fun."

"It was last minute or I would have invited you too," she adds hastily.

"No worries. I'm glad you had fun."

"Yeah." Another long silence.

"Did, um, Mom and Dad call you yet?"

"No," she says sharply. "Ned and Nora forgot like usual."

I sigh. Couldn't they have at least pretended to make an effort? "There's still time, though, they might send you some—"

"Thanks for calling me, Sidney," she cuts me off. "And for the present. It really means a lot. I'd better go."

With a click she is gone, leaving me sadly staring at my phone.

"Well, at least she sounds like she's doing okay, Beans," I say to the dog, who is draped across my feet, snoring. "I bet she misses you, though."

I have barely set my phone down again when it pings loudly.

I heard you got hurt. Does that mean I can ride Oriel again today? Can I go on a short trail ride with Josh and Mia? Puh-leeeeese.

Alice. Groaning, I roll over and stuff my phone under my pillow. This girl is completely relentless.

Ping, ping, ping.

Fine. I sit up again and tap out a few furious lines, then toss my phone aside again.

The truth is that, as annoying and manipulative as she is, Alice is not the worst match in the world for Oriel. She might be stubborn and set in her ways, but in this case that's almost a good thing. Because she never once complains in her lessons and she focuses on everything Elliot says with a laser-like focus that is almost scary.

Another ping of my phone and I make a grab for it again, muttering under my breath.

But to my surprise, it's not Alice. It's a strange number that I don't recognize.

Hope your ankle is feeling better. I'll be there in an hour and I'm bringing breakfast.

That's all it says.

I stare down at the text for a second and then throw the covers back and scramble out of bed, limping down the hall toward the bathroom. I have just enough time to have a shower before boarders start showing up. After that it's off limits until after the barn is closed again.

I'm not even sure that the text is from Josh; it could be from Mia, or Ben, or anyone really. And I also don't know why I'm rushing to make myself look decent. It's not like I care what he thinks about me anyway.

Exactly an hour later, footsteps thump up the steps and Mia bursts in, followed more slowly by her cousin who is laden down with three stacked boxes from the bakery.

"You poor thing," Mia says as she watches me hobble toward them, "you shouldn't be walking when you're hurt."

"It's okay," I say quickly, because by Josh's expression he's about to launch into a lecture. "I have to walk Beans and help Alice tack up Oriel. You're sure you two are comfortable taking her on a trail ride?"

"Of course, but you sit down on the couch. We didn't know what you liked so we brought you one of everything. How do you like your coffee? You look like you could use a cup or two."

I stare at her blankly for a second, a little overwhelmed by her whirlwind personality.

"It's best not to fight her when she's in these moods," Josh says, quirking an eyebrow at me. "Sit, and I'll run Beans out for you."

Beans is already hopping all over Josh's feet anyway so I sit down without arguing.

"There's a small change of plans," Mia says, not looking at me as she works the industrial coffee machine on the counter. "Oliver, Kira and I will take Alice on a short trail ride while Josh keeps you company. I hope that's all right."

"Oh. Um, sure. He doesn't have to do that, though. I'm fine."

I feel a faint blush crawling up my neck and tiny spark of excitement twitches through me for no reason at all.

"I think that he wants to." Mia swoops in and sets a mug down beside me. "He feels so bad about being a jerk before. Let him make it up to you. Besides, he could use a friend."

"Friend, right, of course." I pick up the coffee gratefully and inhale the fragrant scent. They don't use cheap grocery store beans in this place; everything is gourmet, free-trade deliciousness. I feel a little guilty every time I use the machine but Ben had assured me that it was all right.

"Here." Mia sets a box of pastries on the table in front of me and helps herself to a croissant dipped in chocolate. "Have some of these before I eat them all. I have no willpower when it comes to baked goods."

"You don't need willpower." I laugh and pick out a sugar-crusted apple turnover. "You're thin as a rail."

"Yeah, for *now*," she says darkly. "You should hear my mom moan about her hips and love handles. I see my future."

She breaks into laughter and we grin at each other. All my worries that Mia might be secretly be a backstabbing traitor like Zara have disappeared this week. She is genuinely a nice person and I feel grateful to count her as a friend.

"And here's Josh now. Anything we need to know about your horse? Alice will be all right with him on the trails?"

Beans comes clattering into the room, dragging Josh along with him, and for a second I'm distracted. Josh has an actual smile on his face as he kneels to unclip the lead.

"Yes, if you stick to a walk, he'll be really good," I say finally, turning back to Mia. "Alice handles Oriel well in the ring. He likes other horses but don't crowd too close behind him. And watch for overhead branches with Alice. If the woods are too shady then she won't be able to see anything coming at her face. I wish I could go with you."

"We'll be fine. We'll stick to the main trails and keep it short. An hour tops. You two enjoy your date."

"What?" Josh and I say at the same time.

"Your breakfast then." Mia rolls her eyes. "See you." She swoops down and grabs another pastry before flouncing out the door.

"I love my cousin," Josh says, shaking his head. "But she's a *lot* sometimes. She wasn't bothering you, was she?"

"No, she's great. I haven't hung out with anyone in a long time so she's a refreshing change to being alone."

"Ah. Yes."

There is a long silence while we both stare anywhere except at each other.

"So, are you still looking for a second horse?" I ask finally, dredging up the safest topic I can find. "Lena said that you'd tried a few out."

"Nothing yet. But I'm riding Marsha Townsend's horse, Sonata. I'm quite liking her."

"Oh, she's so sweet when I feed her at night. Is she nice to ride?"

"Yes, she's not very confident yet, but I think there's talent waiting to be developed there. Marsha is not a good match for her, though."

"Are you going to put an offer in on her?"

"I'm not sure. You should watch me ride her sometime and see what you think."

"Okay, sure."

Silence falls over us again and I reach down to pet Beans, who has wedged himself on the couch between us.

"Is that book in German?" he says, pointing at the training manual and battered notebook I'd accidentally left on the table last night after he'd left.

I nod, feeling myself blush again. "Er, yes, it's by this famous dressage rider from the nineteen sixties. He's brilliant so I'm working on a translation."

Josh is staring at me so I take a nervous sip of coffee.

"I know it must sound lame to you," I say in a rush, "but –"

"It doesn't. Not at all. I'm impressed. How many languages do you speak?"

"A few." I shrug. "It's no big deal. I'm good with words. I love them."

It's a big admission for me. Most people aren't interested in that part of my life so I rarely share it. I'm not sure why I'm letting my guard down now.

He smiles at me warmly and picks up the book, turning it over so he can study the old grainy photo of the horse and rider on the back.

"Will you read some of it to me?" he asks, handing it back, his fingers brushing against mine.

"What, in German? Or my translation?"

"How about both? We have time."

A warm fuzzy feeling expands in my chest when I look at his gentle smile and I nod, opening the book to my favourite chapter.

CHAPTER 31

ALICE

*T*oday is the best day.

I dress carefully in breeches and my tall boots, layering on a sweater under my jacket.

It's beautiful out, the perfect day for a trail ride. And it's going to be me and Josh, and some other people from the barn. Like a dream come true, really.

I sing a little tune as I practically skip down the hill to the barn. Mia will help me tack up but I can get Oriel's blanket off and do most of the grooming. Sidney's been letting me do a lot of that lately and I feel completely comfortable handling the big horse now.

I'm so caught up in my good mood that I don't even notice that the area in front of the paddocks is full of people.

"I hope you don't mind that I take Jiggs today," Kira calls out before I reach her. "Darla said someone wants to see him next week so I thought I'd give him some light exercise."

"Um, sure." I slow to a stop. "I can catch him. We've been working on…"

"It's okay, Oliver helped me round him up. I've groomed him and am tacking up now."

"Great," I say through gritted teeth. I hadn't even known that someone was booked to try out Jiggs. Nobody had bothered to tell me.

"I have Oriel brushed and tacked up for you already," Mia chirps. "Sidney told me where all his stuff was. I hope you don't mind."

"Uh. No, it's fine," I say in a grudging voice. It's *not* fine, I had been looking forward to doing all that myself. I love grooming Oriel. But it's too late now so there's no point complaining. "Thanks."

"You're welcome. Oliver will be here in a second and then we can go. Josh is going to stay behind and keep Sidney company. They're having a breakfast date. They are so cute and awkward together that I can hardly stand it."

"Josh isn't coming?" I hate how disappointed my voice sounds right now.

"No, he isn't," she says slowly. "Unless you had your heart set on him going with us, I mean. I could always text him and tell him to come."

"No, no, of course not. It's fine. Let's just go."

Oliver shows up leading his mare, Bluebell, and Mia's dark, leggy mare, Nim. Mia insists on boosting me into Oriel's saddle and adjusting my stirrups like I'm a child.

"You stay behind Bluebell," she says, "and I'll ride behind you."

"Uh-huh." For the first ten minutes of our ride, I'm fuming mad even though I don't have a real reason.

It had been my idea for Josh to ask Sidney out in the first place. But I hadn't been prepared for the jealousy and anger that hit me out of the blue the second I realized that he preferred to spend time with *her* rather than me.

These feelings are illogical, I tell myself, which makes the whole thing even more irritating. I hate not being in control of my emotions.

Still, I'm in the woods on a beautiful day on a great horse, so it's only a matter of time before I let out a deep sigh and let go of some of the anger that's been building.

Oriel strides along with his head bobbing, completely unaffected by all the emotions jittering inside of me. I stretch the tension out of my body limb by limb and feel him swaying beneath me, solid and dependable.

Birds dart through the trees overhead, chattering excitedly, and the sunshine cuts through the chill in the air, warming my cheeks as I tilt my head upward.

All the horses are relaxed, except for Jiggs who I can hear occasionally snorting and spooking somewhere behind us.

I don't need to worry about him selling. He's going to act like a psycho for any rider who tries him and they'll hate him. It's a reassuring feeling, because I've been feeling guilty about not asking my dad about keeping him around.

I don't have a proper answer for why I want him to stay. It's not to develop him or make more money off him or to win things. And saying that it's just because I *like* him sounds stupid. Darla would have laughed me out of the barn for being sentimental like that.

My thoughts drift to Oriel and my plans for the future. I've wasted no time in discussing my upcoming show schedule with Elliot. Even though I'm not even cantering off the lunge line yet, I still want a goal to work toward. If I'm going to compete at the BC Summer games and maybe even the Paralympic games in the next few years then I need to get cracking. I need to start showing at local dressage shows, and to get my classification card. Each rider who wants to compete in Para dressage beyond the grassroots level has to get an official assessment done to determine their classification grade.

When we get back to the barn, I make out a familiar figure standing out front, her arms crossed over her chest. I can't see the expression on her face but I can tell by the fact that she's rapidly tapping one boot against the ground that she's not happy. Not that she's ever happy lately.

"Hello, Alice," Darla says stiffly. "Good to see you riding."

"Um, hi." I give Oriel a pat and then swing down, landing lightly beside him.

"I spoke with your father today and he insisted that I tell you the news myself."

"Okay," I say cautiously. "What news?"

Fear washes over me suddenly.

"It's Jiggs, isn't it? He's finally been sold."

"What? No, that pony is a lost cause. I have given your father my notice. I will be leaving next month."

"Leaving?" I say in astonishment. "But you can't."

Three Sisters without Darla is inconceivable. She's been here since the beginning. Since my mom dreamed up the idea of Three Sisters in the first place.

"My sister is dying," she says shortly as if that explains everything.

"Oh, I'm sorry." I'm not particularly sorry about her sister, since I don't even know the woman. I'm thinking about what this is going to mean for Three Sisters.

"She did it to herself. That's what happens when you destroy your liver with alcohol and bad decisions. I'm taking over our family farm and it will be a full-time project to whip it back into shape."

"Oh." I gulp. There is so much that I want to say. About how badly I'd missed her and how much it had hurt when she abandoned me. And how I wished things had turned out differently for both of us. But all the words stick in my throat.

"I will continue with my scheduled lessons here for now, but all my extra energy will be on getting the new farm ready. There is a herd of scruffy school horses there that will need to be assessed and sold off to whoever will take them. The whole place will need a complete overhaul. You'll let your father know that I gave you the news in person?"

"I will." I nod.

"Then good luck with everything, Alice. You were a talented and hardworking rider. I don't see how you'll ever get to jump again; the whole idea seems ridiculous to me. But, if anyone can make it happen, it's you."

With that she's striding away across the parking lot toward her car.

"I think that's as close to an apology as I'm ever going to get, Oriel," I whisper to him, as I hear her car rumble to life and drive away.

And even though Darla hasn't officially stopped working here yet, I feel like I've said my goodbyes now. That part of my life is over.

CHAPTER 32

ALICE

The weeks fly by so fast that I hardly notice them passing. The temperature drops and we have our first brief snowfall that brings the whole city to a standstill before abruptly melting again.

That's the way it is with fall and winters here. You never know if you'll get blazing sunshine, monsoons or three feet of snow overnight.

Thanksgiving break is nearly upon us and I'm excited to have Trin home for four whole days. I've missed having her around.

My rides on Oriel keep getting better even though he's far from a simple ride. I'd graduated from the lunge line but it hadn't been easy. I'd had to learn how to safely navigate the ring at all gaits and to remember the letter placement.

And that had been scary when it came to Oriel's gigantic canter stride because he can make it across the ring in just a few bounds. He is a *lot* of horse when he gets going. When I'm riding at anything faster than a walk, Sidney, or one of the working students like Lena, calls out the letters to me as I approach each one. This is the only way to keep us from getting dangerously close to the rail sometimes.

It's humbling to ride a fully schooled horse who knows more than me. There is nothing I can do to improve Oriel; he's perfect and I just have to do my best not to wreck his training.

I miss having a project horse to school and bring along, and I wish I could start riding Jiggs again because there are lots of things I could teach him. I hadn't realized how many holes I'd left in his training before, but now I think that half of his spookiness was just a lack of education.

My dad is still being stubborn about that, though. So I have to content myself with taking Jiggs for walks around the property while I listen to my podcasts.

Sometimes Sidney and Oriel come with us too. And that's what we are doing on a nippy morning in October, both of us bundled up with scarves and gloves, letting the horses saunter along looking for errant blades of grass. There is no snow today but everything is covered in a fine layer of frost. The ground is hard underfoot and the horses' feet echo against the frozen dirt.

The footing in the outdoor rings is too solid to ride in this morning and the indoor arena is full of Darla's students cramming in their last lessons before she leaves.

I know that we're going to lose a bunch of clients when she goes. Darla has a huge following of riders who are loyal specifically to her and not to Three Sisters.

If her new barn wasn't in the middle of renovations, then I bet a bunch of them would have left already.

We haven't found a new coach yet, which is a bit worrying. Unfortunately, instructors with Darla's reputation and show record don't just grow on trees.

I almost wish there was a way to take Three Sisters in a new direction. Barn A has been so focused on competition and winning that we'd been losing clients. I wondered if there was a way to make our barn more fun and inclusive.

After listening to so many hours of the No Limits podcast, I am dying to help out with the Para show jumping cause. It's so silly that there are barely any opportunities for Para athletes to jump in North America when it is a fully recognized sport in Europe and the UK.

Maybe, someday we could start a program at Three Sisters.

"What are you brooding about over there?" Sidney asks, probably noticing the scowl on my face, but before I can answer, her phone rings.

"Hang on, Alice, I have to get this. It's my sister."

I nod reluctantly and let Jiggs tug at the lead rope so he can reach a tuft of frozen grass. I don't like when Sidney talks to her sister, especially during the hours she's supposed to be spending with me; it always makes her moody afterwards and not much fun.

Personally, I think her entire family sounds crazy and she'd be better off forgetting them altogether. She'd be happier focusing all her energy on me.

"What do you mean they're sending him to Nanna's?" she says sharply. "They can't do that. He will hate it there."

She's silent for a moment, listening, and then she sighs.

"Okay, well, thanks for telling me, Eden. I wish there was something more I could do."

I can hear her sister's voice on the other end but I can't make out the words.

"Damn," Sidney says finally, shoving her phone in her pocket.

"Problems?"

"My parents are shipping my little brother off to live with my Nanna."

"Oh. That doesn't sound too awful."

"She doesn't like kids, especially not Leo. Her house is dark and smells like feet and there are religious shrines everywhere. It's a horrible place for a child."

"Ew, poor kid."

"I'm not sure what I can do to help him. I feel so bad."

"Well, if you sold me Oriel then you'd have lots of money to take care of your brother."

I'd meant it as a half-joke but as soon as the words are out, I know I've made a mistake.

Sidney sucks in her breath with a little cry, like I've just punched her.

"I was kidding," I say quickly, but it's already too late. She marches away with Oriel in the opposite direction, not saying another word.

And the feeling of her walking away from me, taking Oriel with her, is indescribable. Icy fear plunges over me and my throat closes so hard that I can barely breathe.

She could take him away forever if she wanted to. The one good thing in my life could be gone in a heartbeat and I am powerless to stop her.

Powerless. Weak. Useless.

All the things I hate most.

"I can't let her do that, Jiggs," I say softly to the pony who is grazing unconcernedly beside me. "I'll find a way to keep him. No matter what it takes."

CHAPTER 33

SIDNEY

"*A*nd then she said that if I'd sell her Oriel then all my problems would be solved." I jab a fry angrily into the little paper cup full of ketchup and shake my head in frustration.

"She's only a kid," Josh says, sounding way too reasonable. I want him to be full of outrage like I am. "It's not like she can *make* you sell Oriel. She's getting attached to him and saw a way to solve two problems at once."

"You didn't see her face when she said it. It just gave me the creeps, that's all."

Josh puts his burger down and studies me seriously for a second.

"I think I know what you mean. Her sister Clara could be like that too when she wanted something. Look, if Alice gives you any more trouble, then let me know, okay? I'm here to help. Now, where are we going on today's non-date?"

"Well, there's this paleontology lecture at the museum if you're interested. Or we can try that new mini-golf place."

"The museum it is," Josh says, grinning at me.

I am serious about keeping my job at Three Sisters so Josh and I are on a strict no-dating policy, but that has not stopped us from hanging out as friends whenever I'm not working. That first breakfast we'd spent together, where I'd read him my German translation, had shifted things between us.

Last month, I would have never predicted that he'd become the person I'd most want to spend time with. But it turns out that he is fun, smart, and kind underneath that slightly frosty exterior.

I'd also been helping him work with Sonata. He had finally bought her a few weeks ago, and gotten her for a good price too, since her owner, Marsha, had wanted to get rid of the horse fast.

"Good riddance to bad rubbish," she'd said as soon as the mare was sold. "You'll have your hands full with her, that's for sure. You won't be seeing me around here either. My new horse will be going straight to Darla's new stable when he arrives from Germany."

I will not be sorry to see either Darla or Marsha go. I don't have much to do with them myself, but they brought down the whole mood of the barn whenever either of them were around. I have the feeling it would be a much happier place once Darla left and took her followers with her.

"I heard that Darla will be selling all the Happy Acres school horses soon," I say, taking a sip of my root beer. "Poor Val texted and asked me to buy Diva. She thinks I'm rich for some reason."

"We can't save every horse in the world, unfortunately." Josh reaches out and quickly steals one of my fries before I can stop him.

"Yeah, I know. But this horse has potential. She'd make a nice school horse for Barn B once she has some bodywork done and a chance to be reschooled."

"Did you talk to Anna about her?"

"Not yet." I shake my head. "I did ask her about getting Val a spot at camp over winter break, though. She said she'd add her to the list."

"See, I told you it would work out."

"Yes, you did." I grin at him and he reaches across the table to squeeze my hand.

Late that night after all my evening chores are done, I am sitting on my bed working on Alice's lesson plan when my phone begins to vibrate. I glance over to see Eden's number flashing and make a grab for it.

"Hey, Eden, did Leo make it to…"

"No," she snaps before I can finish. "He did *not* make it to Nanna's. He's here."

"What? At your place? How? Why? Is he okay?"

Eden sighs dramatically. "If you'd be quiet for two seconds then I'll tell you. He paid some older kid at school to change his plane tickets and came here instead. Well, he *tried* to go to the old house first because I guess nobody told him that you weren't living there anymore, and then when strangers answered the door, he called me."

"Oh no. He must have been so scared."

"Patrice drove me to pick him up but she's freaking out and he can't stay here. You need to do something."

"Okay, calm down. Did you call Mom and Dad?"

"Of course I did. I left them dozens of messages. They're probably out at some dumb function and not answering."

"Right. Well, we need to figure out how to get him to Nanna's then."

"He won't go," Eden says. "He says he'll run away."

I drop my head into my hand and groan. Just when I'd gotten my life somewhat settled, this had to happen. Couldn't I just have a single month without disastrous complications anymore?

"Eden, I live in a dorm room and I'm not even allowed to have guests in the daytime, let alone overnight. I can't…"

"Well, neither can I," she says sharply. "You're the oldest so technically you're in charge of looking after him since our parents can't be bothered."

"I work two jobs to support Oriel and Beans. I'm saving up for a real apartment and to pay for school and…."

"That's nice. It's too bad you don't work that hard to keep your real family together, Sidney. Your human family, I mean."

"Eden, that's not fair. Beans and Oriel are defenseless creatures who can't look after themselves. They depend on me."

"Yeah, well, I'm barely fifteen freaking years old so I'm a little young to have a kid. This is on you, Sidney. Pick. Him. Up."

"Fine. I'll be there as soon as I can. But it's only temporary, Eden. I can't keep him long term."

"Not my problem," she says and then the line goes dead.

I stare at my phone for a minute, a headache pounding to life somewhere behind my left eyeball.

All right. I inhale and then exhale slowly. *I can do this. I can figure this out.*

Eden's manager, Patrice, lives in a small three-bedroom house outside of town in the suburbs, sitting smack up against the street with barely any front lawn.

Both Eden and Leo are sitting on the front step when my old truck rattles to a stop. She has her arm around his shoulders and he's leaning heavily against her, looking half-asleep.

I leash up Beans who is already squeaking and yapping in eagerness to see them and let him tow me up the cement path toward the house.

Leo's whole face lights up when he sees Beans and he lets the little dog plow right into him.

"Hey, Beans," Eden says, reaching over and giving him a friendly scratch. Which surprises me because she never paid him too much attention when we'd all lived together.

"Are you all right, Leo?" I ask, peering down at him anxiously. He looks pale and skinny with dark circles under his eyes.

"Yeah, I'm fine now that I'm home. I'm never going back to Vegas again. And you can't make me go to Nanna's either, so don't bother trying."

Eden gives me a pointed I-told-you-so look.

"I don't blame you for not wanting to go to Nanna's," I say, crouching down in front of him. "The problem is that neither Eden nor I have our own places. I live in a dorm and they don't let me have guests."

"I'll be quiet," he says, looking at me with big, sad eyes, "they won't even know I'm there."

Tears pool on his lower lashes and suddenly I know there is no way I'm putting this kid on a plane tonight.

"All right, Leo, we're going to figure something out. But for tonight you can stay with me. And I have a surprise for you too. I saved some of your stuff from the old house. Like your telescope."

"Really?" He looks at me warily, his expression wavering between hope and disbelief.

"Yep, I boxed it all up and brought it to the dorm when I moved. I knew how much you cared about your stuff."

I look over to see Eden watching me closely, studying my face like she's trying to figure me out.

"Well, I need my beauty sleep," she says, pushing herself to her feet. "You two have a good time."

"We should all meet for lunch tomorrow," I say, "we could catch up."

"I have appointments all week. See you." And with that she's gone.

"Eden's not coming to the farm with us?" Leo's brow crinkles into a frown.

"No. She has a home with Patrice now. She has a career."

"Yeah, but she's not happy."

"Hmmm." I glance back at the little house but the lights are off and there is no sign of my sister.

Leo is quiet during the drive to the farm. He sits with one arm wrapped around Beans, staring out into the darkness with a worried expression.

But all that changes when we pull up in front of the stable.

"You mean, you live *inside* the barn?" Leo says incredulously, getting out of the truck. "With the *horses?*"

"Pretty much." I laugh at the horrified expression on his face. "It's not so bad and the price is right. It's better than being homeless, right?"

"I guess so." He squinches his face up and puts a hand over his nose as we near the front door. "But it smells like animals."

"You'll get used to it. Would you rather smell horses or Nanna?"

"Horses," he says quickly, dropping his hand to his side and hiking his backpack further up on his shoulder. He juts his chin out in a determined line and takes a deep breath.

He's so thin that his clothes practically hang off of him. Didn't they feed him at all in Vegas?

"Come on, have you had any dinner?" I roll back the front door to the barn and usher him inside.

"No." He shakes his head. "They were having fried chicken and the smell was gross so I didn't eat."

"You know that most kids actually like fried chicken, right?"

"I know." His eyes are wide as he looks at the horses lining the aisle on both sides.

They nicker as I come in, raising their heads and blinking sleepily at us.

"Hang on, Leo. I need to do night check, okay? Sit there on

the steps while I make sure everyone has food and water. It will only take me a second."

I walk down the aisle, peering into everyone's stalls to make sure their blankets are on and their food and water are still full. They've already been fed a late-night snack so this is just the final check to make sure everything looks like it should.

"Good night, everyone," I say, flicking off the aisle light once I'm certain everyone is tucked away comfortably.

Leo shuffles after me up the stairs.

He stops and looks at the kitchen and the small living room with the viewing window that overlooks the now-dark ring.

"Wow, this is nice. Eden said you were poor now."

"Oh, I *am* poor," I say, laughing. "This is the kitchen and lounge for all the clients. I only get to use it when nobody else is around."

"His eyes widen and he follows me wordlessly down the hall.

"This is it." I usher him into my narrow room. "Ta dah."

He stares inside for a second, looking less than impressed, and then suddenly his eyes light up when he sees the pile of cardboard boxes in the corner. "My telescope, my books. You really did get them."

"Yeah, I wasn't making that up. Go on, the top bunk can be yours if you like."

"I don't like heights much, could I have that bottom bunk over there?"

"Sure." I laugh. "Wherever you like."

He drops his backpack in the middle of the floor and runs over to where his boxes of things are, rooting through them excitedly.

CHAPTER 34

SIDNEY

*T*he next morning, I get up early and sneak out of the room while Leo is still snoring softly on his bunk with Beans tucked snugly under one arm.

My parents aren't early risers but this might be my only chance to reach them.

Dad's phone goes right to voicemail, but luckily Mom picks up on the third ring.

"Sweetheart, this is an unexpected surprise. I'm on my way to an early yoga class."

"Fantastic," I mutter, heading down the hall to the viewing area. The lights are off in the indoor arena below and it's like looking into a vast, dark cavern. "Did you know that Leo didn't make it to Nanna's last night?"

"Oh, yes! We got all of Eden's messages. I was so relieved to hear that he's safe and sound with the two of you. I had no idea that he was so resourceful."

"I think he was desperate not to go to Nanna's. But we need to figure out what to do with him now. He can't stay here with me. I'm not allowed to have guests at all here."

"Darling, I think that this is the universe's way of providing a perfect solution for everyone. Leo and Eden have always looked up to you so it's natural that he would want to be with his big sister."

"Are you kidding? I will literally get kicked out of my home if anyone finds him here. And I work all day and most nights. He needs a proper home, Mom."

"Honestly Sidney, your father and I pulled many long hours over the years and the three of you turned out perfectly fine."

"Because you had an army of nannies and housekeepers to raise us," I snap. "There were some months we barely saw either of you at all. I'm not sure you're shining examples of great parenting, Mom."

"Oh, Sidney, that is just hurtful. We only want what's best for all of you. We thought sending Leo to Nanna's was the perfect solution. But, he is on his own life path and we don't want to dictate his choices. If he wants to be with you..."

"No. No way. You need to take responsibility for him."

"Sidney, I don't like your tone and I'm late for yoga class. Your father and I will discuss this tonight, but it would be nice if you could come up with some solutions of your own in the meantime. You've always been a resourceful girl. Maybe meditate on it and the answer will come."

"Seriously?"

"Love you, darling. Bye!"

The line disconnects with a click.

"Arrrrg!" I toss my phone to the other end of the couch and put my face in my hands. What am I going to do? Why do Ned and Nora suck as parents?

I'll just have to convince my brother that going to Nanna's or back to Vegas are his only choices.

But when I tiptoe back to the dorm room and look at his pale, thin face and the dark circles under his eyes, my resolve slips. Even in sleep he looks sad and forgotten. His skinny arms are wrapped tightly around Beans like the dog is a life raft keeping him afloat.

"Sidney?" He blinks a few times and then looks around in confusion. "What time is it?"

"Early. I'm sorry to have woken you up. You look like you could use some sleep."

"That's okay."

"So, here's the thing, buddy. You can stay here for today but you have to keep hidden, okay? I could get in big trouble if anyone finds you here. I could get kicked out and lose my job."

He nods solemnly, his big eyes fixed on my face.

"You can use the shower now before anyone else gets here and then you'll have to stay hidden while I'm at work. Can you do that?"

"Yeah."

"All right, let's get you cleaned up and then we'll figure out breakfast, okay?"

He nods again but he looks so sad that my heart nearly breaks. I can't believe that he came all this way by himself; he's so tiny and frail but he has this inner fierceness too. I just want to protect him.

Just one more person to add to my list of things to worry about, I think with a sigh.

∼

When one day passes and then another without any contact from our parents, Leo and I fall into an uneasy routine. We get up early so he can shower and have breakfast in the lounge area. Then he hides all day and I let him back out at night.

There aren't any real ways to cook things other the microwave and the toaster, but I bought a small supply of muffins and instant waffles for his breakfasts, and soups and crackers for his lunches. Dinners are either instant noodles, take-away or stuff I bring back from the Shrimp Shack.

At least he's eating for me, which is kind of a miracle since he's been notoriously fussy with food his whole life.

I guess the shock of having to live like a vampire, hiding in the shadows, has given him an appetite.

I don't think this is any life for a kid, but he actually seems pretty happy to spend hours reading and playing on my laptop by himself. The dark circles under his eyes gradually fade and he smiles more and more. I can't imagine the stress he must have been under in Vegas if hiding out here is relaxing in comparison.

He's set his telescope up in the window too and I let him stay up as late as he wants, looking at the stars, because he has plenty of time to catch up on sleep during the day.

But, as happy as he is, the stress is killing me. I'm awful at keeping secrets and I hate lying. Especially to Josh. I'd had to come up with some pretty lame excuses not to hang out with him this weekend and I knew that he was already suspicious.

Not for much longer, I tell myself, *I'll figure a way out of this mess soon.*

CHAPTER 35

ALICE

$\mathcal{I}$ try to concentrate on my latest school project but it just isn't the same without Beans' comforting weight on my lap. For the last few days, Sidney has been leaving him at her place in the mornings instead of dropping him off with me when she goes to work at Barn B.

She'd told me that it was because he'd hurt his leg while out playing, but Sidney is the world's worst liar and I know she's hiding something.

"Forget this," I say out loud, pushing back my chair abruptly. "It's in her contract that I get to spend time with him. She can't keep him from me. I need Beans."

Only a few grooms are around when I get to the barn and nobody questions me when I slip upstairs to the lounge. I pause for a second to make sure the room is empty and then creep down the hall to Sidney's dorm.

But, when I get to her room the door is locked. I turn the

handle and hear a thump inside, then Beans' claws clicking on the wood floor toward the door.

"Hey buddy," I say, crouching down outside the door. "It's just me. I came to visit you."

"Who is this?" a small voice says and I jolt sideways, nearly jumping out of my skin. There is a tiny second there where I wonder if Beans hasn't magically learned how to talk.

"Um, it's Alice," I say finally. "I'm, er, a friend of Sidney's. Who is this?"

The door cracks open and a small boy looks out. I can't make out his features but I can tell that he's small and thin.

"You're Alice?" he asks cautiously. "Sidney told me about you."

"Yes, I am. And who are you?

"I'm Leo," he says solemnly, "Sidney's brother."

"Oh." I raise my eyebrows. "I didn't know you were visiting her."

He hesitates and then nods. "Yes, but you can't tell anyone, okay? I'm not supposed to let anyone know I'm here."

Oh, really? I think, *that's interesting.*

"I promise. Your secret is safe with me. But let's not tell Sidney that you met me, okay? She might get worried for no reason."

"Yeah, she worries all the time. Don't you go to school?"

"Not this year. Don't you?"

"I'm supposed to. I hated school in Vegas, though. I miss my old school here and my friends. And I miss learning stuff."

"You could homeschool like I do," I say. "Sidney's actually a good tutor."

"Maybe. I'm doing my own project about planets," Leo says. "I have a telescope too. Do you want to see it?"

"I can't see very much, Leo."

"Oh right, Sidney told me that. You can't see many stars from this room, but Sidney says there's a big flat rock up on the hillside where I can set up my telescope someday."

"Sure, I know the one she means. So, Leo, how long are you staying with your sister?"

"Not long," he says hurriedly, taking a step back from the doorway. "I'm just visiting. I don't think Sidney wants me to stay."

"Oh, I'm sure she does." The idea that has slowly been taking root inside my head suddenly blossoms to life and I can't stop the slow, triumphant smile from spreading across my face. "I think she cares about you very much and would do almost anything to keep you safe."

"Okay," he says in a small, uncertain voice, taking another step backward.

"Look, I should go before Sidney gets back. If you promise to keep our visits secret, then I'll make sure to visit every day. I can tell you all about that star-watching rock."

"Oh, yes, I'd like that."

"I have the feeling that you and I are going to be good friends, Leo."

"Okay, Alice."

I leave the barn feeling a weird mixture of guilt and excitement. It's been a long time since I've been involved in anything sneaky and it feels good to practice my skills again. On the other hand, I like Sidney, and I know that what I'm planning is going to hurt her.

It's for a good cause, I remind myself, *Oriel belongs here with me. And I'll offer Sidney enough money to make her happy. She'll get over it eventually.*

For the next two days, I visit Leo in secret when Sidney goes to work at Barn B.

But even though he is happy to chatter on about his telescope and whatever sciency thing he's interested in, and eat the junk food I bring him, he won't say a word about his family and Sidney.

And, for my plan to work, I'm going to need every bit of information I can get out of him.

It isn't until Trin finally comes home for Thanksgiving break that I get another brilliant idea and everything falls into place.

CHAPTER 36

ALICE

"You promise you can keep a secret?" I ask Trin as she leads me through the darkness down to the barn. It's nine o'clock and I know that Sidney won't be home from working at the restaurant for hours. "Even from your mom?"

"If it's a good secret then I can," she says, tightening her grip on my hand. "As long as nobody gets hurt."

"It's a very good secret. I made a new friend while you were away and he's just your age. He lives above the barn but we can't tell anyone he's there, okay?"

"He lives all by himself?" she asks, sounding worried.

"No, with his sister. But she works all the time so he's all by himself a lot of the time and he's lonely."

"That's sad."

"It is. Very sad. Hopefully you'll like him and you can be friends."

"I'll like him," she says with certainty. "If he's your friend then he's mine too."

"Perfect. But you can only hang out with him after dark when there's nobody around, okay?"

"Why? That's weird."

"Yeah, I know. But his sister works nights so that's when he needs friends the most."

"Oh. Okay. If you say so, Alice."

I smile at her, feeling guilt churn in my stomach. Getting information out of Leo myself is one thing, but roping my little sister into it is probably going a bit too far into crazy-town.

It takes about three seconds for Leo and Trin to hit it off, just like I'd known they would.

I just have to sit back and listen while they play together on the computer. And, around Trin's bubbly energy he lets his guard down and begins to *talk*.

I am practically skipping up the hill as Trin and I head back through the darkness to the house.

This is it. This is exactly what I need. Sidney isn't hiding him while he *visits*. He's a runaway whose parents don't even want him and he doesn't have anywhere else to go.

"Leo is so nice," Trin says as we hurry up the driveway. "Can we go see him again?"

"Absolutely. We'll sneak out and visit him tomorrow night."

By tomorrow my perfect trap will be set. And then Oriel will be all mine.

CHAPTER 37

SIDNEY

"*S*idney, it's your turn to go on break. And there's a boy here for you."

Kumiko glares at me from her workstation like I've mortally offended her.

"A boy?" I look up blearily from where I've been prepping shrimp and rub my eyes in the crook of my elbow. I am bone tired. I took a bunch of extra shifts this week so I could save up for an apartment, but the lack of sleep is catching up with me.

I have made the hard decision that I'm going to keep Leo. In another month I will have enough to afford the damage deposit and first month's rent on an apartment. I hate the idea of keeping him hidden until then, and him missing so much school. But I can't see another way around it.

"Sidney," Kumiko snaps again, "the boy. He's waiting outside, by the back door."

"Oh, right. Sorry, I forgot." My brain has been in a constant fog all week. It's a wonder I'm able to function at all.

I take off my apron and wash my hands and then slowly make my way to the back of the restaurant, stifling a series of yawns on the way there. What I wouldn't do for a good nap right now.

"Sidney." Josh is waiting just outside the door, a frown on his face.

"Josh, what are you doing here? Is everything okay? Is it Oriel?"

"No, no, everything's fine at the barn. I wanted to talk to you. About us."

"Us?" I look at him blankly.

"Come on, I know you've been avoiding me all week. Are we fighting? Have you met someone else?"

"What? No, of course not. I've been...busy." Distracted, over-whelmed, on the edge of a breakdown. All those things.

"Uh-huh." He looks at me skeptically. "Well, you look like hell. Do you mind telling me what's going on? I thought we were, er, friends, at the very least. I thought you trusted me."

"I do. It's not that. I just..."

I look at his honest gaze and let out a heavy sigh. He's right. Keeping secrets is no way to treat him after all we've been through. And, even though he's not a rule-breaker, I don't think he'll tell on me.

"All right. I'm sorry. I have been keeping a secret from you, but it has nothing to do with us. I should have told you before. I..."

"Sidney!" The door bursts open and Vinny sticks his head out. "We're getting swamped here. Break's over; we need you."

"I have to go," I say quickly to Josh. "But I'll tell you everything tonight. Meet me at Three Sisters once my shift is over, okay?"

"Okay, but..."

"Thanks." Impulsively, I lean forward and press my lips against his, sending a little shockwave of warmth through me. "I'll see you tonight."

Then I turn around and run inside, not waiting to see his reaction.

CHAPTER 38

ALICE

$\mathcal{I}$ have set the scene perfectly. Trin is upstairs playing with Leo, completely oblivious to what I'm up to. It's nearly midnight and I'm lying in wait in the barn aisle with all the lights blazing so I can see what I'm doing.

I hear Sidney's truck rumble to a stop in front of the barn and then the sound of footsteps. The door rolls back and I hold my breath in anticipation. *This is happening. I'm really doing this.*

"Hello, Sidney," I say from where I'm leaning against Heck's stall door. I'd picked that particular spot on purpose. Because there is an immature part of me still angry that Josh likes her better than me. Yes, I know that's ridiculous, but standing here gives me the shot of anger I need to carry through with my plan.

"Alice? What are you doing up so late? Is everything okay?"

She sounds so concerned about me that I feel a pang of guilt. *Do it for Oriel, do it for Oriel,* I remind myself.

I take a deep breath and plow forward. There is no going back now. "I know your secret, Sidney."

"Secret?" Her voice wobbles and I pause, waiting for her confusion to clear.

"Yes, Leo and I have become good friends while you leave him alone every night by himself so you can go work your second job. Did you know that it's illegal to leave a kid that young alone on their own? And dangerous too. Anything could happen."

"I know, I know," she says hurriedly, "it's temporary. He's just visiting."

"That's not what I hear, Sidney. I heard that your criminal parents dumped him on you. That they deserted him exactly like they deserted you and your sister."

"Alice, what's going on?" Her breath hitches like she's starting to panic. That twinge of guilt hits me again but I push it away. I am strong enough to do this.

"Oh, don't worry," I assure her smoothly, "your secret is safe with me. In fact, I can make life so much easier for you, Sidney. I can ask my dad for both you and Leo to move into our house with us. Leo will have his own room and can go to his old school like he wants to. He can take those astronomy lessons he dreams about."

"What?"

"I can see how much you're struggling." I lower my voice, aiming to sound sympathetic. "You work two jobs, you try to do everything for Oriel and for your family, but you fall short no matter how hard you try. And your dreams of going to university are fading in front of you."

"No, I…"

"It's okay. It's not your fault that your parents are criminals and that you're poor. But it's time to stop fighting, Sidney. I can help you. All you have to do is sign Oriel over to me."

"What?" she asks incredulously, angrily. "*Give* you Oriel?"

"Sell him to me. I'll give you more than a fair price. It makes the most sense. You can still see him every day and maybe even ride him once in a while. But he'll be *my* horse and you won't be able to take him away. He'll get the care he deserves and an owner who can afford to give him everything he needs."

"No! You're crazy, Alice."

"Maybe I am." I shrug. "I want you to see that this is the best thing for everyone, Sidney. If you agree to sign him over then we can all be happy together. You, Leo, Beans and Oriel will be cared for and I'll get the horse I want. It's simple."

"It's not simple. It's nuts…"

I hold up my hand to stop her. "I'm afraid that if you don't sign him over then I'll be forced to tell my dad that you're keeping Leo here without anyone knowing. You'll be fired, of course. They'll kick you both out of the dorms tonight and you won't have anywhere to go. And then my dad will have to make a call to social services. Leo will probably be put into foster care and you'll never see him again. And…."

"Alice?" a small, disappointed voice says behind me. "What's going on?"

I spin around, my heart suddenly in my throat and my mind whirling.

"Hey Trin," I say brightly, pushing down my panic and plastering on what I hope is a convincing smile. "I thought I told you guys to stay upstairs. Sidney and I are just having a conversation."

"We heard you," she says in a wobbling voice, and I realize that Leo is standing on the stairs right behind her.

"It's not what you think," I say quickly, "we were only joking around. Right, Sidney?"

"It's okay, Leo," she says, brushing past me and heading toward the two kids. "Don't worry. We're going to figure everything out. Trin, why don't you head back to the house, all right? Your mom would be worried if she knew you were out here this late."

Even though she's trying to act calm, her voice is thick with tears as she ushers Leo quickly up the stairs.

Trin stands still for a second and, even though I can't see her well, I can feel her gaze on me.

"I can't believe you would do something like this, Alice," she whispers. "You're just like Clara." Then she bolts down the aisle sobbing so hard that it sounds like her heart is breaking.

"Trin, come back. I can explain."

But she's already gone.

"Alice," a quiet voice says in the darkness. "What have you been up to?"

"Josh?" I gulp. Damn it. Could this night get any worse? My carefully laid plan has turned into a complete nightmare.

Josh is one of the few people whose opinion I care about. And he's just seen me at my very worst. Shame washes over me and I bolt toward the house.

I don't make it more than a few steps past the parking lot before I'm plunged into complete darkness. There is no Trin here now to help me navigate this black void. I can't see a single thing.

I stumble to a halt, heart thundering. Is this my karma coming back on me? Am I going to die out here all alone?

Don't panic. You can do this. You can figure this out. I kick at the gravel and inhale a ragged breath. Yes, that's right. If I start walking upward, the driveway will take me to the house. If I stay on the gravel then I can't get lost.

It's terrifying, though. Time and again I find myself tripping onto the grassy edge of the driveway and having to re-center myself. The lane climbs steadily and suddenly I realize there is a dim light ahead of me on the left.

The house, finally.

I'm nearly sobbing with relief by the time I make it to the front porch. Thankfully, Trin has not locked me out. I slip inside and heave a deep breath, feeling like I've come through some sort of hellish ordeal.

There is nobody around and the house is completely silent, even though the lights are on. I climb the stairs slowly and finally make it to the safety of my room, sitting down on the bed and waiting for my body to stop shivering.

I messed up. Tears prick my eyes. *I've wrecked everything. I'm going to lose Oriel and the people I like best will never speak to me again.*

CHAPTER 39

SIDNEY

"*L*eo, stop, this is not your fault," I say firmly, sitting down beside where he's curled up on the bottom bunk under the covers.

"It is," he mumbles in a shaky voice. "You told me not to tell anyone that I was here and I didn't listen. I've ruined everything."

"No, no. It wasn't fair of me to ask you to do that. I should have figured out something else. Asking you to lie and hide was wrong, even for a short time. You have nothing to be sorry for, okay?"

He nods but I don't like the vacant way he's staring at the wall. He didn't cry after we came upstairs. He'd woodenly answered my questions as he told me all about spending the entire week hanging out with that sneak, Alice. What kind of monster betrayed the trust of a little kid like that? And *my* trust for that matter? I'd actually started to like the little rat and then she pulls something like this.

"Are you fired now?" Leo asks in a small voice.

"Honestly? I have no idea. But this isn't the only job I have, Leo. I need some time to think about everything but we're going to get through this. We'll figure it out."

"I should have gone to Nanna's," he says miserably.

"Well, let's not worry about that now. We'll have a good sleep and figure it out in the morning, all right? It's well past midnight and you should be sleeping."

"Okay," he mumbles. "Hey, Sidney?"

"Yeah, buddy?"

"I really thought Alice was my friend."

"I know, Leo. I thought she was my friend too. Get some sleep, okay?"

I flick the light off and step out into the hallway, not wanting him to hear me when I have my own meltdown. My breath catches in my throat the second I shut the door and my eyes begin to burn.

"Sidney?"

I stare at Josh, waiting to hear what his judgement will be. Will he hate me for lying?

"So that was your secret?" he says quietly. "You're looking after your little brother?"

I nod, not able to talk around the lump in my throat and suddenly he's there, wrapping his arms around me and pulling me firmly against his chest.

For a second, I hold in the tears and then they are coming out in wracking sobs that I can't keep back.

He doesn't say anything, he just rubs my back and lets me cry until I don't have anything left.

"Sorry," I say, pulling back a little. "I should have told you right away. And I cried on your shirt."

"It will dry." He kisses my forehead and then leads me to the couch, pulling me down beside him when he sits. "You're not alone in this. We'll figure it all out."

"I feel so bad for Leo. My parents don't want him and I'd hate to send him to Nanna's. She's awful and he doesn't want to go. And I can barely afford to take care of myself, let alone him. I don't know what to do."

For the first time I think about what Alice had said.

"I don't know, maybe I should sell Oriel to Alice. Maybe she would be a better home for him."

"No way. After what I heard tonight, she is the last person who should get that horse. I am really shocked she'd do something like that. Clara, yes, but not Alice."

"But I have nowhere to keep him now. And I probably just lost my job."

"Let's not panic yet." He squeezes my shoulders a little tighter. "I don't think anyone is going to fire you over this, Sidney. Anna is pretty understanding and you're one of the hardest workers here. This will all get sorted out."

I lean my head against his shoulder with a sigh, closing my eyes. Gradually the tension in my shoulders eases. There is only the feeling of his solid weight against mine, his fingers running through my ponytail in a soothing motion that nearly lulls me to sleep.

"I should go to bed," I say finally, reluctantly, pulling away from him. "And you need to get home. It's so late."

"I can stay on the couch if you want," he says, "if you need a guard dog."

I smile, reaching up to smooth the concerned wrinkles in his forehead. "I don't think I'm in any mortal danger. But thanks for staying with me. And for understanding. It means a lot."

When he finally leaves, I slip back to my room and climb onto my bunk, my eyelids already fluttering closed.

I shouldn't have been able to sleep at all but my exhaustion catches up with me like a tidal wave, washing over me and dragging me down before I've barely pulled the covers up to my shoulders.

I sleep soundly all night long and it isn't until I wake up in the chilly early dawn that I realize that Leo is gone.

CHAPTER 40

ALICE

"*A*lice, get up." Tiffani stands in my bedroom doorway. "Get up this instant."

"What?" I snap awake, rubbing my eyes. "What do you want?"

I realize suddenly that Trin is there beside her, sniffling and trying not to cry. I sit up, suddenly remembering all the events of last night. I am going to be in so much trouble. My dad will probably never let me ride again.

"Sidney's brother is missing. He ran away in the night and you need to help find him since you clearly had something to do with this."

"Leo is missing?" I ask, gulping hard.

"Yes, and the temperature was well below zero last night. He doesn't have proper winter wear. Apparently, something upset him enough that he left his warm bed and decided to take his chances with running away."

"Alice, if he's dead I will never forgive you," Trin says, hiccupping through her tears.

"He's not dead," I say firmly, my fear making me snappish, "that's ridiculous. He's probably hiding in the hay room or something. I doubt he went far."

"He left a note for Sidney saying he was going to live with his grandmother since he'd messed up his sister's life so badly."

I swallow hard. "Well, there you go. Mystery solved. He's going to his grandmother in Alberta."

"He left on foot, without any money or a way to get there. I am so ashamed of you, Alice. This is very serious. Very."

"Okay, I know," I grumble, pulling myself out of bed. "I get it."

"I don't think you do. Triniti told me the whole story. You tried to blackmail that poor girl into giving you her horse. You used a child. You used *my* child to try and get whatever you wanted without thinking about anyone but yourself. These kids trusted you, Alice. They trusted you because you're older and you pretended to be kind. You manipulated them."

"That's not true," I say, feeling truly shocked. "I love Trin. And I like Leo. I never meant for them to get hurt."

"And Sidney? A vulnerable employee of ours who had nowhere else to go and was desperate to keep her family safe. Who has been nothing but kind and patient to you since she got here. Did you mean for *her* to get hurt?"

"Maybe?" I say in a small voice, wilting under Tiffani's glare. She is usually so sweet and meek, I have never heard her like this before. "I just wanted to have something good in my life. Oriel makes me feel whole again. Normal. I didn't want her to take him away."

"So, you decided to help yourself to him? Even though he's not yours?"

"And why shouldn't I?" I ask, suddenly furious at the guilt she's heaping on me. "Sidney has everything I want. Her sight. That horse. Josh. Everyone likes her. And I hate her."

Tiffani is silent for a second.

"Alice, you can't go on like this. You can't go on lashing out and hurting people and crashing your way through life. You deserve more than that and so do the people around you. Especially the people that love you."

And with that she shuts the door and leaves me all alone.

I hate them all, I think viciously. *Nobody understands me. If Clara were here, she would know exactly why I did what needed to be done. She would be proud of me. She'd....*

I put a hand over my mouth, feeling sick. Clara *would* be proud of me. This is exactly the type of thing she would have done herself if she'd wanted something out of her reach. And people would have hated her for it and thought she was some sort of monster.

I sit down on the bed heavily, biting my lip.

"I don't want to be like Clara," I say out loud to my empty room. "But I don't know how to be anyone different."

I don't have any good answers, but I do know that I need to find Leo and make this right.

Where would he go, though? He is afraid of horses and of the outdoors, so I can't see him hiding in the barn or trekking out into the woods.

But there was one place we'd talked about. That star-gazing rock that Isabelle had taken me to once. Leo had seemed really interested and I'd practically given him directions right to it. What if he is trying to make his way there?

I jump off the bed and hurry from my room, heading for the barn.

I can see the whole thing unfolding in front of me like a movie. I will take Oriel and ride bravely up the trail to the lookout rock, galloping the whole way, trusting him to guide me. I'll find Leo there and I'll comfort him and bring him home safe and we will be treated like heroes and Sidney will be so grateful to me that she'll give me Oriel and things will be back to what they were before and everyone will love me again.

I'm so carried away by this fantasy that I'm in the golf cart and driving halfway to the barn before I hesitate.

It's a wonderful, dramatic story. The old me wouldn't have hesitated to do any of it. But it was the old me who created this whole mess in the first place.

I stop the golf cart, chewing my lip as I stare across the pastures, trying to work out what to do.

Finally, I pick up my phone with a sigh.

"Tiffani?" I say quietly when she answers. "I think I might know where Leo went."

Things happen quickly after that. It turns out that I was right and that's exactly where Leo had gone. Or at least tried to get to. The search party had discovered him halfway up the mountain, where he'd fallen and hurt his knee so badly that he couldn't walk. They'd found him shivering with cold and clutching his small telescope to his chest.

I'd listened to the whole thing from my open bedroom window. The search and rescue team carrying him down on a stretcher to the ambulance waiting in front of our house. Sidney's tears as she'd been reunited with him.

And all the while a sick guilt churned in my stomach. He could have died. And it would have been all my fault.

I sit on my bed, not caring about the cold wind blowing across me. I deserve to be cold. What if it had been Trin lost out there in the dark? I would have gone out of my mind worrying about her.

"Alice?" I look up, surprised to find Tiffani is standing in my doorway. "Are you okay?"

"No," I say listlessly.

"Honey, it's freezing in here." She goes over and shuts my

window and then comes and sits down on the bed beside me. "He's going to be okay, you know. He needs to go to the hospital for observation and then they'll release him. Just a twisted knee and mild hypothermia."

Mild hypothermia. My eyes sting with tears and I sniff hard to hold them back.

"You were smart to figure out where he went. It could have been much worse if they hadn't found him so fast."

"Yeah." My voice comes out a croak. "But it would have been better if he hadn't run away at all. I nearly killed him, Tiffani. This is all my fault. You were right."

She doesn't argue with me. We both know that it's the truth. Instead, she reaches out and wraps her arms around me in the world's tightest hug.

I stiffen in shock. Tiffani has never hugged me like this before and there is a part of me that absolutely hates it. She's not my mother. She's just some girl my dad happens to be dating. Nobody can replace my mother. Nobody can...

I sink into her suddenly, tears flowing out of me like a river and I sob and sob, letting her hold me.

"I am so sorry," I say between sobs. "For all of it. For being me. I don't blame you for hating me."

"Alice, you are a smart, brave, strong person who is going to grow into an amazing adult. I don't hate you. I love you. I know I'll never replace your mother. Nobody can do that. But I'd love if you'd let me be your friend."

And that undoes me even more. I have spent so much time resenting Tiffani; plotting against her, making fun of her, treating her like she's garbage, that I didn't even take the time to see who she really was. Somebody who'd been rooting for me all this time. Probably like my dad and Mrs. Pitts have too. They've all been on my side and I was too caught up in my own drama to see it.

"Okay," I say, sniffling. "I really am sorry."

"I know. You should probably start thinking about your apology to Sidney and Leo too."

"I will. Can we go to the hospital?"

"Of course. As soon as we're allowed."

CHAPTER 41

SIDNEY

"*H*ow is he doing?" Eden asks softly from the open hospital doorway. I turn to see her standing behind us, staring at Leo's sleeping form with a soft expression on her face.

"He'll be fine. Just cold and exhausted. They want to keep him overnight to make sure he's okay."

She nods and moves closer to the bed, not stopping until she's standing right next to me.

"You never asked me for money like Mom and Dad did," she says quietly.

"What do you mean? Why would I ask you for money?"

"You were nearly homeless, your horse was nearly homeless, your car was repossessed, Sidney, and you never asked me to help."

"Eden, it's not your job to help me. You work hard for your money, nobody knows that more than me, and I would never dream of taking that from you."

"I know," she says in a low voice. "That's why I'm doing this."

"Doing what?"

"I'm buying a house."

"Eden," I say, barely resisting rolling my eyes. "Houses are expensive. There is no way you make…"

"I do, actually," she interrupts, giving me a withering look. "My accountant says I can afford the down payment on a small house. Nothing fancy. But big enough for me, you and Leo to live in. I've already picked it out."

"Really?" I look at her in disbelief. "I mean, it's a nice offer, Eden, but you really don't have to take on this responsibility. I thought you were having fun living with Patrice."

"Eh," she wrinkles her nose and shrugs, "I'd rather be with my own family. And I consider it an investment anyway, and a place to crash when I'm in town. You're not going to be able to talk me out of this, Sidney, so you might as well give in."

She says the last part gently and then puts her arm around my shoulders and gives me a hug.

"All right," I say in a small, choked voice. "If you mean it."

"I mean it. Just don't expect me to cook. Or clean. Or look after your smelly dog."

"You love that smelly dog."

"Maybe. And no creepy internet boyfriends, either."

"Yuck. I promise. Actually, I do have someone I'd like you to meet. It's not serious yet, but one day it might be. I think you'll like him."

"As long as he doesn't write awful poetry like the last one."

We both laugh and then, before she can escape, I wrap my arms around her and hold her tight. I don't think I'm ever letting go again.

CHAPTER 42

ALICE

I hesitate in the doorway, my heart thumping a million miles a minute. I can hear Sidney and her sister laughing quietly inside which is a great sign, but it makes it even scarier for me to push open that door.

"Um, can I come in?" My voice is too soft and they don't notice me until I'm standing awkwardly in the middle of the room.

"Alice?" Sidney stands up, taking a step toward me, and I automatically flinch backward like she's going to hit me. Not that Sidney is exactly a hitter, but I would deserve it if she did.

"Is this her?" the girl beside her asks in a hard voice.

"Yeah. Eden, can you sit with Leo for a second? We'll go out in the hall so we don't wake him up."

When she puts a hand firmly on my arm and steers me out of the room, my stomach drops. She is never going to forgive me.

"Sidney, I am so sorry," I say, the second we get outside. "I just came here to apologize to you and Leo. I know I messed up badly and that I'm a horrible person. I'm probably the last person you want to see right now. But…"

"Alice," she says firmly. "Shut up." And then she shocks me by pulling me into a hug that nearly squashes all the air out of my lungs. "Thank you for finding him. You probably saved his life."

"No, but I didn't. I…"

"Seriously, shut up right now. I know you're sorry. I've been tutoring you for a while so I have a good idea how your brain works by now. Apologies mean nothing, Alice. Really being sorry means changing things so they don't keep happening. You don't really want to be this person and have people hate you, do you?"

I shake my head, feeling miserable.

"No, I didn't think so. This is your chance to end this now before it's too late. You can be a better human, Alice. I know you can. I've seen how kind and sweet you can be. That's the real you inside."

"I wouldn't be so sure about that," I say in a low voice.

"Oh, so what if you're selfish and impulsive sometimes. At least you know it about yourself. If you were really bad then you wouldn't care. But you do care, Alice. You care so much that it eats you up inside. You deserve to be happy too."

I blink at her, wondering how my attempt to apologize had taken such a weird turn. I'd expected her to rage at me, not tell me that I'm a good person who deserves to be happy.

"Are you going to leave?" I ask in small voice. "Are you quitting?"

"I'm not going to live at the farm anymore. Eden and I are going to share a house with Leo."

"Oh." I gulp. "That's good."

"It is. But I'll still be your tutor this year and I'll work for Anna. Your dad has already said that I can keep Oriel there."

"He's going to stay?" I look up at her in astonishment. If she keeps Oriel there then I'll get to see him every day. Maybe even…

"But you're not going to be able to ride him anymore," she says firmly. "I think you understand why."

"Oh." I take a deep breath and nod. "Yeah. I get that. I messed up."

"You did. But, there's another reason too. I don't think you really love dressage, Alice. It's not where your passion is. And I don't believe that Oriel truly inspires you, either. No matter how much you love him."

I gape at her, not knowing what to say.

"Elliot told me last week that she thinks you should start taking lessons with her on Jiggs. He's so calm now that he might do okay on the flat if you school him slowly. You've done some nice work with him on the ground."

"Really?"

"Yep. And I have one more idea too. A project horse I know has just come available. I think she might be right up your alley. She's calm but will need to be reschooled properly. You're a trainer at heart, Alice. This will be good for you. Get their flat work solid and we'll find a way to convince your dad to let you start jumping."

All I can do is nod, not able to believe how kind she's being to me after everything I've done. And she's right about the dressage thing. I've been pushing myself down a path that was never mine to begin with.

When Tiffani finds me a while later, I'm sitting on a plastic chair in the hall, thinking hard about everything that had happened lately.

"Well, how did it go?" she asks as I get up to follow her.

"It was different," I say slowly, I feel like the grinch in that cartoon at the part where his heart suddenly doubles and triples inside. I feel like a part of me has abruptly unlocked and instead of me being this hard, angry person who hates everyone, I am suddenly somebody else. Somebody I don't even know.

"Well, let's get you home then. It's been a big week."

"Tiffani?" I reach out to grab her arm gently. "Thank you."

"For what, honey?"

"For everything. For putting up with me when I was so awful. For not leaving when we all made your life hell. Dad really loves you, you know. He would have been miserable if you'd left."

"Oh." The breath whooshes out of her. "Well, thank you. That means a lot. I'm glad that I'm still a part of your life."

Still holding onto her arm tightly, I let her lead us outside into the drizzly afternoon.

CHAPTER 43

SIDNEY

"*A*re we almost there? Are you sure we're not lost?" Alice asks for the fifth time. She bounces up and down on the back seat, tilting her head to catch whatever she can of the view skimming by outside.

"Almost there," I say with a smile, sharing an amused look with Josh. He'd been wrangled into driving the horse trailer today, not that he seems to mind. "Jeesh, you're almost as bad as Val."

"I'm not *bad*," Val pipes up, "I'm great. Better than great. This is the best day ever. I can't believe you did this, Sidney. I can't believe you saved her. I can't wait until I get to ride her again."

"Well, you can thank Alice. I'm not the one who bought her. And you'll have to wait until Alice has her tuned up again and then *maybe* she'll let you ride her."

"Yep, I know. She's Alice's project first. And then she gets to be a school horse for Anna. And THEN I get to ride her."

She says the last part at the top of her lungs and I bite back a groan. Why is this kid always so darn loud?

Val had finally convinced her mother to let her ride full time at Three Sisters. It wasn't every day like she used to do at Happy Acres, but at least she could ride once a week for now and more during the holidays. It was something, anyway. And I thought she deserved to be here today.

"We're here, guys," I say as we finally turn into the Happy Acres parking lot.

"Look, there's a new sign," Val says excitedly, "it's not Happy Acres anymore."

"Pinnacle Farms," I say slowly, "that's a nice name."

"And look at the *barn*," Val squeals. "It's brand new."

Not quite new but definitely refurbished. It was amazing what a fresh coat of paint and some repairs could do to improve the look of a place. And it looked like a large structure was being built behind it.

"Looks like an indoor." Josh raises his eyebrows. "Fancy."

"Well, come on, let's go find our project," I say, and we all climb out together.

It feels so strange walking in here again; the time I spent at Happy Acres feels like it happened ages ago, in another lifetime.

"Alice, Josh? What are you doing here?"

Darla is standing in the middle of the barn aisle, a brush in hand as she coats a stall-front with black paint. There is a smudge of black on her chin but she looks happy. Happier than I've ever seen her, anyway.

"We're here to pick up the horse we bought," Josh says when Alice doesn't answer. "The paint mare."

"You bought *that* horse for Three Sisters?" Darla blinks at us in confusion. "She's not much to look at, you know. Not what you're used to at all. I wouldn't use her for a school horse myself, that's for sure."

"We know," I say. "But she's just our type. We like second chances."

"Well, suit yourself. Good luck. She's down at the end there. Last stall on the right."

Alice is quiet as we walk toward the mare's stall and I wonder if she's regretting her choice in projects. If she thinks that Darla is right and that we've made a mistake.

"There you are," Val says, sniffling. "I told you we'd come back for you. I kept my promise."

Diva nickers under her breath, moving toward the door like she recognizes us. It's been months since Happy Acres officially closed down and Diva probably hasn't been ridden in all that time. She looks fat and out of shape, but her expression is softer too and her eyes aren't so hard and guarded. Not being in pain constantly from ill-fitting tack and harsh treatment suits her.

"How does she look?" Alice asks nervously. "Did we make the right choice?"

"Yes, I think we did." I move back to stand beside Josh so Alice can take my place and watch as the mare reaches over and sniffs delicately at her new owner's hands.

Josh gives my ponytail a playful tug, winking at me reassuringly, and my heart gives a happy leap.

After a second, Alice smiles and runs a hand softly down Diva's neck.

"I think we made the right choice too," she says finally. "Let's get her home."

The End

ALSO BY GENEVIEVE MCKAY

Thanks for reading the latest book in the Three Sisters Farm series. I hope you enjoyed it!

Want to read more exciting horse drama? Start your next series today.

Defining Gravity Series

Defining Gravity

Astrid never breaks the rules; she's much too terrified of her overbearing father to step out of line. He controls her weight, her friends, and even her career path. And he doesn't approve of anyone in their family thinking for themselves.

When one impulsive decision ends in disaster, Astrid is grounded for the summer, forced to put her archery career on hold and take a menial job cleaning horse stalls at a posh dressage barn. It takes a little horse named Quarry and a quirky cast of characters to banish Astrid's unhappiness and show her that she is worth something. But when her father steps in, once again, everything Astrid has grown to love is threatened.

Flight

Astrid doesn't argue when she's exiled to the wilds of northern Canada to stay on her long-lost aunt's ranch. It seems like as good a place as any for both her and Folly to heal after their horrific accident. Especially since Folly is angrier and more dangerous than ever.

But life in the country is full of surprises; real-life cowboys, a failing archery team that needs her help, and a funny horse named Red who would rather nap than work.

The path to fixing Folly isn't easy and as Astrid grows increasingly terrified of her volatile horse she realizes she'll need to reach out to the people who care about her if she wants to come out of this situation alive.

Freefall

Moving back to Vancouver Island with her new horse, Red, seemed like a good idea at the time but now Astrid is seriously doubting her decision. Her family is just as crazy as ever, her archery career is taking a path she doesn't like and her best friend Hilary is acting so strange. The only solid thing in her life is the horses and her friend Rob who is turning out to be someone she doesn't want to lose. But when life at home becomes unbearable Astrid has to decide if finally standing up for herself is worth risking everything.

Riding Above Air

Living on the Ahlberg's country estate should feel like paradise now that sixteen-year-old Astrid is finally free from her overbearing parents. But instead, it's just a lot of hard work.

With Hilary still injured, Astrid has a full barn of horses to look after on her own, a failing archery career to rebuild, a flock of bad sheep to keep out of trouble and a young horse to train. Plus, avoiding Miranda's wrath and surviving Hilary's ever-increasing mood-swings has become a full-time job.

When the new coach arrives, and she's not what anyone expected, Astrid is pushed to decide between her archery career and the challenging horse-life she's come to love.

Touching Ground

An invitation to the ranch to prepare the Triple Hill's horses for an upcoming mounted archery clinic seems like a dream come true to Astrid, Rob and Nori. Especially when they can bring their own horses with them too.

It's the perfect distraction Astrid needs to keep from worrying about her parent's new baby and her own uncertain future.

But the ranch is changing, for better or worse, and it's a struggle for the Triple Hill's team to keep up with the never-ending work that farm life demands.

And some people are keeping secrets they'd like to stay buried.

October Horses Series

October Horses

The last thing Bree Connor expected, after being diagnosed with a terminal illness, was a second chance at life. But, somehow, that's exactly what she got. When a fateful encounter at the hospital introduces her to the world of horses, Bree is determined to make them a part of her new life. Things quickly spiral out of control when she becomes the caretaker to a pair of misfit thoroughbreds who also need a second chance. Will her strength and willpower be enough to beat the overwhelming odds that are stacked against them all?

Facing the Fire

Bree can't wait for the endless winter to be over. With snow locking the whole countryside in ice, the long-awaited October Horse project has come to a screeching halt. Only the pending arrival of the racehorses and the thought of finally being able to ride her project horse Ace is keeping Bree's spirits up.

Meanwhile, Angelika has found a rehab project of her own. This time it's not a horse that needs rescuing but a young singer who needs a second chance and a safe place to land.

When the new horses arrive, they are not quite what everyone expected. The team will need to pull together to make their dream a reality.

Keeping Chilly

Everything is finally going perfectly for Bree and the October Horses project. Horses are being adopted out, new racehorses are arriving steadily and her fundraising campaign has brought them some much-needed income. Even the more difficult rehab horses are starting to come around. But when Chloe is sidelined with an injury, Bree is suddenly scrambling to make sure the farm keeps running smoothly. And she'll need to use every trick she knows to keep Jeremy and Chloe from engaging in a full-out war. Meanwhile...Maisy Fletcher has the whole world at her fingertips. She has fame, fortune and a Grand Prix horse that's just about to enter the international stage. But when a terrible accident cuts her partner's life short, Maisy doesn't have the heart to start over with another horse. She doesn't know if she ever wants to ride again. When she's roped into volunteering at a retraining center for retired thoroughbreds and meets a funny horse named Chilly, she begins to remember why she fell in love with horses in the first place.

Greystone Manor Mysteries

The Curse of the Golden Touch

All Jillian Harrington wants is to live a predictable, ordinary life. One where she can ride her horses and read books in peace. And for her haunting memories of the past to stay buried.

But, when life throws her a curveball in the form of her reckless cousin Xander, Jilly is dragged into a deadly adventure. Not only is she forced to face the secrets of her eccentric family, but the creepy mansion they're stranded in has a dark past of its own; along with a resident ghost or two.

With her best friend Gilbert, and her four-legged side-kicks, Morris and Bally at her side, Jilly will have to fight harder than she ever has to make it through this adventure alive.

The Sting of the Serpent's Blade

When one door closes.... another one slams in your face.

Left abruptly to manage Greystone Manor on her own, and dealing with her difficult new ability to see spirits, Jilly struggles to keep her world from falling apart. Gil is moodier than ever, the stable-hands hate her and she's in dire need of money. Only Bally and Morris can keep her laughing when times get tough.

Throw in a murder and some missing artifacts and Jilly will have to use all her wits to stay one step ahead of the killer. Will her strong-willed ghost-horse be able to save the day this time?

ACKNOWLEDGMENTS

Big thanks to my editor, Shannon Page and to James at Go On Write for designing the cover.

Thanks to the Advanced Reader Team for being the first eyes on the page. And special thanks to Mariko Brown and Honey Johnston for the support and excellent feedback.

And a huge shout-out to the patient, saintly horses of my childhood who let me gallop around bareback and barefoot and refrained from bucking me off too often. I was very lucky to have grown up with such amazing teachers.

ABOUT THE AUTHOR

If you would like to keep updated on upcoming releases, contests and other fun news then sign up for the newsletter HERE. Or follow me on Facebook and Instagram

Genevieve McKay is the author of over a dozen books, and most of them are about horses. She was allowed to free-range as a child and spent many hours riding (and reading) in the woods, dreaming up new worlds. She lives on the west coast of Canada with her family, her horses, and an assortment of barnyard animals such as dogs, cats, sheep, chickens and two half-tame ravens.